In From the Shadow

In From the Shadow

Integrating Europe's Informal Labor

Truman Packard, Johannes Koettl, Claudio E. Montenegro

THE WORLD BANK
Washington, D.C.

Library of Congress Cataloging-in-Publication Data
Packard, Truman.
  In from the shadow : integrating Europe's informal labor / Truman Packard, Johannes Koettl, Claudio Montenegro.
     p. cm. — (Directions in development)
  Includes bibliographical references.
  ISBN 978-0-8213-9549-3 (alk. paper) — ISBN 978-0-8213-9550-9
  1. Informal sector (Economics)—Taxation—Europe. 2. Taxation—Europe. I. Koettl, Johannes. II. Montenegro, Claudio. III. World Bank. IV. Title.
  HD2346.E85P33 2012
  331—dc23

2012011903

Contents

Boxes

Figures

Tables

Acknowledgments

This book is a product of the World Bank's analytical and advisory services to the Baltic and central European "new member states" that joined the European Union (EU) in 2004 and 2007. In joining the Union, these countries have made a profound commitment that has had a transformative impact on their political, social, and economic institutions and will continue to do so. This commitment is to converge with the welfare and development level of their partners in western "Old" Europe. In working toward that goal, four are already members of the Organisation for Economic Co-operation and Development (OECD). For these reasons, although the focus of the book and its intended audience are the governments of Bulgaria, the Czech Republic, Estonia, Hungary, Latvia, Lithuania, Poland, Romania, the Slovak Republic, and Slovenia, we have, wherever the available data permitted, extended our analysis to include countries such as the Netherlands, Greece, Portugal, Spain, the United Kingdom, and others not typically covered by World Bank reports but that set the most relevant benchmarks. Many of these countries have traveled a path of development very similar to the one that the new member states are on today. Some only graduated from World Bank financial assistance in the 1980s and 1990s. All provide valuable lessons.

The book was prepared by a team of researchers and World Bank staff. The authors are Truman Packard (Lead Economist, Human Development Economics, Europe and Central Asia Region, World Bank); Johannes Koettl (Economist, Human Development Economics, Europe and Central Asia Region, World Bank); and Claudio E. Montenegro (Economist and Statistician, Poverty and Inequality Unit, Development Research Group, World Bank). Research assistance and much of the quantification of the arguments presented were provided by Isil Oral (Junior Professional Associate, Human Development Economics, Europe and Central Asia Region, World Bank).

The book draws on primary research conducted by leading specialists from the region and elsewhere. The researchers who contributed to this volume are as follows:

Kamila Fialova	Economist	Charles University, Czech Republic
Mihails Hazans	Professor	Economics Department, University of Latvia
Willi Leibfritz	Consultant	Former Head of Division Economics Department, OECD
Eva Militaru	Researcher	Institute for Labour and Social Protection, Romania
Christina Mocanu	Senior Researcher	Institute for Labour and Social Protection, Romania
Michal Palenik	Economist	Inštitút Zamestnanosti, Slovak Republic
Filip Perthold	Economist	Center for Economic Research and Graduate Education, Czech Republic
Friedrich Schneider	Professor	Department of Economics, Kepler University of Linz, Austria
Ondrej Schneider	Senior Economist	Institute of International Finance
Benno Torgler	Professor	School of Economics and Finance, Queensland University, Australia
Mateusz Walewski	Research Fellow	Centre for Social and Economic Research (CASE), Poland

The World Bank team received administrative and logistical support in Washington from Regina Nesiama (Program Assistant, ECSHD), Annie Milanzi (Information Specialist, ECSHD) and Carmen Laurente (Senior Program Assistant, ECSHD), and at the World Bank's Warsaw Office from Katarzyna Popielarska (Senior Executive Assistant, ECCPL).

The team worked under the direction of Tamar Manuelyan Atinc and Mamta Murthi (prior and current Directors, Human Development, Europe and Central Asia Region, World Bank); Orsalia Kalantzopoulos and Peter Harrold (prior and current Country Director, Central Europe and the Baltic States Region, World Bank); Gordon Betcherman and Jesko Hentschel (prior and current Sector Managers for Human Development Economics, Europe and Central Asia Region, World Bank); and Alberto Rodriguez (Country Sector Coordinator for Central Europe and the Baltic States, Human Development, World Bank). Indermit S. Gill (Chief Economist, Europe and Central Asia Region, World Bank) provided critical intellectual guidance.

The peer reviewers of the book were William Maloney (Lead Economist, Development Economics Group, World Bank) and Omar Arias (Lead Economist, Human Development Economics, Europe and Central Asia Region, World Bank), who provided helpful insights at the outset of the task and held the team to a high technical standard of quality.

About the Authors

Truman Packard is a lead economist in the Human Development Economics group of the World Bank's Europe and Central Asia Region. Trained as a labor economist, he has focused primarily on the impact of social insurance on household labor supply decisions, saving behavior, and risk management. Since 1997 Truman has worked for World Bank programs in Latin America and the Caribbean, East Asia and Pacific, and in central and eastern Europe. He served as co–deputy director for the *World Development Report 2009*, "Reshaping Economic Geography," leading the analysis of labor migration. Truman holds a PhD in economics from the University of Oxford.

Johannes Koettl is an economist in the Human Development Economics group of the World Bank's Europe and Central Asia. He has been working on issues related to labor markets, migration, health, and social protection at the World Bank since 2004. Previously he completed an MA in international relations at Johns Hopkins University's School of Advanced International Studies and a PhD in economics at the University of Vienna and the Institute for Advanced Studies (IHS), Vienna. His current work focuses on—among other topics—labor market diagnostics and policies, informal employment, social insurance, long-term care for the elderly, and social protection for international migrants.

Claudio E. Montenegro is an economist and statistician with the World Bank's Development Research Group. He has held positions at the University of Chile, in Santiago, where he currently is an adjunct professor, the Inter-American Development Bank, and the World Bank. His research interests are labor economics, international trade, poverty, and applied statistical methods. His research on topics as diverse as trade, labor, water accessibility, and econometrics has been published in academic journals and several books. He has been a contributor to several *World Development Reports* and also to several *Human Development Reports* of the United Nations Development Program. Claudio holds a bachelor's degree from the University of Chile, a master of arts in economics from the University of Maryland at College Park, and a master of science in statistics from George Washington University.

Abbreviations

ATO	Australian Taxation Office
CASE	Center for Economic and Social Research
EC	European Commission
EMTA	Estonian Tax and Customs Board
EPL	Employment Protection Legislation
ESS	European Social Survey
EU	European Union
EVA	(Hungary) Simplified Entrepreneurs Tax
FTR	Formalization Tax Rate
GDP	Gross Domestic Product
ILC	International Labor Conference
ILO	International Labour Organization
METR	Marginal Effective Tax Rate
MIMIC	Multiple Indicator Multiple Causes
OECD	Organisation for Economic Co-operation and Development
PPP	Purchasing Power Parity
SME	Small and Medium Enterprise

Overview

Magda dresses the hair of a very select and discerning clientele: women in her neighborhood "of a certain age" who want their rinses and perms done just so and who don't like all the glitz and loud music at the salon that opened last year just three streets away from Magda's small apartment. She has been attending to these ladies from her kitchen for most of her adult life and spends much of the day listening to their family news, gossip, and complaints as she washes their hair, trims away split ends, and sets curlers. Most of her customers see her every week. For some of her elderly clients, who find it difficult to come as often, Magda sends her husband, Dawid, out in their car to ferry them to and from their appointments. She admits that some keep coming more for the company than because they actually need their hair done.

Magda was certified as a hairdresser years ago, and she's very proud of the salon apprenticeship she did shortly after. She learned a lot and made good friends but was never fully comfortable working for somebody else. When her daughter was born, she found it easier to set her own schedule than to work salon hours. Magda earns a modest income from her ladies and keeps the notes they pay her in tightly rolled bundles squirreled away in an old cookie tin. She sometimes struggles to manage the cost of her weekly grocery shopping, but on the whole she is content. While friends have lost jobs and struggled to find new employment, she knows that her ladies "…will always want their hair done." Magda receives child allowances, and given that what she earns from hairdressing is not officially recorded income, she could probably qualify for additional benefits from the municipality. "But those are for poor people," she says, "and we're not poor." She's also worried that the local authority would force her to renew her certification, or worse, to stop hairdressing from her kitchen.

Magda's neighbor three doors down, Jacek, has his own business too, in construction. "No job is too big *or* too small" is written in bright red letters across the side of his van, right above the web address he has set up for his company and through which he gets most of his customers. Jacek was the first person in his family to go to university. He did well in college but stayed only three years. He already had a wife and a child and didn't have the patience to finish his engineering degree. "I prefer getting out and working with my hands." For several years it was easy to find jobs. Jacek even struggled to keep up with the demand for repairs and extensions, and he had to double the number of workers he picked up down by the parking lot each morning to take to his work sites. Times are tougher now, and there are always more men waiting for work in the mornings than he needs. But business is steady.

Jacek's clients pay him in cash, and he pays his men in cash as well. He sometimes needs to show a license to get the trade price on parts and materials. But he can keep it up-to-date by declaring only part of what he actually earns to the tax office. He doesn't feel at all guilty about not declaring his full income. "They'll just waste it, or steal it!" he says, nodding in the direction of the municipal offices across the street. Jacek offers to invoice his clients for taxes if they want to pay the extra 23 percent. He is sure his clients would trust him to actually pay the taxes to the authorities, but none accept. And the building inspector who signs off on plans and drops by sites to check on progress never asks any questions. But what about pensions and security for the men who work for him? "Pensions pay pennies. The guys have families and houses to pay for. They need their money now. When they want to work, they show up. When they don't, they don't, and I have to spend time finding new guys."

This book is about Magda and Jacek and millions of others like them, who earn a living working full- or part-time in Europe's untaxed markets for goods, services, and labor. Their activities are not registered as part of the economy, and because they go unrecorded, they are also unregulated. This makes them *illegal* although not in essence *criminal*. Some call this the "underground economy," the "black market," or the "shadow economy." As governments in Europe struggle to manage the fiscal legacies of the global financial crisis and the prospect of a rapidly aging population, the circumstances that lead people to work and trade in the shadow economy have grown in importance. This book is about the policies that governments might consider to bring these men and women in from the shadow.

What Is the Shadow Economy?

Few of the phenomena that occupy the time of governments, economists, and others in the business of crafting and executing policy are as ambiguously defined and as difficult to measure as the shadow economy. Professor Friedrich Schneider, of the University of Linz, who has dedicated most of his professional career to doing both, likes to point out that it is inherently difficult to observe that which, by definition, is activity people are trying to hide. It is a form of economic activity that first captured the interest of anthropologists and sociologists in the 1950s and that came under the scrutiny of development economists in the early 1970s with a seminal report by the International Labour Organization (ILO). It became a central focus of policy in the late 1980s and early 1990s, when sufficient data were available to show that the shadow or "informal" economy was far more than cottage industry, taxi drivers, and kids selling candy on street corners.

So what is the shadow economy? Definitions change according to who is asking and what motivates their question. A minister of finance might ask so as to know how many untapped sources of additional tax revenue can be found, and where. This particular motivation has risen to the forefront of discussion as governments across Europe and elsewhere struggle to close budget deficits and slow the growth of public debt. But a minister of labor or the leader of a trade union might ask in order to gain a better idea of where to concentrate efforts to ensure that the rights and protections of labor market regulation are upheld. A minister of trade and industry or the head of the local chamber of commerce might ask to learn where opportunities might lie to expand sales, ensure fairer competition, and improve productivity. A neighbor, frustrated by the time it takes to get his satellite service installed, might want to know who could do the job sooner, faster, and probably for less if paid in cash. And from each of these perspectives, a different definition can be drawn of what exactly the shadow economy is.

In 2002, at the 90th Session of the International Labour Conference (ILC), the term "informal economy" was defined as "all economic activities by workers and economic units that are not recognized, regulated, or protected by existing legal or regulatory frameworks and non-remunerative work undertaken in an income producing enterprise" (ILO 2002).[1] Although the 2002 definition seems comprehensive, it can be unwieldy. The Organisation for Economic Co-operation and Development (OECD 2004; 2008) offered a more parsimonious definition of the informal sector as "employment or other economic activity engaged in producing legal goods and services where one or more of the legal requirements associated with employment and production are not complied with." This is a more widely applicable definition and is consistent with what the European Commission (EC) calls "undeclared work ... or other paid activities that are lawful as regards their nature but not declared to the public authorities."

In this volume, we use the overarching term "shadow economy" to refer to market-based production of goods and services that are in essence legal under prevailing laws, which is concealed to avoid payment of income taxes and social insurance contributions and to escape product and factor market regulation. We measure the shadow economy as a percentage of a country's registered gross domestic product (GDP) using a set of internationally comparable indicators constructed for this volume by Schneider, Buehn, and Montenegro (2010) (figure O.1). We count as the shadow or informal workforce the nonprofessional self-employed and employers who employ five or fewer workers; workers without a written employment contract; unpaid family workers; and those who do not make social insurance contributions (figure O.2). We present statistics prepared from Hazans (2011) showing how Europe's labor force is distributed across those categories, as well as "formal" dependent employment, professional self-employment, employers whose firms engage more than five workers, job seekers, and the discouraged who would be happy to work but have given up trying to find a job.

Why Does It Matter?

Why should policy makers be concerned about informal employment and the shadow economy? People work and do business outside the confines of social, labor, and business regulation for a variety of reasons. Some exit the structures of the formal economy to escape regulatory costs or to enjoy greater flexibility, whereas others are excluded by lack of opportunities to advance and by actual barriers to better-protected, higher-productivity jobs (Perry et al. 2007; Oviedo, Thomas, and Karakurum-Ozdemir 2009).

Figure O.1   The Shadow Economy as a Percentage of Recorded GDP, Various Countries, 2007

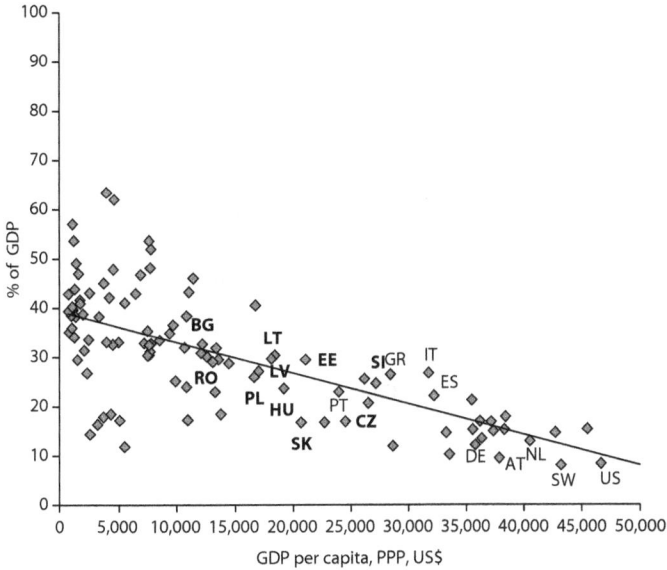

Source: Schneider, Buehn, and Montenegro 2010.
Note: EU new member states are in bold.

Figure O.2   Informal Work as a Percentage of the Labor Force

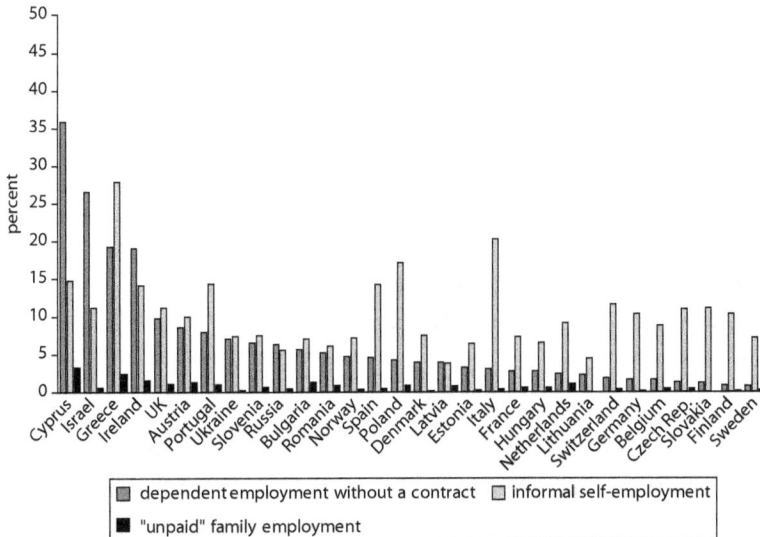

Source: Hazans 2011a.

But whether they are working informally because they exited formal jobs or because they are excluded from them, widespread informal employment in a large shadow economy is evidence of inadequate and unsustainable social institutions—the very institutions that the state puts in place to help households build, sustain, and protect their investment in human capital as they enter the labor market to seek a return on that investment. Indeed, a large and growing shadow economy can be seen as the consequence of a mass opting out of institutions by firms and individuals and "a blunt societal indictment of the quality of the state's services provision" (Perry et al. 2007).

Informal employment in the shadow economy has long worried policy makers for several reasons:

- First is the problem of the individual and her family. People working informally in the shadow economy, and their dependents, face explicit and implicit barriers to publicly and privately provided insurance instruments to manage potentially impoverishing shocks to their income. Even if people are able to manage many risks to their well-being without the help of the state, they may find it difficult to assess the costs of certain needs accurately, for example, their health care, or to make sufficient provision for losses far in the future, for example, securing adequate income in old age when they can no longer work. Nor do people who work informally have easy recourse to their rights and legal protections when things go wrong.

- Second is the problem of the firm. In countries with large shadow economies, bigger firms are often overtaxed to make up for revenue lost to the government through widespread tax evasion. That can discourage investment and hinder growth. Moreover, firms that operate within the rules face unfair competition from those that operate outside them. Firms that operate informally in the shadow economy can be constrained to a small size to escape detection by the tax authorities and may have to forgo a more efficient scale of production. And like households in which the main breadwinner works informally, those informal firms also have limited access to credit and limited recourse to legal protection when they need it.

- Third is the problem of society. A large shadow economy imposes heavy costs to society—costs that deteriorate public services and goods. This is what economists like to call a "free rider" problem and in extreme cases can corrode civic structures so greatly as to contribute to state failure. As a specific example of this corrosive process, a country's social "risk pools"—such as public social security for old age, unemployment, and health insurance; and the tax and transfer system—become fragmented, inefficient, and too expensive to remain viable.

What to do about the extent of informal employment and the size of the shadow economy is a dilemma that has been gaining urgency, particularly in Europe. The forces that accompany globalization put a premium on mobility and skill renewal. Rapid population aging will require that people work longer and be far more productive. For that to occur, social institutions have to be more "pro-employment," encouraging greater participation in the formal sector. And looking ahead, public financial resources will be increasingly scarce, giving urgency to measures that can significantly and sustainably increase tax revenue.

This book focuses on the objective of policy makers in the EU's new member countries to bring as much economic activity in from the shadow economy as they can.[2] Deriving specific policy guidance and recommendations for 10 countries at various levels of economic and institutional development from a multicountry study is impossible. Thorough country studies are the only instrument that can take full account of specific structural incentives and institutional contexts and draw from them detailed recommendations. A good example is the World Bank's (2008) report on reducing undeclared work in Hungary. That said, a multicountry study can nevertheless offer valuable insights. From the conceptual framework and empirical evidence presented in this book, a set of general policy suggestions can be formulated that are relevant for all the EU's new member states, those that aspire to join the EU, and indeed for upper-middle-income and high-income countries in other parts of the world. The findings on which these general suggestions are based are substantiated in 10 background papers (identified in the references). For those short of time and with little inclination for econometrics, the findings and broad policy suggestions are summarized in the following sections of the overview.

Who Is Working Informally in Europe's Shadow Economy?

The primary research conducted for this book shows significant differences in the composition and profile of the informal workforce across the different regions of Europe, and even within the new member states of the EU that are the book's core focus. In Bulgaria, Romania, and Slovenia the informal workforce is about evenly split between dependent workers without a legal contract and the nonprofessional self-employed (see box O.1 for a discussion of the different definitions of informal employment). In the Czech Republic, Hungary, Lithuania, Poland, and Slovakia, informal self-employment is the dominant form of unregulated work. That is also the case in the EU's southern members, Greece, Italy, Portugal, and Spain.

Those working informally in Europe are predominantly men. That is apparent in simple descriptive statistics but also from analysis that controls for the relatively lower rates of labor force participation among women. While some significant differences appear in the gender of the informally self-employed and informal dependent workers, among the new members, only in Romania are informal dependent workers mostly women. Informally self-employed people tend to be older, whereas the age profile of informal employees is more diverse.

Undeclared work—whether informal dependent employment or informal self-employment—is generally not something that immigrants with-

---

Box O.1

The Shadow Economy and Informal Employment: Terms Used in This Book

Shadow economy. Estimates of unregulated, undeclared production as a percentage of recorded GDP, using the multiple-indicators-multiple-causes approach (see Schneider, Buehn, and Montenegro 2010; and box 1.1 in chapter 1).

Informal work. Any form of unregulated, unregistered, or undeclared work, as a dependent worker, unpaid family member, or an own-account or self-employed worker.

Informal dependent employment. Undeclared, dependent, salaried employment, proxied in the book with three measures: employees in firms of 10 or fewer or five or fewer workers; employees not contributing to social insurance; employees without a written employment contract in their main job.

Informal self-employment. Own-account, independent work as a sole trader or employer, distinguished from "formal self-employment" and "professional self-employment" by (a) nonprofessional occupation, or (b) employment of five or fewer workers.

out the legal right to work are engaged in. Particularly in the new member states, those working informally are predominantly locals. However, in several of those countries, those employed without a contract—our preferred proxy measure of informal dependent employment—are likely to be part of a native-born ethnic and linguistic minority group. That raises concern that native minority groups, such as the Roma, might be excluded from certain forms of social protection or from pathways out of poverty that start with formal employment. Because of limitations in the available microdata, that is a concern that the book is unable to address. However, the World Bank is working with partner agencies to extend the coverage of available microdata to Roma communities. Informal dependent workers tend to have less education than those in formal employment and are also more likely to be in manual, low-skill jobs. In contrast, people who are informally self-employed are as likely to be doing skilled as to be doing unskilled work.

The differences in the face and profile of the informal workforce and those working formally are starker in the older, southern and western member countries of the EU than they are in the new member states. For example, a person employed without a contract in Spain is far more likely not to have gone to university than a similarly employed person in Estonia. And an informal worker in Greece or Portugal is far more likely to be an immigrant without the legal right to work than a similar worker in any of the new member states. That is an important observation, as it indicates that the labor markets in the posttransition countries of the EU are more integrated and the movement of people across different sectors and forms of work is more fluid. "Segmentation" appears to be a more significant feature of labor markets in the older member countries, particularly on the EU's southern flank, than in the new member states of the EU.

Structural Incentives Are Important, Particularly Taxation

Most firms in the new member states of the EU cite taxation as the biggest obstacle to doing business. That provides a compelling reason to look first to the manner in which people and firms are taxed for structural explanations for the extent of informal employment. Drawing on case studies of structural reforms of taxation, Leibfritz (2011) points out that quite apart from the size of government and the tax take, the mix of tax instruments deployed in most of the EU's new members creates strong incentives to evade taxes and to underdeclare labor. For example, the predominant means of financing social insurance—labor taxes—combined with personal income taxes pushes the tax burden disproportionately onto earnings from work. With the objective of attracting internationally footloose capital for investment, the new member countries have kept taxes on capital income and real estate very low in comparison. And although several studies draw from global good practice to advocate shifting some of the burden of labor taxes onto other instruments, such as a value-added tax (VAT), those instruments are already intensively used in the new member countries.

The background work for this book concludes with respect to the structure of taxation that incentives for declaring labor could be increased with a shift in the tax mix away from taxing labor earnings to less-distorting and more easily enforced taxes. The already-high levels of tax on consumption limit the extent to which the shift away from labor taxes can be made up with greater use of VAT. Given the mix of tax instruments currently deployed, a more promising shift could be made to a progressive tax on real estate—a reform option that would need to be carefully explored in each country context.

Governments might also consider improving the incentive to declare labor by lowering the rates of effective marginal taxes through "smoothing" the structure of tax rates. That could be achieved, for example, with the introduction of a flat rate structure—a step already taken by several of the new member states and one to which Estonia's success in containing and reducing undeclared work is often attributed. However, a smoother rate structure can also be achieved by introducing intermediate rates where current effective marginal rates spike and in so doing increase the incentive to evade. Similarly, spikes in the marginal effective tax rate (METR) can occur through the withdrawal of social benefits such as child allowances at certain income thresholds. A phased-in withdrawal could smooth disincentives around these thresholds.

But the gains made in containing and reducing the size of the shadow economy and the extent of informal work may arise not from a flat tax per se, but rather from the measures that have typically accompanied such structural reforms. Governments that have reformed the structure of tax rates have also simplified the tax structure by removing minor taxes and minimizing exemptions and loopholes. Those steps not only reduce compliance costs for firms and households but can broaden the base of the more effective tax instruments. More mundane, but no less important, are reforms in the ways that taxes are collected and administered. Gains can be had from automating administrative processes and interactions between the tax authorities and taxpayers, taking advantage of e-filing and other Internet-based procedures to lower transaction costs and increase the effectiveness of monitoring. Furthermore, compliance can be improved by integrating collection and auditing of taxes and social insurance contributions, to reap the benefits of administrative synergies and to enable cross-checking and verification. These types of changes in the ways that taxes are collected and administered have been supported by the World Bank in several of the new member states.

More controversial from a political standpoint, and also far more difficult, the pure tax component of mandatory social insurance plans can be reduced by tying benefits closely to contributions and shifting the financing of benefits with a primarily redistributive objective to general taxation. That has already been done to a substantial extent with the structural reforms of old-age pension plans in Latvia, Poland, and elsewhere. Given the formidable deficits between benefits being paid and contributions in most social insurance plans in the region, and keeping in mind the shrinking size of the labor force, a closer alignment between benefits and contributions will likely require reconsideration of what benefits can continue to be offered sustainably by state-organized social insurance plans.

Formal Work Should "Pay" for Low-Wage Earners

In collaboration with the OECD, we extended that organization's Tax and Benefits Model to the new member states of the EU that have not yet become members of the Paris-based club. We used the OECD's model to examine the incentives created for firms and workers from the interaction of labor taxation and noncontributory forms of social protection. A purely synthetic representation of these incentives—what we call the "formalization tax rate" and the better-known "marginal effective tax rate"—shows how the most common social protection structures in the EU's new member countries (and in several of the older member countries) create a powerful impetus for informal employment and even for inactivity. Those disincentives to formal work coincide with actual observed rates of informal employment at critical inflection points in the incentive structure.

The exercise highlights how, for low-wage earners in particular, the value of being covered by the social and employment protection that come with formal employment would have to be enormously high to offset the opportunity costs of reporting their income. That leads to the conclusion that formal (part-time) jobs at low wage levels—so-called mini-jobs and midi-jobs—may not in fact be an economically viable option for low-productivity job seekers. When one looks at the actual earnings potential of informal workers, it is apparent that most of them are indeed low-wage earners. Making formal work more economically viable for those workers could help bring them in from the shadow economy.

The policy literature identifies two main levers to make formal work pay for low-productivity workers: (a) decreasing the labor tax wedge at lower wage levels and (b) smoothing incentives with changes to taxes, contributions, social assistance, housing, and family benefits. Regarding the tax wedge, the current social protection financing structures in several countries discriminate against lower earners. For example, Hungary applies a minimum social insurance contribution at very low wage levels (less than 20 percent of average wage). Among the EU-15 countries, only the Netherlands uses the same approach. A minimum contribution floor at such a low wage increases the tax burden considerably for those in low-paying, part-time jobs.

Other options for reducing the labor tax wedge include incentives linked to wage subsidies, social insurance contribution credits, or so-called in-work or employment-conditional benefits—cash benefits or refundable income tax credits conditional on formal employment—for low-wage earners. Germany introduced a phased social insurance contribution schedule as part of the Hartz IV reforms that came into force in the early 2000s. Monthly wages less than €400 are not subject to social insurance contributions. For monthly incomes between €401 and €800, the contribution rate rises gradually to the full share. Another way of improving incentives is to channel credits and subsidies to workers via their personal income tax returns. In the United States, for example, refundable ("non-wastable") tax credits (the "earned income credit" and the "making work pay" credit) are available to low-wage earners and their families.

The drawback of these types of measures is that they can carry a certain amount of stigma for workers who benefit. They also bring a fiscal cost. However, the costs have to be weighed against the benefits of having people who were working informally (or not working at all) in formal jobs.

With regard to reforming the design of social assistance, housing, and family benefits, the key is to keep the marginal effective tax rate in mind when designing eligibility conditions and the way that benefits are withdrawn. In other words, those who receive social assistance and housing and family benefits should gain from additional formal work—that is, any additional formal wage should increase their net income, including benefits. Otherwise, additional formal work does not pay, and beneficiaries will prefer to not work at all, to work informally, or to underreport their earnings.

The extent to which targeted forms of social assistance create disincentives to formal work is probably limited in the new member countries of the EU. Programs are usually tightly targeted to a small group of beneficiaries, so that coverage, even among the poorest people, is low. Categorical benefits—those available regardless of income and means, such as family allowances—are far more prevalent. Nevertheless, provision of targeted, "last resort" assistance has increased across the region as part of countries' response to the recent economic crisis. To the extent that income-targeted forms of social assistance gain importance as a permanent feature of social protection systems in the region, policy makers should take these considerations into account.

To make formal work pay for the lowest earners who are receiving income-tested social assistance, the withdrawal of benefits has to be gradual as their income increases. Sudden drops in net income have to be avoided. Eligibility criteria that restrict, for example, family benefits to those below a certain income threshold—often around 50 percent of the average wage—result in very high marginal effective tax rates and a considerable drop in net income once the income threshold is crossed. The German Hartz IV reforms again offer a good example of how that can be avoided and how benefits can be gradually withdrawn. However, although these measures are clearly good social protection policy, the impact of smoothing the marginal effective tax rate, on its own, should not be oversold. Empirical evidence of a positive reaction to this type of reform, that is, the formalization of more workers, is still scarce.

Most of the reforms that make formal work pay have immediate fiscal costs. Given the current fiscal constraints on governments across the EU, little space may be available to push through such measures. In particular, wage subsidies, tax credits, and other such measures can considerably reduce tax revenues, including social insurance contributions, or increase public expenditures. In this regard, though, the new EU members are in a relatively favorable position: their tax systems are relatively nonprogressive. Making a relatively nonprogressive tax system more progressive could make any future reforms along these lines fiscally neutral to a large extent.

Labor Market Regulation Should Promote Formal Job Creation

Most people accept that minimum wages distort the labor market and increase labor costs for firms, but they also understand the benefits of a more equitable distribution of income that that policy tool can offer. Textbook models and evidence from several countries show that past some critical threshold level, a minimum wage can prevent firms from offering formal employment to workers whose marginal productivity does not exceed the minimum. The results presented in this book indicate a more nuanced process at work (Hazans 2011b, Flalova and Schneider 2011). In country-level panel estimations on a sample restricted to the EU's new member states, the level of the minimum wage has an unanticipated negative impact on the scale of informal production, measured as a share of GDP. We infer from this unanticipated result that the minimum wage is acting as a lever of fiscal policy, containing the extent of informal employment and the size of the shadow economy by setting the minimum amount firms have to declare.

However, when one uses more precise measures of informal work, that is, the share of the labor force in employment without a contract and informal self-employment, similar panel estimations reveal that in the new member states and southern member countries of the EU, raising the minimum wage increases informal employment as the textbooks predict. In the western and northern older member countries, however, the impact of an increase in the minimum wage is exactly opposite: a higher minimum wage lowers the amount of employment without a contract. Our inference from this contrasting result from the western and northern member countries is that the imposed minimum could be acting as an "efficiency wage" that attracts workers into formal jobs. Evidence presented in this book showing that the minimum wage is often more binding on informal labor contracts could also explain why a higher minimum wage reduces informal employment in the western and northern member countries: the higher minimum could be pricing low-productivity workers out of any form of employment, formal or informal. With a pooled sample of all EU countries, however, raising the minimum wage increases informal self-employment. That indicates that policy makers must take care to strike the right balance in what can sometimes be a trade-off between ensuring a socially suitable minimum level of earnings and encouraging offers of formal employment, even for the least productive workers.

The second area of labor market regulation examined in the empirical research for this book is employment protection legislation (EPL)—essentially, restrictions on dismissal that raise firing and hiring costs for firms. Once a country's level of development has been taken into account, EPL is the variable that is most consistently, significantly, and positively associated with the size of the shadow economy as a share of GDP and the extent of labor informality proxied by various measures. Although it was not examined explicitly in the papers commissioned for the book, the negative impact of EPL on the availability of formal employment has been found to be greater for younger job seekers.

Undoubtedly, with greater diversity and the rise of services, stringent restrictions on dismissal that once were important to protect workers in the highly monopsonistic labor markets of economies with a dominant manufacturing sector may have outlived their purpose. In the southern member countries of the EU, where EPL is the most restrictive, all but the most educated new entrants to the labor market are limited to part-time and informal work. The need to loosen the constraints of EPL on the labor market lies at the core of Denmark's renowned "flexicurity" model, which shifts protection away from jobs to the people who lose employment through intensive deployment of active programs such as retraining and job search assistance. Indeed, our results indicate that spending on these "active" intervention measures seems to reduce the extent of informal employment in OECD member countries and northern and western EU member countries. Spending on active programs significantly reduces informal self-employment (as well as unemployment and discouragement) both in western and northern Europe and in Europe at large. The lack of a measurably robust significant effect of spending on these programs in the (non-OECD) new member states may reflect an inappropriate program mix (for example, more training and less job search assistance), design problems, or weaknesses in implementation of the interventions.

The impact of "passive" interventions—unemployment insurance—also varies across Europe. In the southern and new member states, spending on unemployment insurance benefits is relatively modest but seems to help keep job seekers from having to accept informal work. The same is true for long-term social assistance to the unemployed, as long as its five-year average net replacement rate (including unemployment insurance benefits) does not exceed 55 percent. However, raising the replacement rate of long-term assistance (unlike unemployment insurance) also tends to increase the unemployment rate. In contrast, in western and northern European countries, higher spending on unemployment benefits (other things equal) increases informal dependent employment as well as unemployment, whereas higher net replacement rates of social assistance benefits over five years seem to reduce the extent of informal work without increasing unemployment. Passive interventions such as unemployment insurance are designed to enable better matching of job seekers with employers offering jobs. It appears that in southern and new member states unemployment insurance may perform that function without creating undue moral hazard in the form of informal work and unemployment. By contrast, in western and northern European countries, unemployment insurance might be encouraging—and even subsidizing— informal work.

Drawing policy guidance for the labor market from cross-country analysis is perilous. As mentioned earlier, important context-specific factors can only be examined in adequate depth in country-specific reports, such as the World Bank's (2008) report on undeclared work in Hungary. Nevertheless, we venture the following general points of guidance. First, policy makers should maintain nonmarket minimum wages for low-skill jobs at a low level relative to average market wages. In doing so, the minimum wage is more likely to serve the social function of guaranteeing a socially suitable minimum consumption ability from work without choking off the creation of jobs, particularly for younger workers and those with less education, whose marginal product is low.

Second, a "flexicurity" approach of protecting people rather than protecting jobs can greatly improve incentives for firms to offer formal employment. Although some level of labor market regulation is necessary to prevent abuses, restrictive EPL may do more damage than good for employment outcomes in competitive, internationally integrated economies. The less monopsonistic and the more globally integrated labor markets are, the more important it is to provide income security in case of job loss and to enable workers to move between jobs.

Third, governments can improve the incentive structure of income support programs for the unemployed to better match the risk of unemployment and implementation capacity. In this book we present evidence that modest programs of unemployment insurance can have a positive impact on outcomes in countries where governments have more implementation capacity. However, where benefits are relatively generous and administrative capacity is weaker, the risk of perverse incentives has to be taken carefully into account. The benefits of providing income support for the unemployed could be had, and perverse incentives (moral hazard) could be minimized, by introducing an individual savings element into unemployment insurance plans.

Building Institutional Credibility and Trust in the State Is Critical

This book ventures a general conclusion about what policy makers can do to bring more economic activity in from the shadow: Although it may be necessary to improve the structural incentives created by taxation, social protection policies, and labor market regulation, doing so is not sufficient for substantive improvement to be achieved. To back up this general conclusion, the book presents a large body of evidence indicating that much more than the fairly mechanical incentive structures of taxation, social policy, and labor market regulation is at work in shaping the circumstances that lead people into the shadowy unregulated and untaxed markets for goods, services, and labor. A government's performance and the credibility it has in carrying out the state's critical role of providing and maintaining public goods are fundamental (Torgler 2011a and 2011b).

The process of improving governance and increasing institutional credibility is long and difficult, as policy makers in all of the new EU member countries can already attest. Although the gains are difficult to measure with precision, according to the best available and most widely recognized indicators, all of the new member states have made substantial progress in increasing government effectiveness, controlling corruption, strengthening the rule of law, and improving the quality of regulation. Yet despite that progress and the measurable impact that it has had on improving how citizens perceive their obligation to contribute to public goods—what the literature refers to as "tax morale"—as well as shrinking the size of the shadow economy, governments are eager to achieve more.

Much of the policy literature on how to improve and sustain tax morale suggests starting with a shift in how taxation itself is conducted. Tax morale rises when tax officials treat taxpayers with trust and with respect. The inverse is also true: tax morale falls when tax administrators treat taxpayers as suspicious and requiring coercion to pay taxes. Suspicion and coercion on the part of the tax administration can crowd out people's intrinsic motivation to act as good citizens. If tax administrators start with trust and a presumption of good citizenship and establish transparent payment procedures, taxpayers are more likely to respond positively. Where citizens hold positive attitudes toward the tax authority and the tax system, tax morale and collection are significantly greater. Respectful and fair treatment of taxpayers induces respect for the tax system and leads to cooperation. In contrast, opacity, inefficiency, and unfairness in interactions between the tax administration and the taxpayers reduce citizens' intrinsic motivation to pay taxes.

Instead of a preponderant focus on compliance management, risk control, and enforcement, better results are likely when the tax administration becomes more focused on service, customers, quality, transparency, and making the process of compliance as painless as possible. Where the tax administration tries to be honest, fair, informative, and helpful, acting as a service institution and thus treating taxpayers as partners and not inferiors in a hierarchical relationship, tax morale increases and taxpayers are more willing to pay taxes honestly.

Control and elimination of corruption are also critical to improving tax morale. In countries where corruption is systemic, the obligation to pay taxes is quickly dropped as a social norm. Corruption generally undermines the tax morale of citizens because they feel cheated if they perceive that the public finances are being squandered or used for ill gain. At the extreme, people can feel strongly entitled to evade taxes and the structures of the formal economy. A good place to begin cleaning house is the tax administration itself. In many formerly centrally planned economies, the tax administration retains a relatively higher degree of discretionary power over how tax liabilities are assessed and resources are collected, and that can create greater opportunities for corruption.

Hand in hand with control of corruption, the quality of institutions and the degree of citizens' participation clearly matter to improving and sustaining high levels of tax morale. Good governance and a high level of institutional quality allow people to express their social preferences with confidence through involvement and participation in the political process. That enhances the identification of citizens with the state's institutions and can counteract inclinations to be noncompliant. Participation and identification therefore reduce free-rider problems.

Not surprisingly, many studies have found that a participatory political process is key to raising and sustaining tax morale. The possibility of taxpayers' voting on fiscal issues, and thereby being involved directly in the political decision-making process, enhances their sense of civic responsibility. Direct democracy helps to ensure that taxes are spent according to citizen preferences, and the motivation to pay taxes may increase. Several studies show that a higher level of direct democracy leads to higher tax morale and that allowing voting on tax issues has a positive effect on compliance.

Some countries have had a positive experience with active information campaigns that attempt to influence social norms, with the ultimate objective of increasing voluntary compliance by raising the "moral costs" of evasion. Such campaigns are designed to raise social awareness and nurture a culture of high tax morale and rule of law. The campaigns typically inform the public about the negative implications of undeclared work for social insurance and the negative consequences of undeclared work for solidarity, fairness, and society at large. In 2006, the United Kingdom focused on positioning tax evaders as a minority who damaged the interests of the majority. Some campaigns have targeted high-informality sectors. An example is the Canadian construction industry campaign, which focused on consumers, informing them of the legal and financial disadvantages of "cash deals" and linking quality and professionalism with registered contractors. Hungary's "Fair Play" campaign in 2007 emphasized, among other messages, the damage that tax evasion does to the country's financial situation. Tax morale specialists point out, however, that campaigns are usually more effective in countries that have made the broader efforts to improve governance, curb corruption, and strengthen the rule of law. The state, in other words, has an obligation to deliver first and build credibility before citizens can accept the message.

In summary, a growing body of empirical and policy literature clearly indicates the importance of accountability, democratic governance, efficient and transparent legal structures, and therefore trust within the society to increasing participation by households and firms in the structures of the state. Citizens' perceptions of how governments work and how compliant other citizens are have a strong impact on their willingness to comply. Although effective governance improvements and measures to strengthen institutional credibility and ultimately raise tax morale are obviously country and context specific, from the literature and case studies presented here broad policy suggestions can be drawn.

First, a good place to target efforts to reduce corruption, increase transparency, and establish effective accountability structures is the tax administration. Taxation is how citizens feel the weight of their responsibilities in the social contract with the state. It is as good a place as any to focus efforts to strengthen that contract and is likely to be where those efforts can have a quick and valuable return. Ensuring that the "rules of the game" are enforced, even for the economically and politically powerful, is particularly effective.

Second, institutional strengthening of tax administration can be accompanied by a shift in the stance of tax authorities from purely monitoring and enforcement to client service and a presumption that when paying taxes is made easy, taxpayers will act in good faith. Most people want to do the right thing most of the time. Changes that make paying taxes and fulfilling regulatory obligations easier and friendlier experiences can build on people's innate desire to be good citizens.

Third, and probably most important to encouraging more firms and people in from the shadow economy, governments can strengthen the structures through which households can take part in decisions about how public resources are used. Delegation of functions and responsibilities to locally elected government can be effective in reducing the distance between the taxpayer and the state, closely identifying taxation with democratic decisions about the provision of benefits and services.

Notes

1. Informal employment, according to ILO, includes own-account workers and employers employed in their own unregistered enterprises; unpaid family workers, irrespective of whether they work in formal or informal sector enterprises; members of informal producers' cooperatives; own-account workers engaged in the production of goods exclusively for own final use by their household; and finally, employees holding informal jobs in formal sector enterprises, informal sector enterprises, or as paid domestic workers employed by households. For this last category, informal jobs are those where the employment relationship is not subject to legislation, income taxation, social protection, or entitlements to codified benefits such as advance notice of dismissal, severance pay, or paid annual or sick leave (ILO 2002).

2. We use the terms "new member states" and "new members" to refer to the 10 countries that joined the European Union from the Baltic region, Central Europe, and the eastern Balkans in 2004 and 2007. They are Bulgaria, the Czech Republic, Estonia, Hungary, Latvia, Lithuania, Romania, Poland, Slovakia, and Slovenia. Although Cyprus and Malta, which also joined in 2004, are sometimes included in the cross-country statistics and analysis, the book is not directed at them. Many of the arguments presented here are also relevant to aspiring members of the EU, such as Croatia and other countries in the western Balkan region.

References

Hazans, M. 2011. "Informal Workers across Europe: Evidence from 30 European Countries." Background paper for "In from the Shadow: Integrating Europe's

Informal Labor." Policy Research Working Paper 5912, World Bank, Washington, DC.

ILO (International Labour Organization). 2002. "Effect to Be Given to Resolutions Adopted by the International Labour Conference at its 90th Session (2002), (b) Resolution Concerning Decent Work and the Informal Economy." Governing Body, 285th Session, seventh item on the agenda, Geneva, November (doc. GB.285/7/2).

Leibfritz, W. 2011. "Undeclared Economic Activity in Central and Eastern Europe: How Taxes Contribute and How Countries Respond to the Problem." Background paper for "In from the Shadow: Integrating Europe's Informal Labor." Policy Research Working Paper 5923, World Bank, Washington, DC.

OECD (Organization for Economic Cooperation and Development). 2004. *2004 OECD Employment Outlook*. Paris: OECD.

———. 2008a. *2008 OECD Employment Outlook*. Paris: OECD.

Oviedo, Ana Maria, Mark R. Thomas, and Kamer Karakurum-Ozdemir. 2009. "Economic Informality: Causes, Costs and Policies—A Literature Survey." World Bank Working Paper 167, World Bank, Washington, DC.

Perry, Guillermo E., William F. Maloney, Omar S. Arias, Pablo Fajnzylber, Andrew D. Mason, and Jaime Saavedra-Chanduvi. 2007. *Informality: Exit and Exclusion*. Washington, DC: World Bank.

Schneider, F., A. Buehn, and C. Montenegro. 2010. "Shadow Economies All over the World: New Estimates for 162 Countries from 1999 to 2007." Background paper for "In from the Shadow: Integrating Europe's Informal Labor." Policy Research Working Paper 5356, World Bank, Washington, DC.

World Bank. 2008. "Reducing Undeclared Employment in Hungary." World Bank Country Report No. 47777-HU, May, World Bank, Washington, DC.

CHAPTER 1

Informal Employment in Europe's Shadow Economy

Although the size of the shadow economy has shrunk slightly in the years since 2000, among the new members of the EU its relative size has remained fairly stable, even as they have moved from middle to higher income levels. Those most likely to be in the informal economy are men, younger workers, people who have only completed basic education, and people doing manual, low-skill work. In addition, a significant share of informal employees consider themselves part of a group that suffers discrimination, and a greater share of informal employees than of formal workers report experiencing long spells of unemployment. That could indicate that, at times, informal employment is a substitute safety net, especially informal self-employment. At the same time, however, in most of Europe informal dependent employment falls as unemployment rises, indicating that informal dependent workers are the first ones to be fired when economic growth slows.

Europe's Informal Employment in Context

Estimates of the size of the shadow economy as a share of recorded GDP in the EU's new member states present few surprises, given those countries' levels of income (measured in purchasing power parity [PPP] GDP per capita). And although the shadow economy has shrunk slightly since 2000, its relative size among the new members—as well as their peers in the EU and the OECD—has changed little, even as they have moved to higher income levels.

When measured in employment rather than production, as in figure 1.1, the extent of the shadow economy—or specifically, informal or undeclared labor in the shadow economy—appears different across countries according to how those engaged informally are identified. Because people who are self-employed are easily identified in most surveys, the main differences in measurement arise from how those in "dependent" employment are categorized. Three criteria are typically available to proxy for an informal working arrangement: (a) if a person is employed in a firm with five or fewer workers (the firm size criterion); (b) if a person is employed and their employer is not contributing to social insurance (the social insurance criterion); or (c) if a person is employed without a legal employment contract (the contract criterion).

The first of these proxies is probably the easiest to find and use in cross-country comparisons, but is also the crudest and least satisfactory measure, as it can exaggerate the extent of informal work. That is particularly the case in economies with rapidly growing service sectors, where small firm size is commonplace even among fully registered, certified, regulated firms with all their taxes up-to-date. But as Fialová and Schneider (2011) show, the firm size proxy is not entirely without merit, as the correlation between employment in small firms and the estimated size of the shadow economy as a percentage of GDP is positive and statistically significant. Hazans (2011) shows that one-third to three-quarters of employees working without a contract are employed in firms of five and fewer workers. However, a substantial remainder are in larger firms—in fact, in Belgium, the Czech Republic, Denmark, Finland, Israel, Romania, Slovenia, and the United Kingdom, one out of four employees without a contract works in an establishment with 100 or more workers. Despite its imperfection, a portion of the primary research conducted for this book relies on the firm size criterion for lack of a better alternative.

The second proxy, although it directly measures the gap in social insurance coverage—which is among the main motivations for researching informal labor arrangements—is information not widely collected. When questions about social insurance are included in labor and household surveys, moreover, they are notoriously prone to misreporting and other measurement errors. However, as with the first proxy, important empirical

Figure 1.1 Estimates of the Size of the Shadow Economy as a Percentage of GDP

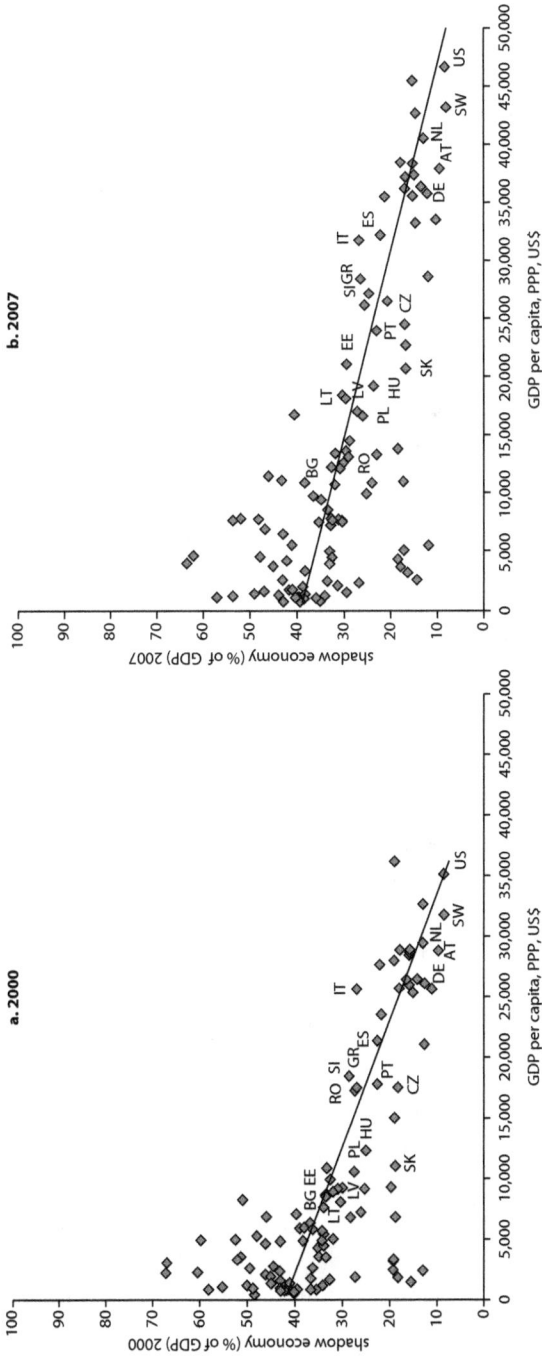

a. 2000

b. 2007

Source: Schneider, Buehn, and Montenegro 2010.

exercises conducted for this book rely on this measure, as will be presented in later sections.

The third measure—employment without a legal contract—is our preferred proxy of informal dependent employment and is among the most reliable for comparisons across countries and world regions, as it is less ambiguous and far more observable to survey numerators and respondents. Where used, the contract criterion refers to a respondent's main job. However, it too has a drawback: the contract measure fails to

---

Box 1.1

Grasping at Shadows? The Shadow Economy as a Percentage of GDP

Measuring the size of the shadow economy has been characterized as a "pursuit for knowing the unknown," precisely because all those engaged in unrecorded and untaxed activities want to keep them that way. Although a large academic literature exists on measuring the shadow economy, the subject remains controversial, as disagreement exists about theoretical concepts and definitions, proxies, the comparability of data, and estimation procedures.

The measure of the shadow economy as a percentage of GDP in figure 1.1 was constructed by Schneider, Buehn, and Montenegro (2010) for this book, using a structural equation Multiple Indicator Multiple Causes (MIMIC) procedure on data from 162 countries. The MIMIC procedure is designed to explain the relationship between *observable* variables and a latent, *unobservable* phenomenon—in this case, the shadow economy. The main benefit of this approach is that it captures what the literature shows are multiple causes and the multiple effects of the shadow economy.

Formally, the MIMIC approach is taken in two steps: the structural equation model and the measurement model. The first step in the MIMIC model estimation is to confirm the hypothesized relationships between the shadow economy (the latent variable) and its theorized causes (for example, a high level of taxation, or burdensome factor and product market regulation), with observed indicators (such as the circulation of cash in an economy and the labor force participation rate). The structural equation quantifies the relationship between observable "causal" and "indicator" variables. Once the relationships are identified and the parameters estimated, the model results are used to calculate the MIMIC index. But since the index only provides relative values—how the size of the shadow

(continued next page)

Box 1.1 *(continued)*

economy varies in one country in relation to another or in the same country over time—a further step is required to arrive at measures of the absolute size of the shadow economy from country to country. To do that, the index is applied to a benchmark: specifically, already available demand-for-cash estimates of the size of the shadow economy for Australia, Austria, Germany, Hungary, India, Italy, Peru, Russia, and the United States.

The MIMIC approach is controversial and is criticized for several reasons. The complexity of the procedure has led many to describe it as a "black box." The choice of causal and indicator variables is considered by some to be too subjective and not sufficiently grounded in theory. Differences in the availability of input data to quantify the causal and indicator variables across countries make the comparability of estimates questionable. Finally, the estimates can be unstable when even small changes are made to either the period or the group of countries being examined.

Schneider, Buehn, and Montenegro (2010) attempted to address those criticisms by presenting a detailed, step-by-step road map of the procedure; by grounding their selection of causal and indicator variables in a discussion of the theoretical and empirical literature; and by bringing to bear the cross-country uniformity of the World Bank's World Development Indicators (WDI). Although still not ideal, the resulting measure of the shadow economy as a percentage of GDP is highly correlated with measures of informal employment and alternative estimates of the size of the informal sector, including the proportion of the labor force that is self-employed (correlation coefficient 0.62, sig. 1 percent) and the proportion of the labor force not contributing to social insurance or pensions (correlation coefficient 0.66, sig. 1 percent).

We do not attempt to sidestep the controversy around the MIMIC approach, but rather, given how widely the method is now employed, to face it head-on. We do so by using several measures in our econometric analysis and avoiding placing undue reliance on any single measure. The cross-section and time series descriptive statistics used in this chapter rely mainly on microdata indicators of the extent of informal work engagement. The deeper explanatory models presented in chapter 3 use several different dependent variables, including the MIMIC measure.

In any case, and whatever the exact indicators used, a healthy degree of caution and care should be taken in interpreting the results of multicountry studies of this nature. For crafting effective policies, they cannot compare with the value of country-specific quantification of the shadow economy and microeconometric analysis that can capture key contextual factors.

capture working arrangements in which employers pay legally contracted workers mostly in cash and declare their wage bill only up to
the minimum wage. Anecdotally, this is a form of informal employment that is especially prevalent in the EU's new member states, where
many are paid above a reported wage in cash "envelope payments."
Unpaid family employment—also easy to measure in labor force surveys—is the least prevalent form of informal engagement in Europe's
shadow economy. It is treated separately in the statistics for this book
because, although this form of work is not remunerated in monetary
form, family workers are likely to be residual beneficiaries of farming
and household enterprises.

When countries are ranked by the share of their labor force employed
in small firms (the least satisfactory proxy of informal dependent employment), as in figure 1.2, four of the EU's new members—Poland, Cyprus,
Slovakia, and Latvia—appear in the top 10, alongside "old" members from
the EU's southward expansion—Portugal, Greece, Spain, and Italy, plus
Austria and Ireland. "Unpaid" family work is highest in Romania and
otherwise appears to be significant only in Poland, Greece, Bulgaria, and
Italy. Alternative microdata, presented and discussed later, allow the
informal self-employed to be separated from those more likely to be
active in taxed and regulated markets. Without the benefit of this differ-
entiation, in figure 1.2, self-employment appears higher in older EU
members (Greece, Netherlands, and Italy) and in the new members from
the East, although Romania is a clear exception.

Use of reported contributions to social insurance to sort informal from
formal dependent workers reduces the set of countries we are able to
compare to just 12 (figure 1.3). Among those, the data from the United
Kingdom should be treated with particular caution.[1] Poland remains in
first place when countries are ranked by the share of the labor force in
dependent employment and not contributing to social insurance. Spain,
Portugal, Latvia, and Greece also remain among the top 10, but are now
joined by Bulgaria, Estonia, and Slovakia.

Using the same data source (Eurostat 2008), Koettl and Weber
(2012b) give a detailed profile of informality rates across individual and
job characteristics for six new member states. Defining informal
employment as dependent workers who do not pay social security contributions and nonprofessional self-employed in small firms (less than five
employees, or none), they found an overall informality rate of 28 percent,
varying from 7.7 percent in Estonia to 39.5 percent in Poland (see
table 1.1). Interestingly, informality in the new member states is largely a

Figure 1.2 Percentage of the Labor Force in Informal Employment: Firm Size Criterion for Dependent Employed

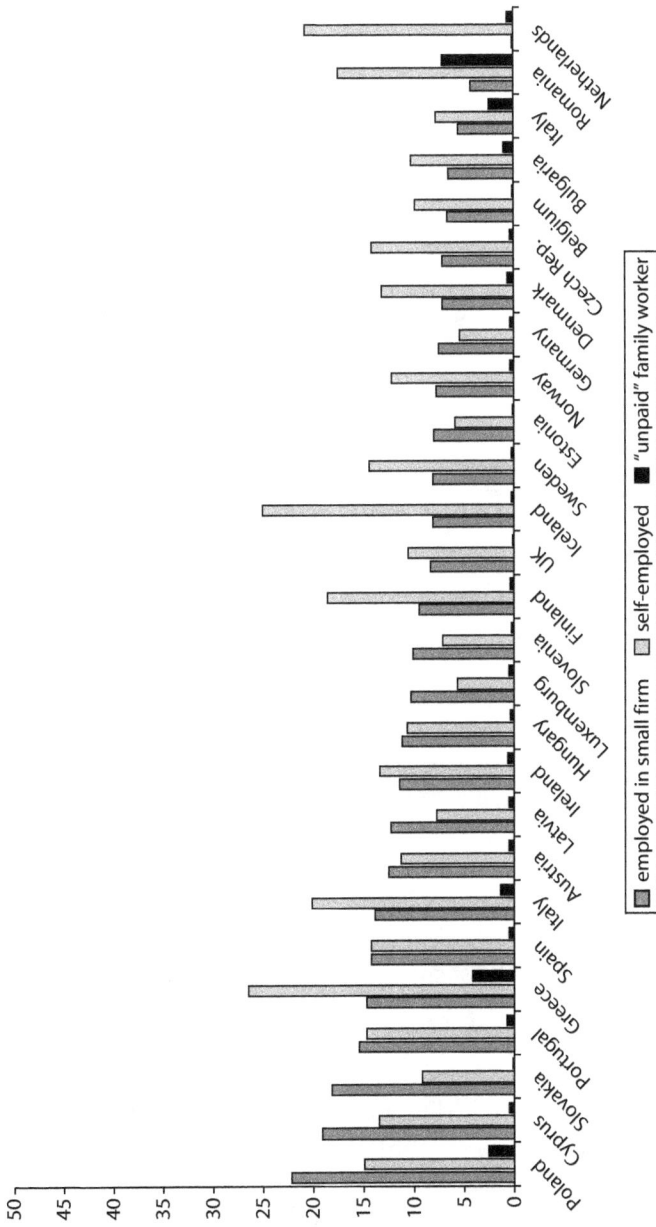

Legend: employed in small firm | self-employed | "unpaid" family worker

Source: Authors' estimates, based on Eurostat 2008.

Figure 1.3   Percentage of the Labor Force in Informal Employment: Social Insurance Criterion for Dependent Employed

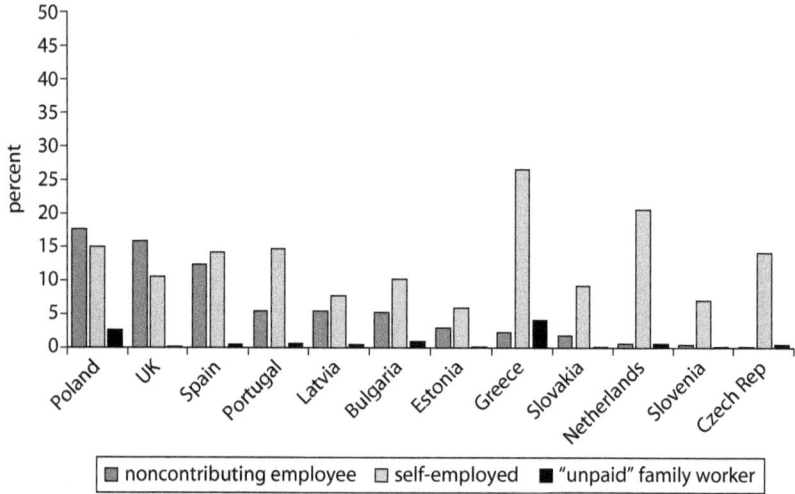

Source: Authors' estimates, EU SILC 2008.

male phenomenon, in contrast to findings from Latin America (see Perry et al. 2007). In age distribution, informality seems to be higher at the fringes of the labor market, that is, among the young and the old. In terms of job characteristics, informality is concentrated among the low-wage earners—unpaid family workers and those earning less than 50 percent of average wage. Informality is lowest in the public sector, including health and education services, and highest in agriculture, construction, trade and repair, and accommodation and food industries. The next section elaborates further and provides a detailed profile of the informally employed.

When countries are ranked according to our preferred proxy for informal employment—the share of the labor force in dependent work without a contract—a new picture emerges. Only two of the EU's new members are among the top 10: Cyprus and Slovenia. Greece, Ireland, the United Kingdom, Austria, and Portugal all have higher shares of employment without a labor contract. Figure 1.4 has two panels, designated a and b. Hazans (2011a) argues that because the theoretical and empirical literature indicates that the drivers of informal labor arrangements can also have an impact on unemployment and discouragement (occurring when people who would like to work postpone or stop searching for a job), indicators of informal employment should be presented as

Table 1.1   Informality Rates across Different Groups in Six New Member States, 2008 (percent)

	Bulgaria	Czech Republic	Estonia	Latvia	Poland	Slovakia	Overall
By employment status							
Self-employed	71.4	82.8	71.5	70.9	87.1	81.5	**83.9**
Employees	7.3	0.1	3.3	6.3	27.1	2.2	**16.2**
By sex							
Male	19.5	17.1	10.8	15.9	42.6	14.2	**31.5**
Female	12.9	8.9	4.6	8.6	35.5	6.0	**23.7**
By age							
15 to 24	19.3	7.8	6.9	11.0	44.6	7.7	**30.2**
25 to 39	15.4	12.2	7.4	12.6	35.6	10.2	**26.2**
40 to 54	15.7	15.8	7.8	13.4	40.5	11.0	**28.8**
55 to 64	17.9	13.2	7.2	9.7	45.2	10.5	**28.0**
65 or above	34.4	30.8	13.2	11.1	73.7	25.2	**48.4**
By income (Percent of AW)							
0	79.8	100.0	67.8	82.8	92.7	80.5	**91.7**
1 to 24	37.6	23.3	29.1	29.0	66.6	18.5	**55.4**
25 to 49	17.1	14.9	5.9	15.2	40.4	11.8	**30.0**
50 to 99	11.8	10.3	3.0	9.7	29.2	8.0	**19.5**
100 to 200	11.2	13.7	6.9	7.1	29.3	10.9	**20.9**
200 or greater	29.8	27.1	24.2	9.8	25.7	21.6	**25.4**
By sector							
Health services	3.3	2.1	1.9	2.6	17.8	4.2	**11.2**
Mining, manufacturing	7.6	7.7	3.9	7.8	27.5	8.3	**18.3**
Construction	22.6	31.2	14.4	21.1	49.7	27.4	**38.2**
Trade and repair	24.4	19.0	8.4	10.9	42.9	13.7	**32.0**
Transport and storage	13.6	9.2	10.3	11.0	40.1	8.1	**26.7**
Accommodation and food	19.0	19.1	6.8	10.9	49.8	7.6	**28.1**
ICT	10.0	13.0	9.4	4.5	25.6	6.5	**18.0**
Financial services	1.3	22.6	7.1	5.1	24.1	15.6	**20.1**
Professional services	14.1	17.8	5.0	10.8	31.7	12.2	**24.4**
Public sector	1.6	0.7	1.0	2.5	21.1	2.1	**11.5**
Education	1.1	2.0	1.1	1.8	15.8	2.7	**10.2**
Agriculture	54.3	26.9	33.2	46.7	93.2	15.4	**80.6**
Overall	**16.5**	**13.6**	**7.7**	**12.3**	**39.5**	**10.4**	**28.0**

Source: Koettl and Weber 2012.

a share of an "extended" labor force, in which discouraged job seekers are included (as in panel b). Readers will note that doing this does not change the relative ranking of countries very much.

As alluded to earlier, the European Social Survey (ESS) data, from which the third proxy for informal dependent employment is drawn, also

Figure 1.4   Extent of Informal Work by Contract Criterion

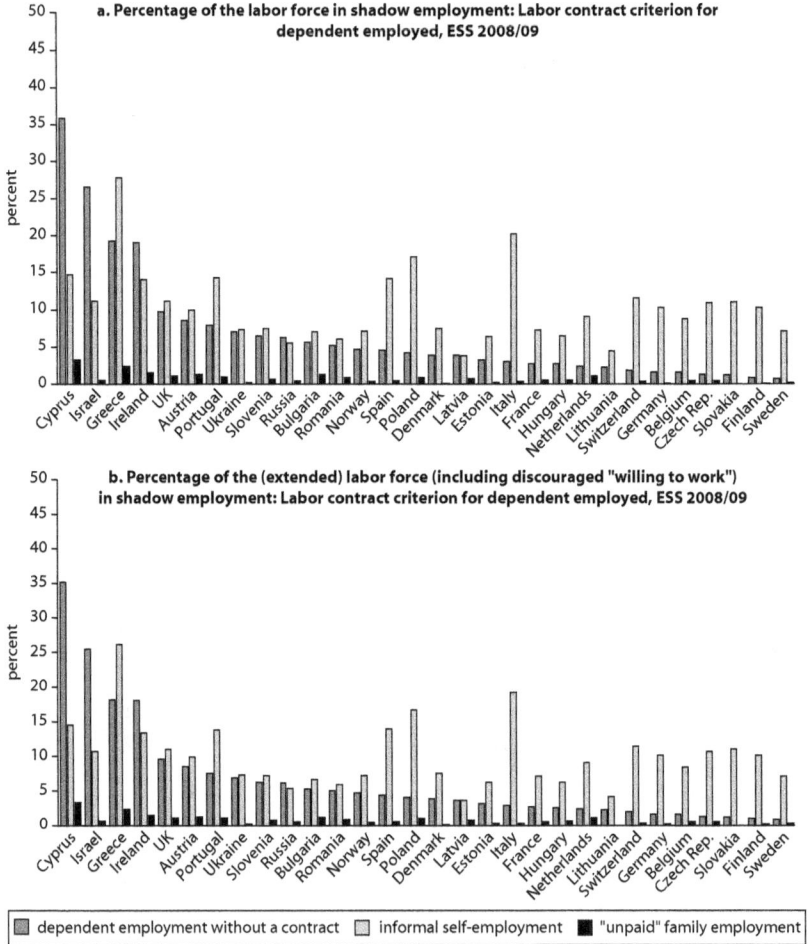

a. Percentage of the labor force in shadow employment: Labor contract criterion for dependent employed, ESS 2008/09

b. Percentage of the (extended) labor force (including discouraged "willing to work") in shadow employment: Labor contract criterion for dependent employed, ESS 2008/09

| ☐ dependent employment without a contract   ☐ informal self-employment   ■ "unpaid" family employment |

Source: Hazans 2011a, for this volume.

allow a more refined measurement and categorization of those in self-employment. The ESS asks the self-employed and employers how many people they employ, if any. Then, by using the ILO's firm size criterion and combining it with the respondent's occupation, "informal self-employed" (those in nonprofessional occupations who employ five or fewer workers) can be separated from the professional self-employed and those with more than five employees, whose activities are more likely to be regulated and taxed. Only three of the EU's new members—Poland,

Cyprus, and Slovakia—are in the top 10 ranked by informal self-employment. That list is led by Greece and Italy but also includes Spain, Portugal, Ireland, Switzerland, and the United Kingdom.

Profile of People Working Informally

The informal labor force as a whole is made up mostly of men, particularly in the new EU member states (figure 1.5). Regression analysis for this book that controlled for the higher rates of participation of men than women in the labor market confirms this result.[2] In Bulgaria, Estonia, Hungary, Latvia, and Slovakia, the proportion of males employed without a contract is much higher than that in formal employment. But this is also the case in Denmark, Greece, Norway, and the United Kingdom. In the 12 EU countries for which a social insurance criterion can be used to sort informal from formal dependent employees, nine have a higher percentage of noncontributors who are men. As has been found in other regions (see Perry et al. 2007, for Latin America; and Oviedo, Thomas, and Karakurum-Ozdemir 2009 for other world regions), a significant difference in gender composition appears among formal work, informal self-employment, and informal dependent employment. In all European countries except Latvia, the proportion of males among the informally self-employed is higher than among formal employees. But the difference is less stark in the EU's new members. The prevalence of men in informal self-employment is greater among the wealthier EU members in the North and South and particularly in the West.

The part of the labor force that is informally engaged shows a significantly different age profile than the part in formal employment (figure 1.6). The age profile of formal workers is noticeably more homogeneous, with the majority in the 25–54 age group across Europe. Workers without a contract are more likely to be younger (under 25). The prevalence of youth is less obvious when the social insurance identifier is used, but in six of the 12 countries for which it is available, half or more of noncontributing workers are age 35 and under. In Slovenia 97 percent of noncontributing workers are 35 and under, and of those, 67 percent are 25 and under. Researchers sometimes attribute the youthful profile of employment without a contract to the costs of providing formal employment pricing out workers with lower productivity; it can also reflect informal apprenticeship structures. People who are informally self-employed are, in contrast, more likely to be older that those in dependent employment, informal and formal. In the formerly planned economies of

34

Figure 1.5 Informal Work in Europe Is Mainly Taken Up by Men

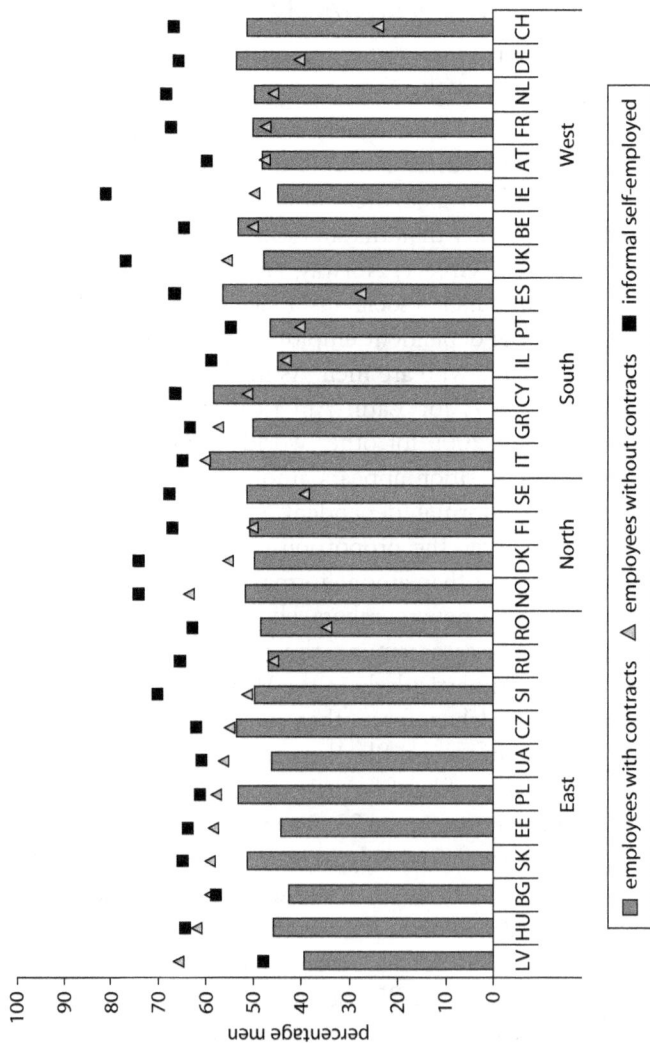

Source: Hazans 2011a.

Figure 1.6   Age Profile of People in Formal and Informal Employment

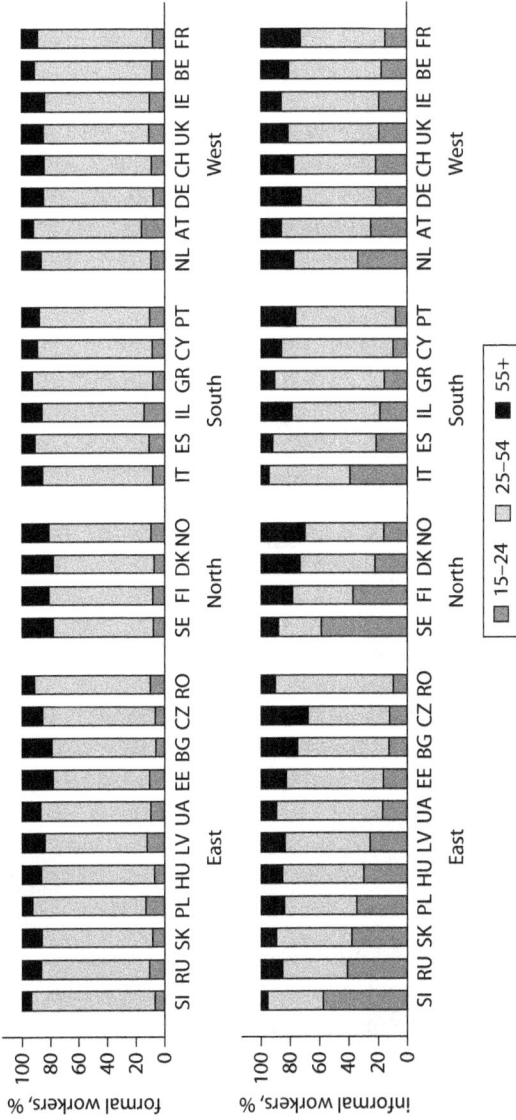

15–24   25–54   55+

Source: Hazans 2011a, using ESS data.
Note: Formal: employee with a contract; informal: employee without a contract.

the East, a part of this segment of the labor force is made up of workers displaced by privatization of state-owned enterprises and downsizing of public administration. However, the significantly older age profile of self-employed people can also reflect the time it takes to build skills and contacts and to raise start-up capital, particularly in places where credit is dear or has been constrained.

Educational attainment differs significantly between people in formal and in informal jobs (figure 1.7). Across Europe, people who have only completed basic education are more likely to be informally employed. Yet the pattern is far more pronounced in southern and western European countries than among the new members from the East. In the new member states most of those employed informally (about two-thirds) have completed secondary education. With the exceptions of Poland and Romania, the share of the informally employed who have completed secondary education is about the same as the share of the formally employed. However, in Belgium, Cyprus, France, Greece, Israel, Romania, Russia, Ukraine, and the United Kingdom, 20 percent to 30 percent of informal employees hold university degrees. When the social insurance criterion is used to identify informal dependent workers, the share of noncontributing employees in the new member states (Bulgaria, Czech Republic, Estonia, Latvia, Poland, Slovenia, and Slovakia) who have at least a secondary education is 70 percent and higher. In Spain, 60 percent of employees who are not contributing to social insurance have higher education.

Among those employed informally, a larger share are doing manual, low-skill jobs than among those employed formally. However, those who are employed informally are also more likely to be doing skilled manual work. A higher share of people employed formally than of the informally employed are doing high-skill, nonmanual work. But in the Czech Republic, Hungary, Romania, and Slovenia, a substantial share of those employed informally are engaged in high-skill, nonmanual work. The distribution of manual and nonmanual work between the informally and formally employed is more pronounced in some of the southern members of the EU than among the new members. For instance, in Italy, Portugal, and Spain, a greater share of informally employed people are engaged in manual, low-skill work than in any of the new member states (figure 1.8).

The limited sample sizes of the ESS constrain the extent to which the distribution of formal and informal employment across economic sectors can be examined (figure 1.9). But even with a reduced set of sector

Figure 1.7 Educational Attainment of People in Formal and Informal Employment

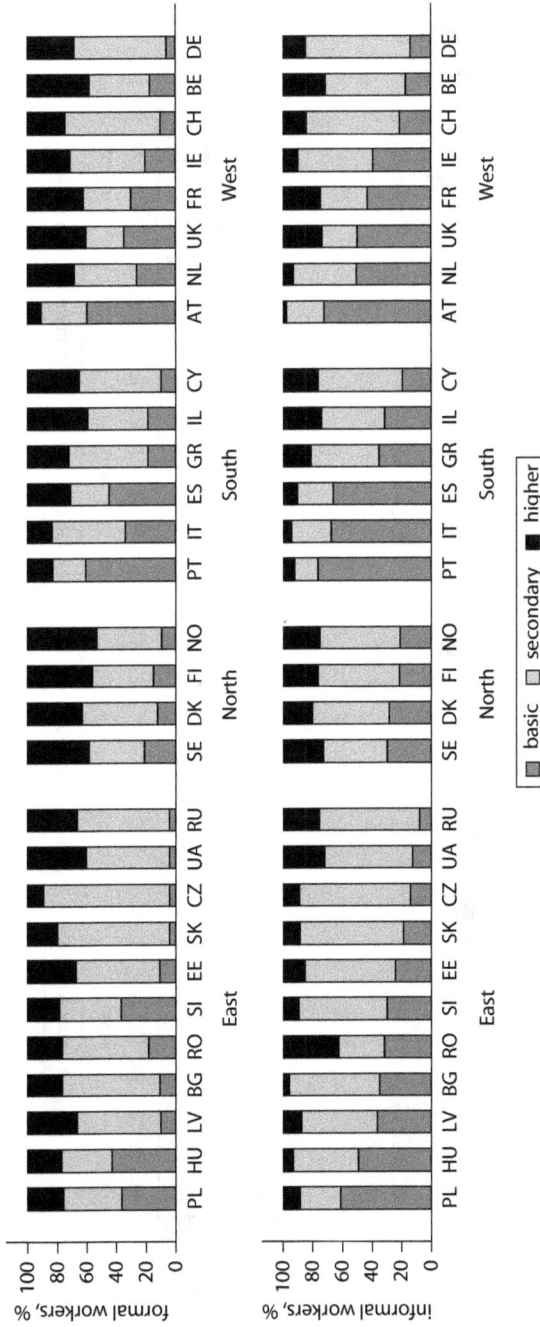

Source: Hazans 2011a, using ESS data.
Note: Work status refers to the survey week. Formal: employee with a contract; informal: employee without a contract; self-employed excluded.

Figure 1.8 Distribution of the Formally and Informally Employed across Skilled and Nonskilled, Manual and Nonmanual Work

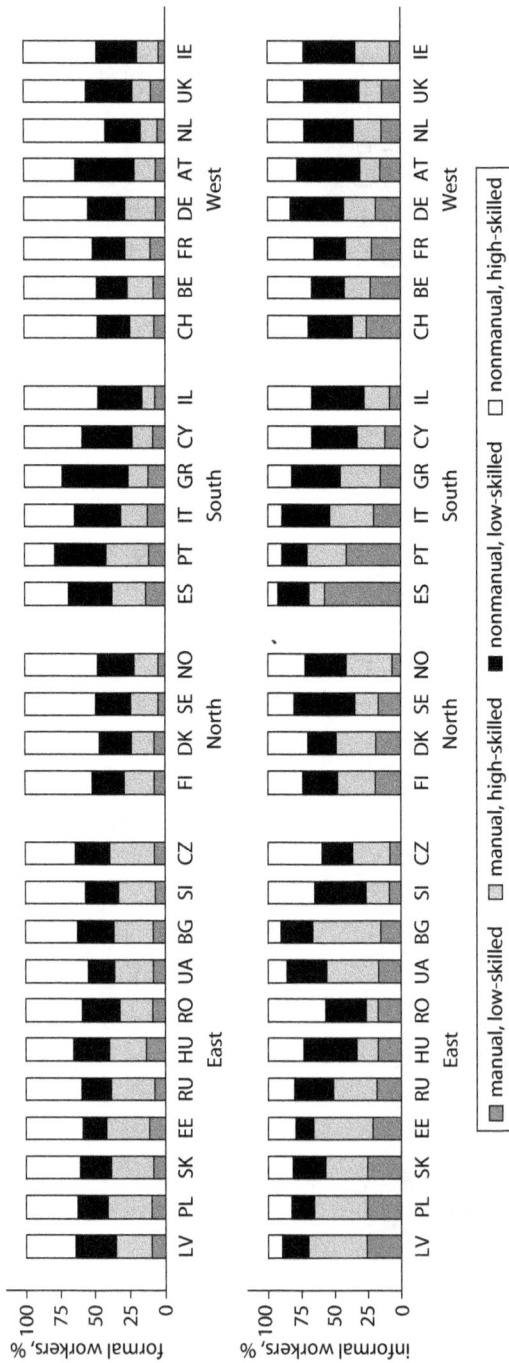

Source: Hazans 2011a, using ESS data.

Note: Formal: employee with a contract; informal: employee without a contract; self-employed excluded.

Figure 1.9 Distribution of Formally and Informally Employed across Economic Sectors

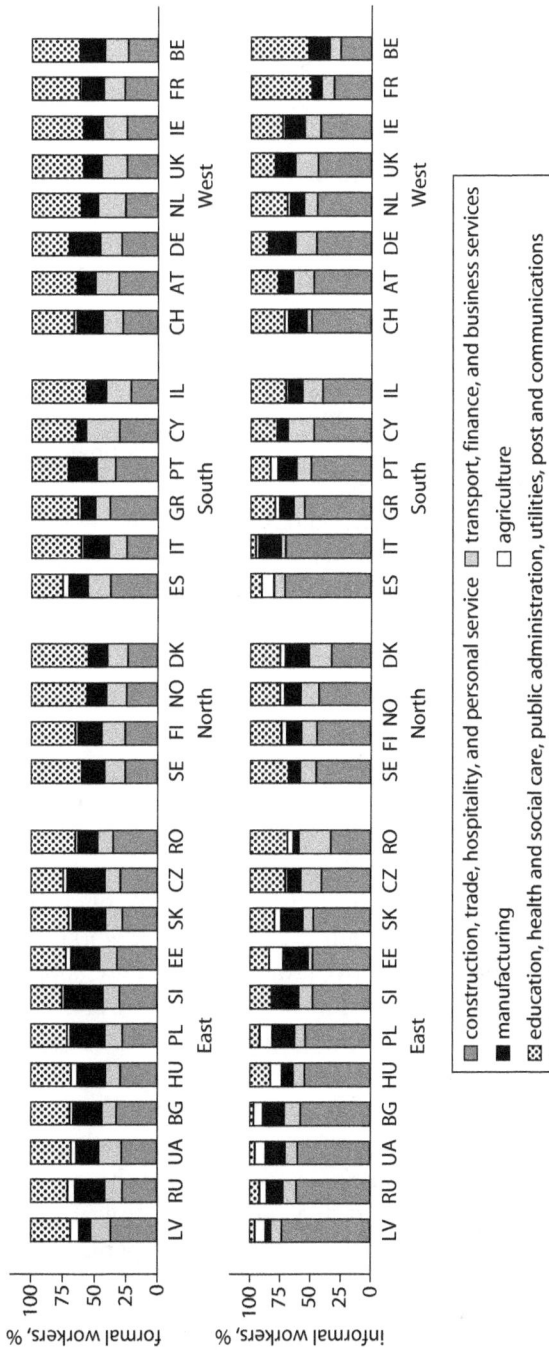

Legend:
- construction, trade, hospitality, and personal service
- transport, finance, and business services
- manufacturing
- agriculture
- education, health and social care, public administration, utilities, post and communications

Source: Hazans 2011a, using ESS data.
Note: Formal: employee with a contract; informal: employee without a contract; self-employed excluded.

classifications, patterns similar to those found in other regions emerge. Informal employment is most prevalent in construction and hospitality. Workers in auto repair and other personal and household services are also more likely to be informally employed. Although a significant share of those employed informally work in agriculture in the new member states, it is only a minor segment (less than 5 percent) and compares with the shares in Portugal and Spain.

The ESS also includes questions that allow a dimension of analysis not often explored in discussions of the informal labor market: groups suffering from different forms of discrimination. Figure 1.10 shows the percentages of formally employed workers, the informally employed, and the informally self-employed who report belonging to a group that suffers from discrimination. The ESS question is phrased, "Would you describe yourself as being a member of a group that is discriminated against in this country?" and specifies discrimination on the grounds of race, nationality, religion, language, ethnicity, age, gender, sexuality, and disability. Responses indicate that a significantly higher share of informal employees consider themselves part of a group that suffers discrimination than is observed among formal employees and the informally self-employed (Russia is a notable exception). But once again, these differences appear greater in some of the southern members of old Europe, Greece, and Spain. The difference is greatest, however, in Finland.

Although undoubtedly subjective, the responses depicted in figure 1.10 provide some food for thought. They act as a segue to a discussion of minorities and people of an immigrant background—both categories into which respondents can more objectively sort—and how these groups are reflected in the formal and informal portions of the labor force. Figure 1.11 presents the share in each category of workers who are part of a native, nonmigrant minority group. Immediately apparent is a substantially higher portion of nonmigrant minorities working informally in the EU new member states (and countries in Europe's extended eastern neighborhood) than in the northern, southern, or western countries. The data do not identify exactly which native minorities, and their identity is likely to vary greatly from country to country, depending on the geography. From anecdotes, one might expect Roma to be disproportionately represented among noncontracted workers in Bulgaria and Slovakia. However, in Hungary and Romania, where the population of Roma is substantial, native minorities appear as likely to be formally as to be informally engaged in the labor market. The available data do not allow us to examine this dimension of informal work in greater depth. However, the

Figure 1.10   Informal Workers Who Say That They Belong to Groups Suffering Discrimination

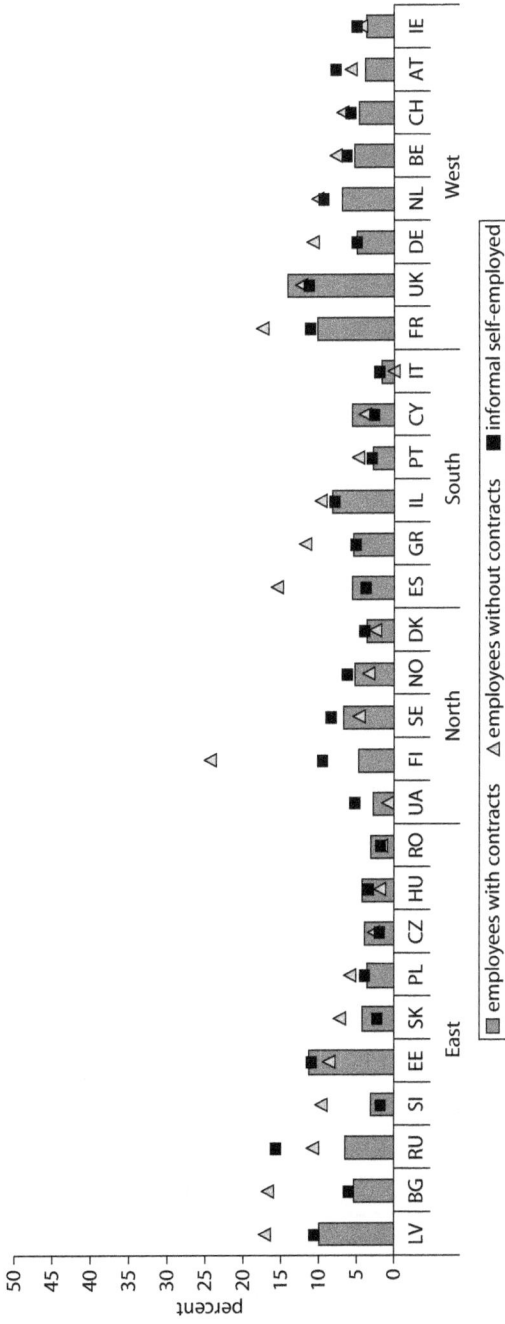

Source: Hazans 2011a, for this volume.

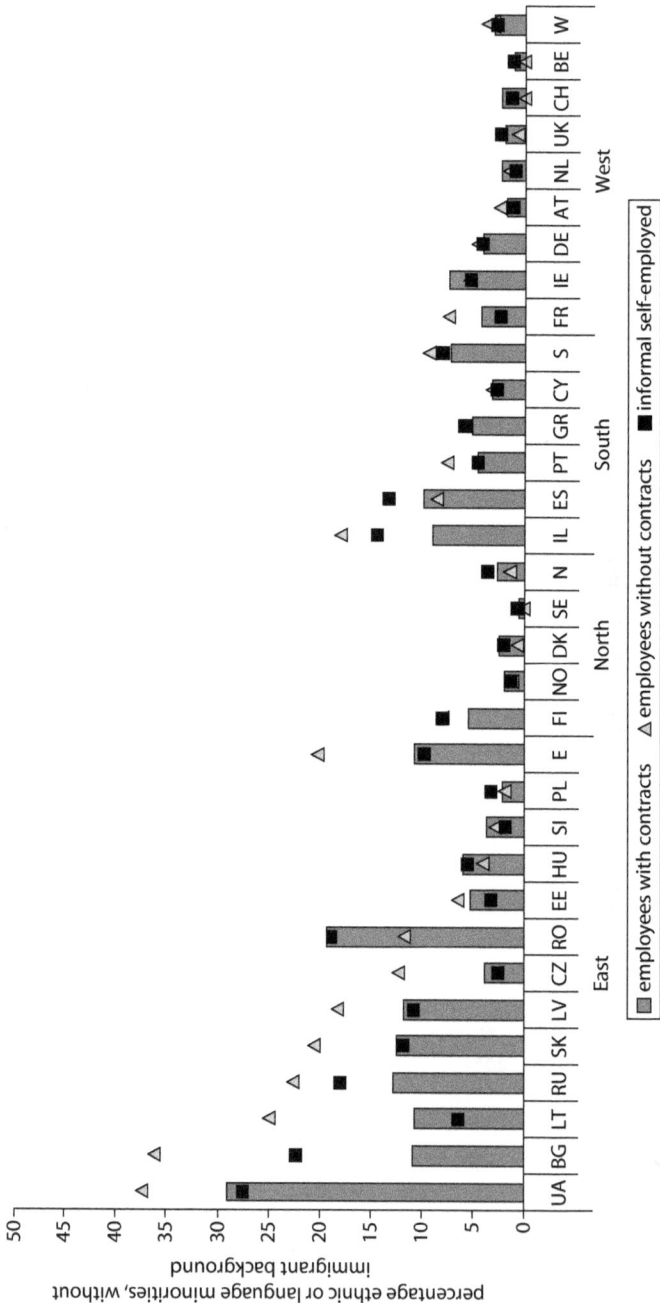

Figure 1.11   Are Those Working Informally More Likely to Belong to a Native Ethnic Minority?

Source: Hazans 2011a.

World Bank is currently participating in efforts to increase the microdata available that would allow a closer look at the extent to which informal work is a manifestation of, or a contributor to, the exclusion of Roma communities in Europe.

Figures 1.12 and 1.13 present the extent to which informal employment is a form of labor market engagement closely associated with immigration. Across the wealthier countries of Europe, the West African street vendor, the East Asian beautician, the Antipodean "man with van," the South Asian owner of a refreshment stand, and the Latin American selling cigarettes in the metro are popular stereotypes. The Polish plumber, the Latvian fruit picker, and the Romanian housekeeper are more recent additions to the list since the EU's eastward expansion. It is reasonable to expect that restrictions on immigration and the right to work would be reflected in the profile of informal employment and self-employment. But that profile might also reflect the power of community networks and clusters of particular nationalities that can offer opportunities for employment and influence prospective emigrants' choices of where to go. These networks develop quickly, can persist over generations, and influence the character of some forms of employment even among naturalized citizens or those with an immigrant background but born with a right to work.

Immigrants without the right to work—measured by Hazans (2011a) as the rights withheld or conferred on an individual in a given country (and in a given year) because of that person's nationality—are indeed more likely to be in informal dependent employment in Spain, Greece, and Portugal, but not elsewhere in the wealthier member countries of the EU. The eastern flank of the EU does not yet appear to be a popular destination for migrants, and its informal labor market appears dominated by local talent. When the social insurance criterion is used to identify informal dependent workers, 99 percent of noncontributing workers in Bulgaria, the Czech Republic, Poland, and Slovakia are native born, as are 85 percent of noncontributing workers in Estonia and Latvia. In the Netherlands, Portugal, Spain, and the United Kingdom more than 90 percent of noncontributors are natives. Only in Greece is there a substantial non-native portion of noncontributing workers: 10 percent are immigrants from other EU countries, and 33 percent immigrated from farther afield.

Among the new member states, immigrants who have the right to work and those born locally from an immigrant background are more commonly found in informal employment only in the Czech Republic, Estonia, and Slovakia. In Romania, this group makes up a significantly

Figure 1.12 Share of Immigrants without the Right to Work because of Nationality in Formal and Informal Employment

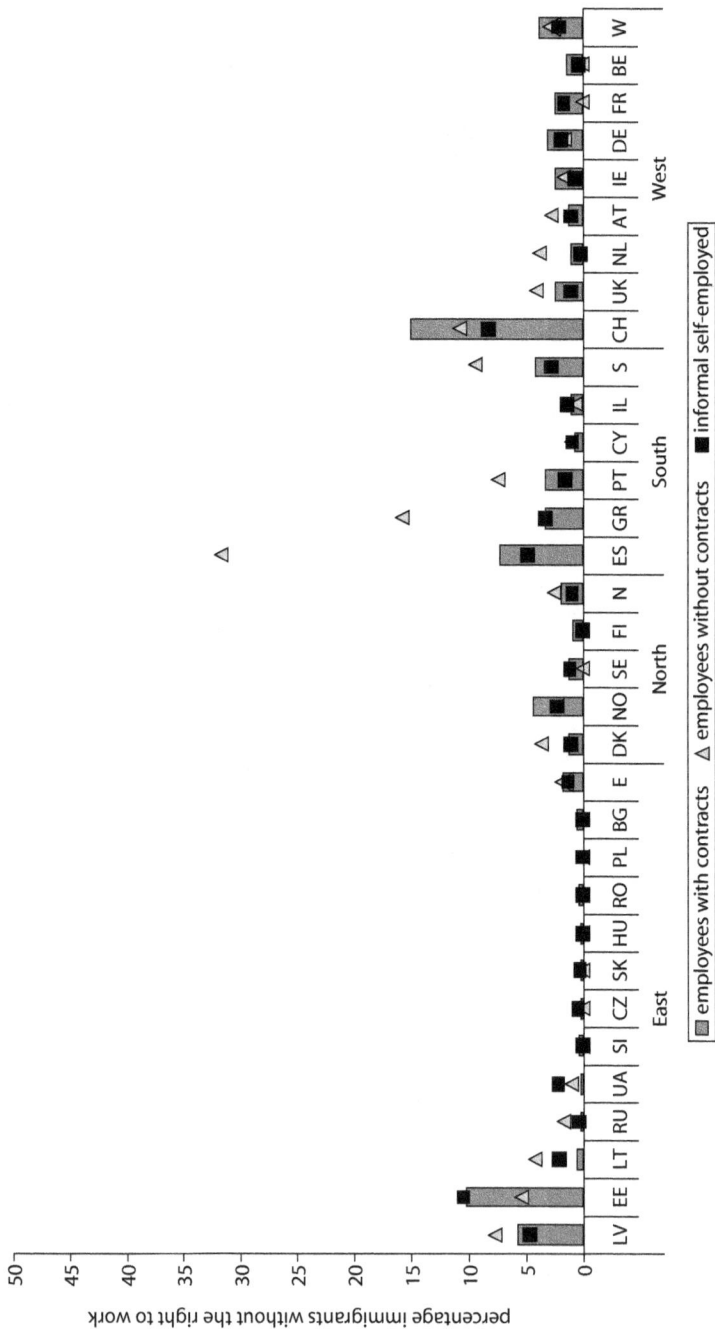

Source: Hazans 2011a.

44

Figure 1.13   Share of Natives with Immigrant Background and Immigrants with the Right to Work because of Nationality in Formal and Informal Employment

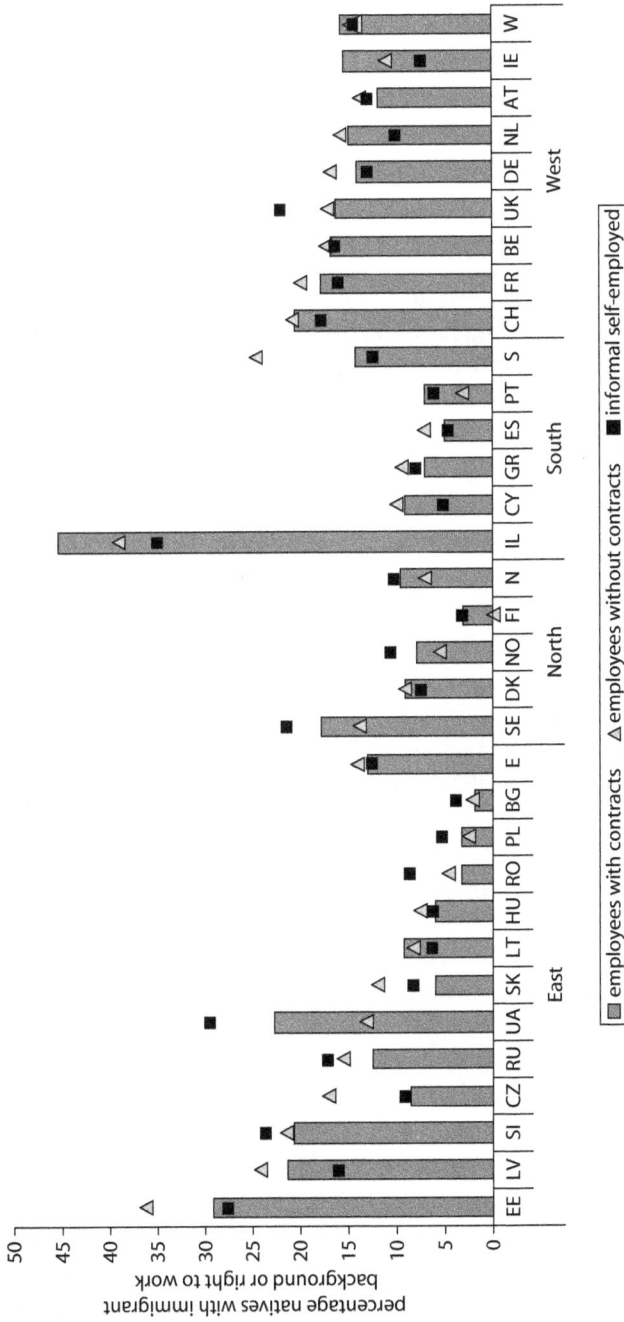

Source: Hazans 2011a.

greater share of the informally self-employed. In the EU's western members, although first- and second-generation immigrants with the right to work make up between a tenth and a quarter of informal dependent and self-employed workers, their representation does not appear significantly different than that in formal work. The caricatures mentioned previously may be fading over time.

The Economic Cycle and Movement across the Labor Market

Many believe that entry to the market for informal labor can be a way of coping that firms and households resort to when economic growth falters and during crises when economies actually contract. It is sometimes characterized as a "safety net" where unemployment insurance does not exist or fails to serve a significant part of the workforce. However, the theoretical and empirical literatures are fairly ambivalent on this matter: The share of undeclared work can vary with the economic cycle, depending sometimes on the extent of segmentation in the labor market, the degree to which informal work arrangements are more prevalent in the "tradable" sectors (such as manufacturing, agriculture, mineral extraction, and tourism) relative to "untradable" household and business services (hairdressing, cleaning), and circumstances peculiar to a given country at a given time. Here we present statistics describing how the portions of the labor force that are engaged formally, engaged informally, or unemployed have moved in the years leading up to and including the global financial and economic crisis.

First, however, figure 1.14 shows that a greater share of informal employees (than of formal workers) report experiencing long spells of unemployment. Their experience is also significantly different from those currently in informal self-employment, perhaps indicating that informal employment is a substitute safety net. People's experiences with unemployment vary more in the wealthier members of the EU than in the new member states. Only in Latvia and Bulgaria does the share of people currently employed without a contract who have experienced long-term unemployment compare with the share in Belgium, the Netherlands, the United Kingdom, Portugal, and Italy, where it ranges from one-quarter to a third of informal dependent workers.

Figure 1.15 exploits repeated waves of the ESS that were collected during Europe's high-growth period (2004–07), and its observations extend into the first year of the economic slowdown (2008) and then actual contraction (2009) in many European countries. The data show an

Figure 1.14 Informal Workers Who Have Experienced Long-Term Unemployment

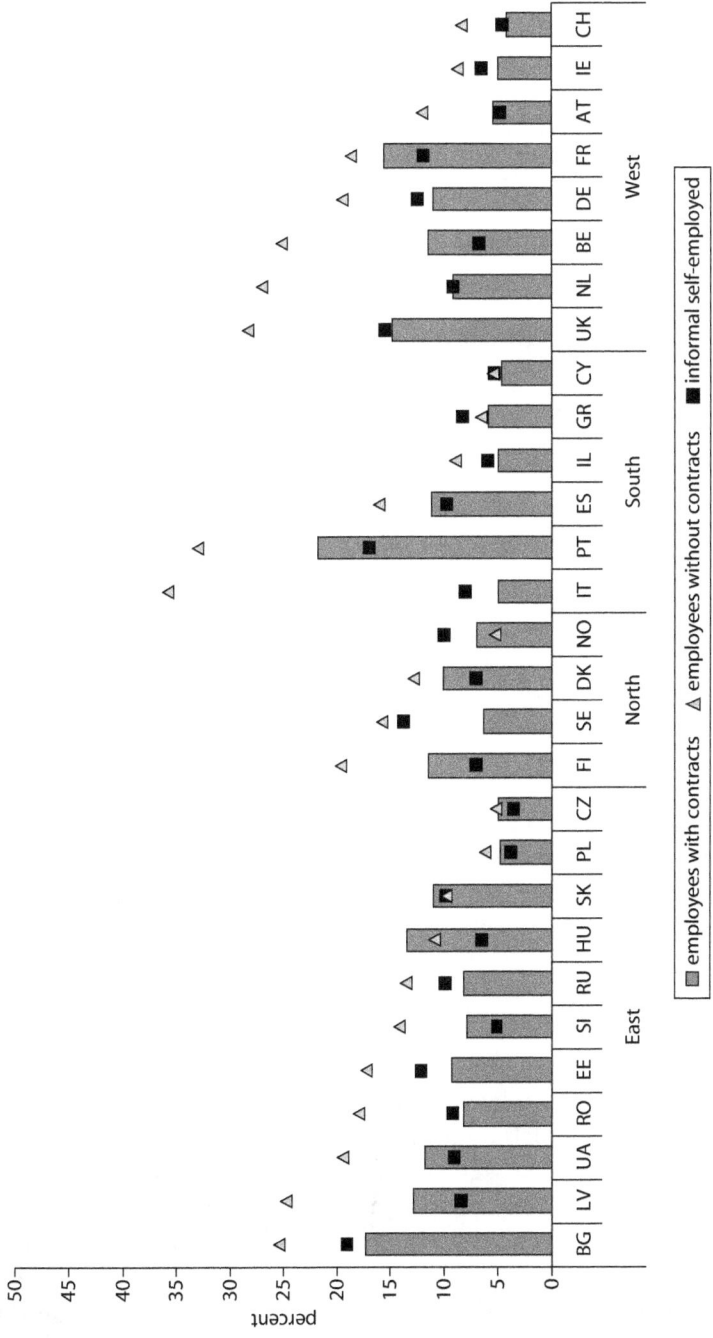

Legend: ■ employees with contracts △ employees without contracts ■ informal self-employed

East: BG, LV, UA, RO, EE, SI, RU, HU, SK, PL, CZ
North: FI, SE, DK, NO
South: IT, PT, ES, IL, GR, CY
West: UK, NL, BE, DE, FR, AT, IE, CH

percent (y-axis): 0, 5, 10, 15, 20, 25, 30, 35, 40, 45, 50

Source: Hazans 2011a.

Figure 1.15   In Most of Europe, Informal Employment Falls as Unemployment Rises

within-country changes in unemployment and informality rates,
ESS rounds 3 (2006–07) vs. 2 (2004–05); 4 (2008–09) vs. 3 (2006–07)

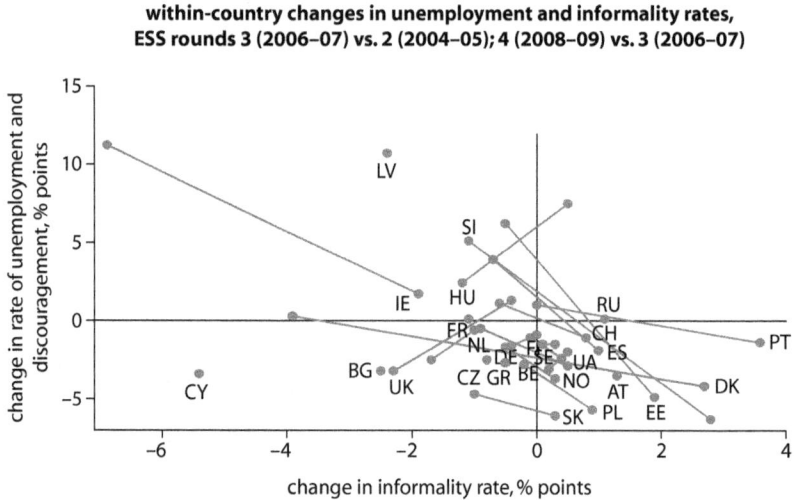

Source: Hazans 2011a.
Note: Informality rate excludes self-employed; connected points correspond to the same country, with the country label at the earlier point; single points, for countries observed only twice, show round 4 vs. round 3 (round 2 for GR and CZ); base-labor force extended to include discouraged workers.

inverse relationship between the changes in the share of the labor force that is unemployed (and discouraged) and the share that is employed informally (without a contract). The pattern of the scatter plot is downward-sloping from left to right, illustrating this relationship across countries. When unemployment rises, informal employment does not appear to expand to fill the gap—the positive quadrant of figure 1.15 is virtually empty. The connected points—showing how the relationship has changed in the same country over time—also slope downward from left to right, with few exceptions. Only for Hungary, the Netherlands, and the United Kingdom are there observed positive slopes, which suggest that in those three countries, after accounting for time-invariant country-specific factors, unemployment and informal work are positively related, as the textbook models predict.

A cyclical informal segment of the labor force could show a "rapid scale-up" effect. When the economy is growing as quickly as it was in almost all of the new member states of the EU, firms may not be able to afford the time to comply with rules and regulations if they are to remain competitive (Hazans 2011a). A complementary explanation might be that prior to the global financial crisis and the onset of contraction late in

2008, the sectors where growth was fastest across Europe were nontrad-able (construction and housing) services where—as shown in the prior section—informal work is most prevalent. To the extent that informal work arrangements were also prevalent in tradable sectors, such as agri-culture (fruit picking) and tourism (hospitality), liberalization and inte-gration could also explain the expansion of informal work during the years of economic boom and its rapid contraction as unemployment soared during the crisis.

Changes in the aggregate shares of the labor force in informal depen-dent work, in informal self-employment, and unemployed (including discouraged) are presented in greater detail in table A.1 in the statistical appendix. The data distinguish between changes over the years of growth (2004–07) and in the slowdown and recession (2008–09), indicating where the changes are statistically significant. Between the second and third rounds of the ESS (a period extending from 2004 to 2007) the share of employees without contracts increased significantly in Portugal (3.6 points), Denmark (2.7 points), Estonia (2.0 points), and Spain (1.0 points). In Portugal and Estonia the increase was accompanied by a com-parable decrease in the share of informal self-employment. In Denmark and Spain, however, informal self-employment rose with the increase in informal dependent work. A significant fall in total informal employment during the period of rapid growth in Europe is observed only in the United Kingdom (3.3 points) and in Slovenia (2.6 points).

As growth slowed and economies began to contract in most parts of Europe (in table A.1, the change from round three to round four of the ESS), there was a significant decrease in the extent of informal dependent work from 2006/07 to 2008/09. In contrast, informal self-employment increased significantly in Estonia, the Netherlands, and Poland; elsewhere, the increase in informal self-employment was small and not statistically significant. That could indicate that informal dependent workers are the first ones to be fired when economic growth slows, which would not be surprising given that they represent the most flexible part of the labor market, where no employment protection is afforded to workers. Informal self-employment, however, seems to be more of a substitute safety net during times of crisis than informal dependent employment.

Using the profile of informally engaged workers drawn from a specially designed survey of informal employment in Poland, conducted by the Centre for Economic and Social Research (CASE), Walewski (2011), for this volume, constructed a pseudopanel of informal employment extending from 2003 to 2008. Because the regularly deployed Polish labor force survey does not include the rich set of identifiers that CASE used to examine informal work in Poland, Walewski used propensity score matching to piece together three profiles of people working informally and showed how the share of individuals in the labor force who match the profiles shifted over the years. For all three profiles of informal work, the probability of informal engagement in Poland grew rapidly during the years of high economic growth, up to 2006 when the economy started to slow, and fell sharply thereafter (see figure 1.16).

When they applied the same tools of analysis that Bosch and Maloney (2008) used to examine worker movements in Argentina, Brazil, and Mexico, the analysis by Militaru and Mocanu (2012) of labor force transitions by workers in Romania revealed similar patterns, as did the analysis of the Czech Republic and Slovakia by Nikolovova, Perthold, and Vosar (2012) (both for this book).

In Romania, the analysis benefited from superior microdata that allow for the preferred contract criterion to identify informal dependent workers. However, the small sample sizes do not permit a separate analysis of movements in and out of self-employment. The probability of various transitions in Romania—from formal to informal employment or from

Figure 1.16   Probability of Informal Work in Poland Grew in the High-Growth Years

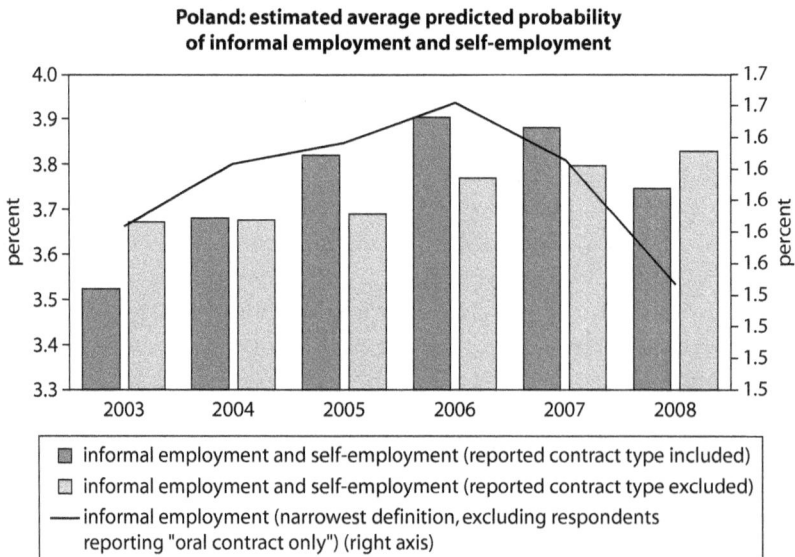

Poland: estimated average predicted probability of informal employment and self-employment

- ▣ informal employment and self-employment (reported contract type included)
- ▢ informal employment and self-employment (reported contract type excluded)
- —— informal employment (narrowest definition, excluding respondents reporting "oral contract only") (right axis)

Source: Walewski 2011, for this volume.

either of those to unemployment, as well as in and out of the labor force—are presented in figure 1.17. As panel a shows, the probability of moving from informal to formal employment rose in the growth years prior to 2008, as did the probability of moving from unemployment into formal work (panel b). But during the same high-growth period, the probability of moving from unemployment into informal work (panel d) rose higher and faster, exhibiting the "rapid scale-up" suggested earlier.

Unlike the Romanian case, for the Czech Republic and Slovakia, only the (least satisfying) firm size variable is available to proxy for informal dependent employment. However, the sample sizes of the Labor Force Surveys (LFS) in both countries allow for a differentiated look at movements in and out of self-employment. From 1998, unemployment in the Czech Republic and Slovakia followed the cycle with the customary lag, although it appears more pronounced in Slovakia. The share of the labor force working informally (proxied in figure 1.18 by employment in small firms, or "SW10," and self-employment) in Slovakia appears to have moved relentlessly upward during the growth period and to have dropped only slightly as growth contracted in the recent crisis. In the Czech Republic, employment in small firms followed a path more apparently countercyclical to growth, while the share of the labor force in self-employment seems more procyclical up to 2005 but countercyclical thereafter.

By linking the 18-month rotating panels of respondents in both the Czech and Slovak labor force surveys, using matching techniques, Nikolovova, Perthold, and Vosar (2012) estimated transition probabilities across types of labor market activity, including unemployment and movements in and out of the labor market. During the high-growth period from 2004 to 2008, the probability of movement into formal work was highest. However, the growth period also raised the likelihood of movements into both forms of informal work. The speed and depth of the economic contraction similarly raised the probability of movements out of all types of employment into unemployment and out of the labor market.

Within these extreme movements, however, less-obvious patterns can be detected. In the Czech Republic from 2001 up to 2008, the probability of people's transitioning from employment in a small firm to formal employment oscillated seasonally between 2 percent and 4 percent, with little apparent relation to GDP growth. The likelihood of movement from self-employment to formal employment moved within a similar range but appears to have been even less responsive to GDP. In Slovakia

Figure 1.17   In Romania Movement from Unemployment into Informal Work Was Greater and Faster than into Formal Work

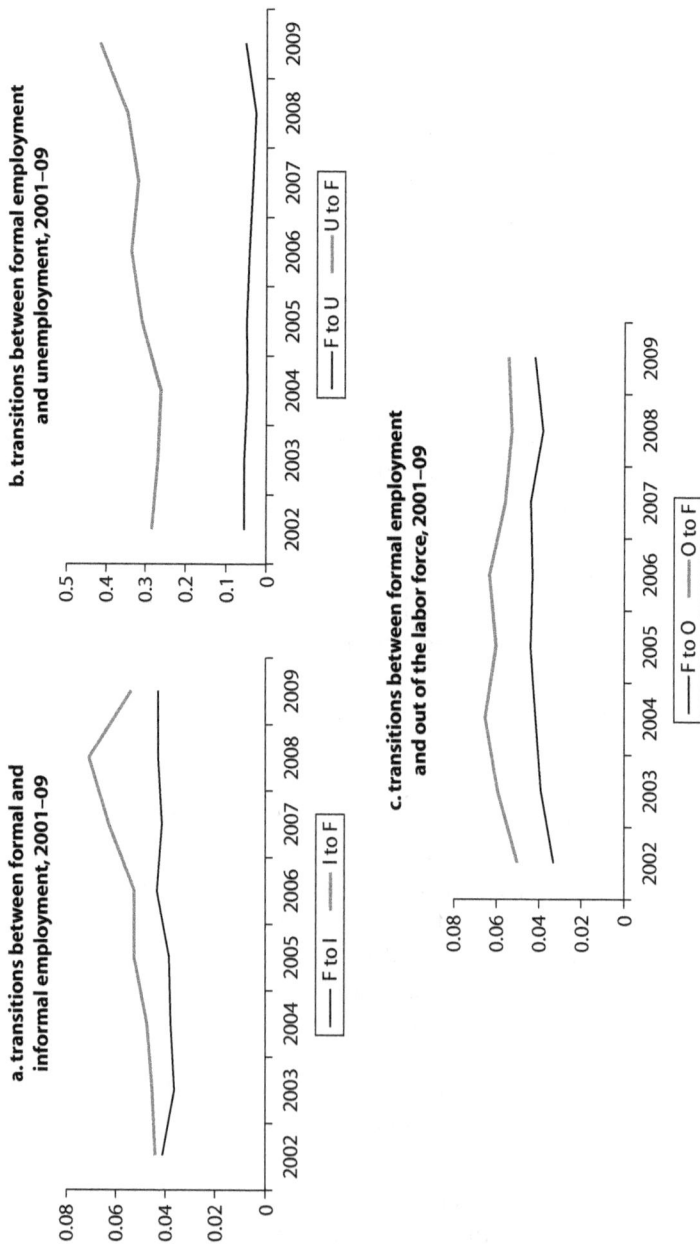

a. transitions between formal and
informal employment, 2001–09

b. transitions between formal employment
and unemployment, 2001–09

c. transitions between formal employment
and out of the labor force, 2001–09

(continued next page)

d. transitions between informal employment and unemployment, 2001–09

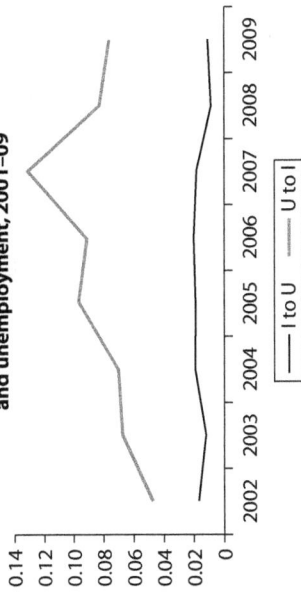

— I to U   — U to I

e. transitions between informal employment and out of the labor force, 2001–09

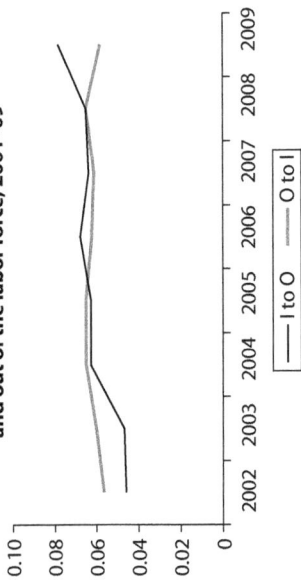

— I to O   — O to I

f. transitions between unemployment and out of the labor force, 2001–09

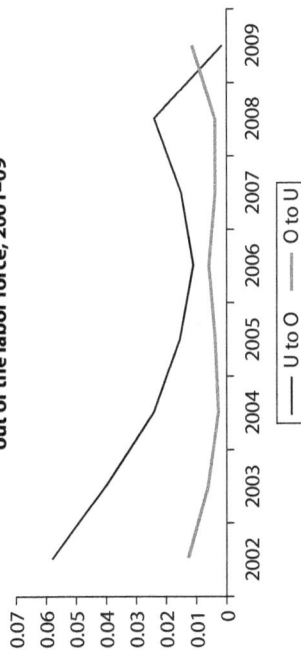

— U to O   — O to U

Source: Militaru and Mocanu 2012, for this volume.
Note: Transition probabilities are instantaneous transition rates for each two consecutive years.

53

Figure 1.18   The Share of the Labor Force in Informal Work Was Relatively Stable in the Czech Republic and the Slovak Republic

a. GDP growth and unemployment

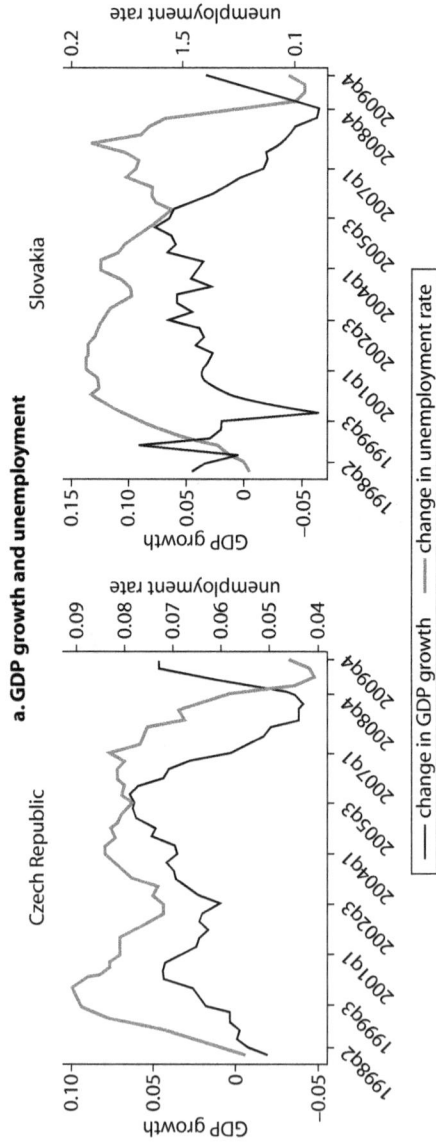

(continued next page)

b. GDP growth, informal dependent (SW10), and self-employment (SE)

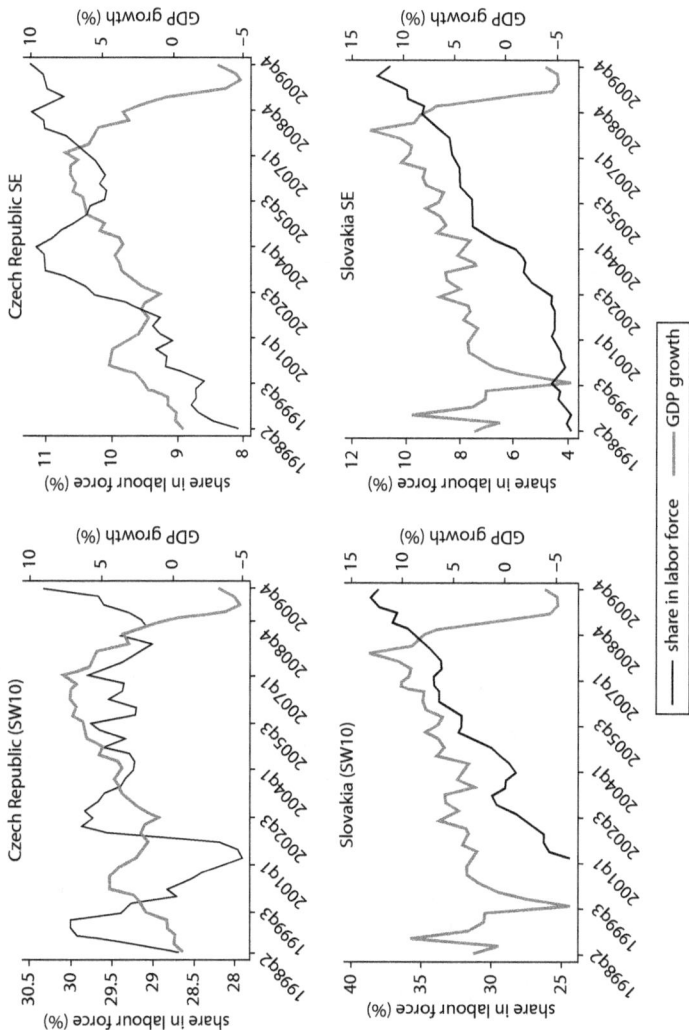

Czech Republic (SW10)

Czech Republic SE

Slovakia (SW10)

Slovakia SE

share in labour force (%)

GDP growth (%)

— share in labor force   — GDP growth

Source: Nikolovova, Perthold, and Vosar 2012, for this volume.

55

Figure 1.19   The Probability of Moving from Formal Employment and Informal Employment to Unemployment Was Similar in the Czech Republic and the Slovak Republic

a. Transitions to unemployment from employment in formal sector and small firms

Czech Republic (SW 5)

Slovakia (SW 5)

b. Transitions between employment in formal sector and in small firms

Czech Republic (SW5)

Slovakia (SW 5)

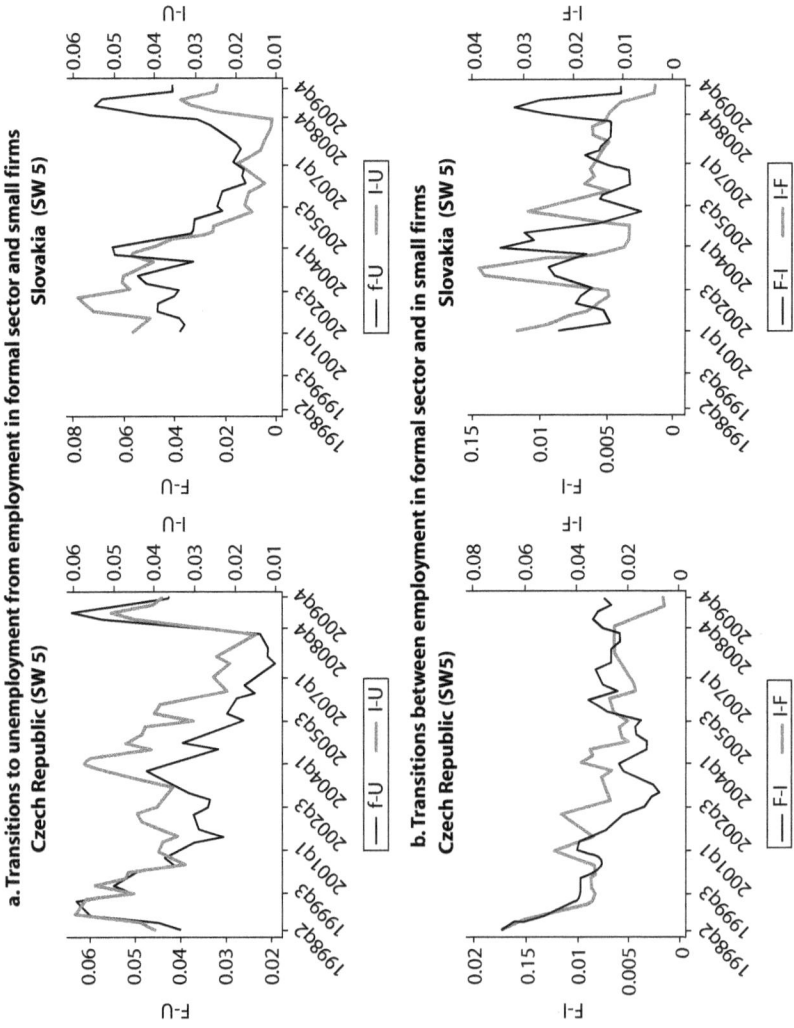

(continued next page)

c. Transitions out of the labor force from employment in formal sector and small firms

Czech Republic (SW 5)

Slovakia (SW 5)

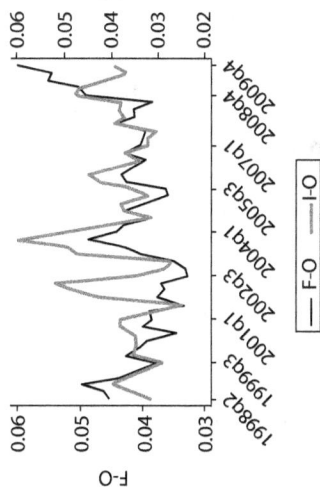

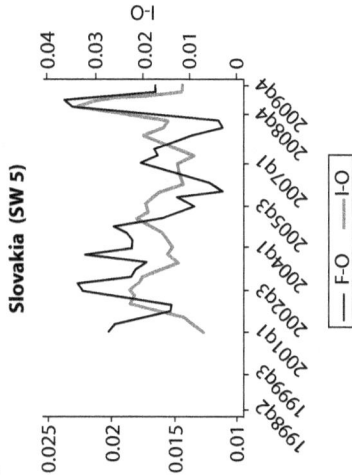

Source: Nikolovova, Perthold, and Vosar 2012, for this volume.

Notes: a. F–U; transitions from formal sector into unemployment. I–U; transitions from informal sector into unemployment. The underlying transitions are computed from the intensity matrices computed separately for every quarter and denote the raw instantaneous probability of transitions between the respective states.

b. F–I; transitions from formal sector into informal sector. I–F; transitions from informal sector into formal sector. The underlying transitions are computed from the intensity matrices computed separately for every quarter and denote the raw instantaneous probability of transitions between the respective states.

c. F–G; transitions from formal sector into informal sector. I–G; transitions from informal sector into formal sector. The underlying transitions are computed from the intensity matrices computed separately for every quarter and denote the raw instantaneous probability of transitions between the respective states.

throughout the same period, the likelihood of movement from both forms of informal employment into formal work was even lower and more stable.

The likelihood of movements in and out of the labor market, and between formal work and unemployment, was far more sensitive to the economic cycle than were movements between different forms of work (figure 1.19). When a smaller firm size ("SW5" indicates five and fewer workers) is used to distinguish informal from formal employees, in both the Czech Republic and Slovakia the likelihood of movement from formal work into unemployment and the likelihood of moving from informal work to unemployment follow nearly identical paths.

Notes

1. Responses to the pension contribution question in the European Union Statistics on Income and Living Conditions (EU-SILC) data from the United Kingdom made available by Eurostat suffer from irregularities and inconsistencies that make it suspect. However, we have chosen to present it, as the relative ranking of the United Kingdom according to this measure of informality is similar to others from other survey data sets.

2. As shown in table A.2 in the appendix, the correlation of informal work with sex stands out clearly as significant and negative. That is, women are clearly less likely to work informally. The results regarding the employment status of the spouse in the same table are somewhat surprising: there is a clear positive correlation between working informally and having an informally working spouse. That suggests that households are not making strategic decisions along the line of one partner working formally (and receiving employment and social protection, including that for dependents) while the other one works informally.

References

Bosch, Mariano, and William F. Maloney. 2008. "Cyclical Movements in Unemployment and Informality in Developing Countries." Policy Research Working Paper 4648, World Bank, Washington, DC.

Bosch, M., W. F. Maloney. 2010. "Comparative Analysis of Labor Market Dynamics Using Markov Processes: An Application to Informality." Labour Economics.

Eurostat. 2008. *EU-SILC—European Union Statistics on Income and Living Conditions.* Luxembourg: Eurostat. http://www.eui.eu/Research/Library /ResearchGuides/Economics/ Statistics/DataPortal/EU-SILC.aspx.

Fialová, K., and O. Schneider. 2011. "Labor Institutions and Their Impact on Shadow Economies in Europe." Background paper for "In from the Shadow: Integrating Europe's Informal Labor." Policy Research Working Paper 5913, World Bank, Washington, DC.

Hazans, M. 2011. "Informal Workers across Europe: Evidence from 30 European Countries." Background paper for "In from the Shadow: Integrating Europe's Informal Labor." Policy Research Working Paper 5912, World Bank, Washington, DC.

Koettl, J., and M. Weber. 2012. "Does Formal Work Pay? The Role of Labor Taxation and Social Benefit Design in the New EU Member States." *Research in Labor Economics* 34: 167–204.

Militaru, E., and C. Mocanu. 2012. "Informal Employment in Romania: Microeconometric Analysis of Labor Force Transitions." Background paper for "In from the Shadow: Integrating Europe's Informal Labor." Policy Research Working Paper, forthcoming, World Bank, Washington, DC.

Nikolovova, P., F. Perthold, and M. Vosar. 2012. "Self-employment and Small Workplaces in the Czech and Slovak Republics: Microeconometric Analysis of Labor Force Transitions." Background paper for "In from the Shadow: Integrating Europe's Informal Labor." Policy Research Working Paper, forthcoming, World Bank, Washington, DC.

OECD (Organization for Economic Cooperation and Development). 2008. Benefits and Wages Database. www.oecd.org/els/social/workincentives.

Oviedo, Ana Maria, Mark R. Thomas, and Kamer Karakurum-Ozdemir. 2009. "Economic Informality: Causes, Costs and Policies—A Literature Survey." Working Paper No. 167, World Bank, Washington, DC.

Perry, Guillermo E., William F. Maloney, Omar S. Arias, Pablo Fajnzylber, Andrew D. Mason, and Jaime Saavedra-Chanduvi. 2007. *Informality: Exit and Exclusion*. Washington, DC: World Bank.

Schneider, F., A. Buehn, and C. Montenegro. 2010. "Shadow Economies All over the World: New Estimates for 162 Countries from 1999 to 2007." Background paper for "In from the Shadow: Integrating Europe's Informal Labor." Policy Research Working Paper 5356, World Bank, Washington, DC.

Walewski, M. 2011. "An Attempt to Measure the Trends in Shadow Employment in Poland and the Transition Probabilities out and into Shadow Employment Using the LFS Data Augmented by the Results of Dedicated Survey Performed by CASE in 2007." Background paper for "In from the Shadow: Integrating Europe's Informal Labor." Policy Research Working Paper 5910, World Bank, Washington, DC.

CHAPTER 2

Conceptual Framework: More than Structural Incentives

Informal employment is conventionally conceptualized using a two-sector labor market pricing model. The model describes the mechanics of "segmentation" into a formal labor market and an informal one, brought about by regulations such as minimum wages and restrictions on dismissal, or by the financing of government interventions, particularly the contributions mandated to finance social insurance plans for unemployment, health, and old age pensions. Although it may indeed be necessary to minimize structural distortions caused by taxation, product and factor market regulations, and social protection policies, that alone is not a sufficient condition to shift economic activity to regulated and taxed markets. The nature of governance, institutional credibility, and social norms of compliance have to be factored into the discussion to arrive at truly effective policy solutions that will bring more firms and workers in from the shadow economy.

In the conventional framework, the rigidities in the labor market introduced by regulations and interventions can create what labor economists call dualism. The mechanics of the dualistic models are particularly good at depicting the "exclusion" view of informal employment—including informal self-employment—in which those working informally are presumed to be standing in line for preferred, formal jobs with nonpecuniary benefits and social protection but are priced out of that form of employment.

In a two-sector model, segmentation happens when a floor is placed under wages—either through an actual, legislated minimum wage or because of the strength of labor institutions, such as collective bargaining and the power of labor unions—forcing a wedge between the earnings of workers not covered by these arrangements and those who are (see figure 2.1).

Firing restrictions, labor taxes, and mandatory social insurance contributions (whether in a purely risk-pooling arrangement or to an individual savings account, although the distinction can be important, as will be discussed) can cause a shift in the demand curve for formally hired labor, leading to a larger share of informally employed workers even without segmentation (see figure 2.2).

The two-sector labor pricing models have yielded important insights on the nature of informal work. Complementary and sometimes opposing views of informal employment—and especially informal self-employment—as a voluntary exit from the formal sector of the economy, after an individual (or firm) weighs the advantages and disadvantages

Figure 2.1   The Conventional Labor Pricing Model Shows Segmentation Caused by a Floor on Wages

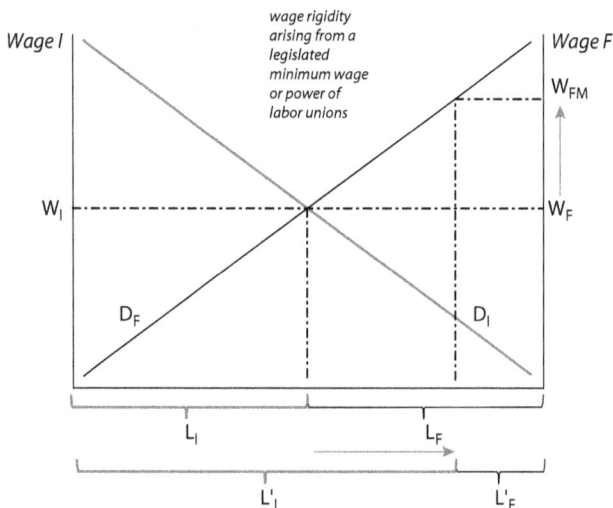

Source: Adapted from Perry et al. 2007.
Note: In a two-sector model, the size of the formal labor force is shown by L_F and the informal labor force by L_I. Imposition of a minimum wage (or the power of unions representing formal workers) pushes the formal wage from W_F to W_{FM}, causing L_F to contract to L'_F and L_I to expand to L'_I. All else equal, similarly qualified workers would prefer employment in L'_F.

Figure 2.2   Labor Taxes and Mandatory Contributions Are Expected to Increase Informal Employment

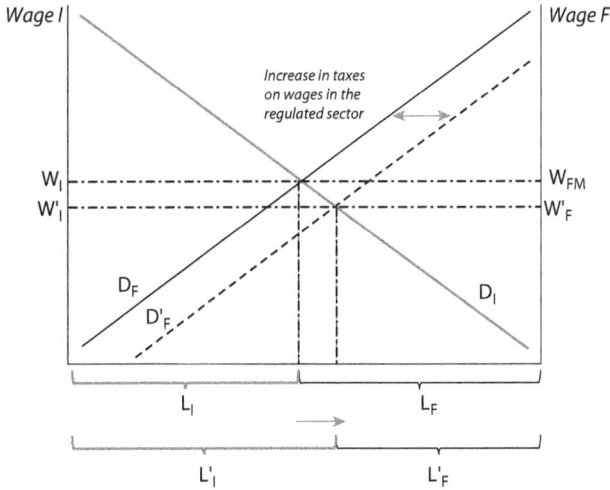

Source: Adapted from Perry et al. 2007.
Note: Restrictions on firing and/or increasing taxes on labor shift the demand curve for formal labor, causing L$_F$ to contract to L'$_F$, and LI to expand to L'$_I$.

of taking (or offering) a formal job, can also be captured in these models. Much of the academic and policy literature oscillates between the "exclusion" and "exit" portrayals of informal forms of work, from country to country and in the same country over time. A finding that seems to recur even across countries at very different levels of economic development is that people in self-employment appear to exhibit greater self-determination and choice, whereas the choices of those in informal dependent employment appear far more constrained. As argued by Perry et al. (2007), in most cases exit and exclusion are complementary perspectives and can amount to the same thing. If an entrepreneur chooses to evade regulation and taxation because the costs of compliance would make her business uncompetitive and unviable, is she exiting or is she excluded? If public pensions are so paltry that the only way a tradesman can earn a decent return on saving is to make sure his kids get a good education or to put an extension on his house, is he exiting or excluded from social insurance coverage? Many of the hypotheses that the conventional models yield have been empirically verified, including in research on the new member states of the EU conducted in the past and for this volume.

However, the conventional labor pricing framework leaves several important questions unanswered. For example, what explains substantial differences in the shares of the labor force in informal employment in countries that have similarly regulated labor markets or where governments deploy similar interventions? Why, for example, is informal employment so much less pervasive in Belgium and Sweden than it is in Portugal and Spain, when Belgium and Sweden have the highest tax wedge on employment in the EU? And although the minimum wage as a share of the average wage in Ireland and the United Kingdom is similar to its share in Portugal and Spain, why is informal employment so much more prevalent in the latter two countries? Differences in capacity to enforce regulations and implement interventions in otherwise similar countries can explain some of the difference, but not much. And as institutions in the EU's new member states—such as parliamentary democracy, a pluralistic political process, and accountability structures such as an independent judiciary and free news media, as well as the role of social partners—grow in importance, they have pushed convergence with the wealthier, "old" members in the sort of labor market regulations and interventions that are in place. Yet the contrast in employment outcomes between the old and newer members remains, in many cases, as stark as ever.

The conceptual framework we have chosen to help shed light on this paradox is adapted from the economics of corruption (see Andvig 1991; Bardhan 1997). Our intention is not to taint all the activities that take place in the unregulated and untaxed market as corrupt. This model was chosen as a way of capturing the important influence that history and the sociopolitical environment can have on the development and legitimacy of institutions and in consequence on the choices of households and firms.

The framework we have chosen builds on a repeated game structure to capture the idea that informal or shadow economic activity is an example of what is referred to in the economic literature as "frequency-dependent equilibria" and "intertemporal externalities." In this framework, the expected gains from transacting in the informal economy depend critically on the number of other economic agents (workers and firms) that an individual expects also to be operating informally.

To illustrate this approach, both Andvig (1991) and Bardhan (1997) use a simple Schelling diagram, which we have adapted in figure 2.3. In figure 2.3, the distance between the origin and any point along the horizontal axis is the proportion of a given total number n of economic agents (or transactions) that are known to be informal. At the origin, no one is informal, and at the end point n all agents (or transactions) are informal.

Figure 2.3   The Benefits and Costs of Working Informally Depend on How Many Other People Are Informal

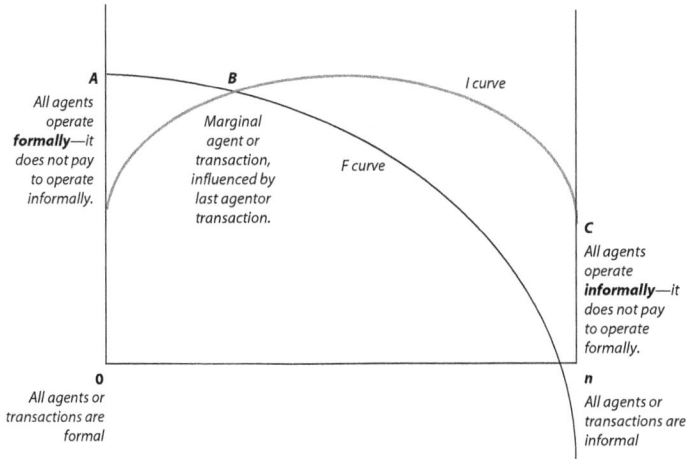

Source: Author's adaptation of Andvig 1991; and Bardhan 1998.

The curves *I* and *F* show the marginal benefit for an informal agent and a formal agent, respectively, given the remaining allocation of agents in each of the two categories.

The *F* curve shows that the marginal benefit to the formal economic agent is greater than that of an informal economic agent when very few other agents are informal. But it declines as the proportion of informal agents increases, and even becomes negative when all other agents are informal. In contrast, the *I* curve slopes upward at the beginning, as an increasing number of agents operate informally. At the margin, lower losses if detected, lower probability of detection, and lower search costs of finding other informal agents to do business with all increase the benefits of informal economic activity. However, at some point the marginal benefit of informal activity will decline—for example, when many other agents bid down informal prices—even if at the endpoint the benefits remain positive.

As in Bardhan (1997), figure 2.3 shows three equilibrium points, A, B, and C. Points A and C are stable, but point B is not. At point A all economic agents are operating formally, and it does not pay to engage in an informal transaction. In direct contrast, at point C all agents are transacting informally, and it does not pay to engage in formal transactions. At point B any given economic agent is indifferent between transacting formally or informally. However, if just one more agent enters into an informal trans-action, it pays for that once-indifferent agent to do the same. Similarly, if just one other agent enters into a formal transaction, it pays the once-indifferent agent to engage formally.

In this way, the Andvig-Bardhan framework captures the importance of initial conditions (history) to the eventual outcomes observed in a country at any given time. If an economy begins in—or, as Bardhan puts it, "is jolted into"—a high level of informal activity, it will move fairly relentlessly toward the high-informality, stable equilibrium at point C. And the farther away from point B the economy moves, the harder it is to return to a path toward less informality. However, if the initial level of informal activity is low, the economy will gravitate toward the equilib-rium point A. In this manner, the framework captures how even small changes can have a large impact on the eventual level of informality if an economy starts at points close to B.

This framework has also been used to take account of learning in the process of belief formation and social norms (Sah 1988). Suppose, for instance, that individuals and firms all start off with some prior notion of the likelihood that other individuals and firms they meet will be willing to transact informally. Those who would prefer to transact informally want to meet individuals and firms that are similarly inclined. For each additional informal agent they meet, their estimate of the likelihood of meeting people willing to engage in informal transactions grows. At some point in the process, people anticipate informality and become more likely to initiate an informal transaction. Bardhan suggests that that is how beliefs about the economic environment are formed and a culture, or social norm, of economic informality is nourished.

The framework can also show how the persistence of informal eco-nomic activity in a society might similarly be explained in part by the col-lective reputation of previous generations (Tirole 1996). Younger generations can inherit the reputation of previous generations, with the consequence that they have little incentive to transact formally. If for some temporary reason—or in the wake of a substantial shock to the economy—informal economic activity increases, it can have lasting effects. Bardhan writes, "[C]ollective reputation once shattered is difficult to rebuild," and in refer-ence to concerted efforts to correct the situation, "[I]t may take a mini-mum number of periods without [informal economic activity] to return to a path" leading to an equilibrium of primarily formal economic activity. Indeed, a recent World Bank report on undeclared employment in Hungary (World Bank 2008) made reference to a "tipping point" that lies between a "bad equilibrium," where transactions on the informal market for goods, services, and labor are the norm, and a "good equilibrium" where engaging in informal transactions "becomes a deviant and socially unacceptable position." The unstable equilibrium point B in figure 2.3 is a formal presentation of that tipping point.

We find this framework particularly compelling, as it can capture how individuals and firms form expectations from their behavior and the behavior of others in their institutional environment. Those expectations are arguably more powerful in driving choices and outcomes than the relatively mechanical structural incentives operating in the conventional labor pricing models. By capturing history and how it sets initial conditions, the framework can offer insights into determining factors such as institutional credibility and the formation of social norms. Furthermore, the framework is arguably more salient to countries in central and eastern Europe, given the "jolts"—Bardhan's term—to institutions and social norms in their recent history that may have pushed their economies closer to the tipping point illustrated in figure 2.3. Depending on how far back one looks, the jolts include the imposition of socialism; years of coping to make up for the shortfalls of a planned economy; the sudden collapse of that model and exposure to market forces; the headlong rush to reform and create institutions to gain entry to the EU; and the impact of the recent global financial crisis. Relative to other middle-income countries where policy makers are grappling with the challenges of widespread informal economic activity, the second half of the 20th century and the first decade of the 21st have been tumultuous for the European Union's newest members.

However, the Andvig-Bardhan framework is not a substitute for the conventional labor pricing models. Those models still offer helpful, testable hypotheses with clear implications for policy. The framework complements these models by allowing researchers and the policy makers they advise to look deeper than the simple mechanics of how their decisions affect supply and demand to include people's perceptions and how those become deeply held beliefs, and eventually widespread social norms that then govern individual and collective behavior.

A good illustration of how the two approaches complement one another is the predicted impact on the incentive to formalize—alluded to earlier—from shifting social insurance away from a purely risk-pooling arrangement to one that is primarily based on individual savings, actual or notional. That sort of shift has been made in social insurance plans that cover losses from unemployment, but it is far more common across EU's newest members in plans designed to smooth consumption in retirement. The two-sector labor pricing model predicts that, at the margin, a higher contribution rate for social insurance distorts labor allocation when benefits are only loosely related to contributions, as is often, but not necessarily, the case in publicly administered risk-pooling arrangements. In the case of retirement pensions, where the payoff to workers' investment in the plan lies far in the future, the distortion is more onerous if preferences for consumption today are felt more keenly because of limited access to credit.

The conventional model predicts that a change that links benefits more closely with contributions (a parametric change or an outright structural shift to individual savings) will lower distortions, as a greater share of contributions is perceived as fully owned, albeit deferred, wages. Thus, whether or not there is an absolute lowering of contributions, the pure-tax element falls, and so too should the distortions to the contract between employers and workers. However, the behavioral response of employers and workers to this type of shift depends critically on whether workers perceive the link between contributions today and benefits far in the future to be strong and credible. In many developing and transition countries, public institutions such as social insurance lack that credibility, but so do the institutions that shape the market for financial services, where property rights are weak, competition is stifled, and available financial investments lack transparency. In these institutional settings, workers will heavily discount that they will receive a pension at all, increasing the perceived tax burden of mandatory contributions, no matter how tightly they are linked to benefits on paper. Furthermore, in societies where people place relatively greater value on the redistributive role played by social insurance, this type of shift could signal a deterioration of the social contract, create disillusionment with mandatory risk management structures, and provoke employers and workers to opt out.

These are the conceptual arguments from which we draw the preliminary conclusion that, although minimizing structural distortions caused by taxation, product and factor market regulation, and social protection policy may be necessary, it is not a sufficient condition for substantial gains to be made in shifting economic activity to regulated and taxed markets within the formal institutional structures of a society. The nature of governance, institutional credibility, and social norms of compliance have to be factored into the discussion for truly effective policy solutions to be offered that will bring more firms and workers in from the shadow economy. In this same vein, Perry et al. (2007, p. 19) concluded that "informality is a canary in the coal mine—the symptom of poor policies and, *more profoundly, a lack of confidence in the state and perhaps in our fellow citizens*" (italics added).

References

Andvig, Jens Christopher. 1991. "The Economics of Corruption: A Survey." *Studi Economici* 43: 57–94.

Bardhan, Pranab. 1997. "Corruption and Development: A Review of the Issues." *Journal of Economic Literature* 35 (3): 1320–46.

Perry, Guillermo E., William F. Maloney, Omar S. Arias, Pablo Fajnzylber, Andrew D. Mason, and Jaime Saavedra-Chanduvi. 2007. *Informality: Exit and Exclusion*. Washington, DC: World Bank.

Sah, R. K. 1988. "Persistence and Pervasiveness of Corruption: New Perspectives." Yale Economic Growth Center Discussion Paper 560, 48, August.

Tirole, Jean. 1996. "A Theory of Collective Reputations (with Applications to the Persistence of Corruption and to Firm Quality)." *Review of Economic Studies* 63 (1): 1–22.

World Bank. 2008. "Reducing Undeclared Employment in Hungary." World Bank Country Report No. 47777-HU, May, World Bank, Washington, DC.

CHAPTER 3

Structural Drivers of the Shadow Economy and Informal Work

In the new EU member states the most frequent reasons for engaging in undeclared work are low formal salaries and high taxes and social security contributions. The wrong mix of tax instruments can reduce growth by distorting the choices of firms and households, including creating incentives to shift the demand and supply of labor to the unregulated and untaxed market. In addition to the tax wedge, the withdrawal of social benefits can substantially increase the opportunity costs of taking up formal work. To understand the structural incentives encountered in the labor market, it is helpful to distinguish among regulations, interventions, and institutions and how each influences the extent of informal employment in its various guises. The importance and impact of these structures on the choices of people and firms varies widely across Europe.

The Structural Incentives of Taxation

In a survey conducted by the European Commission, individuals in EU member countries were asked to report on undeclared work, defined as all remunerated activities (in-kind or cash) that are in principle legal but are not declared to tax authorities or social security institutions (EC 2007). According to that opinion poll, the most frequent reasons for taking part in undeclared work in the new EU member countries are that salaries in the regulated sector are too low. Taxes and social security contributions are also often mentioned as being important motivators for working informally. In Hungary and Lithuania about 30 percent to 35 percent of survey respondents mentioned taxes as the most important reason for undeclared work, whereas taxes were the most important determinant for less than 10 percent of respondents in Slovenia, Romania, Slovakia, and Bulgaria (figure 3.1).

In his review of taxation structures in the EU's new member states, Leibfritz (2011) points out that relatively low formal salaries, together with relatively high taxes on labor, may explain why in the new members of the EU undeclared work often takes the form of underdeclaration of income through payment of part of registered workers' wages in cash or through false registration of workers as self-employed. Both methods provide opportunities to evade. Employers who pay "envelope wages" not only evade labor taxes but will also have to conceal some of their

Figure 3.1   What, in Your Opinion, Are the Primary Reasons for Doing Undeclared Work?

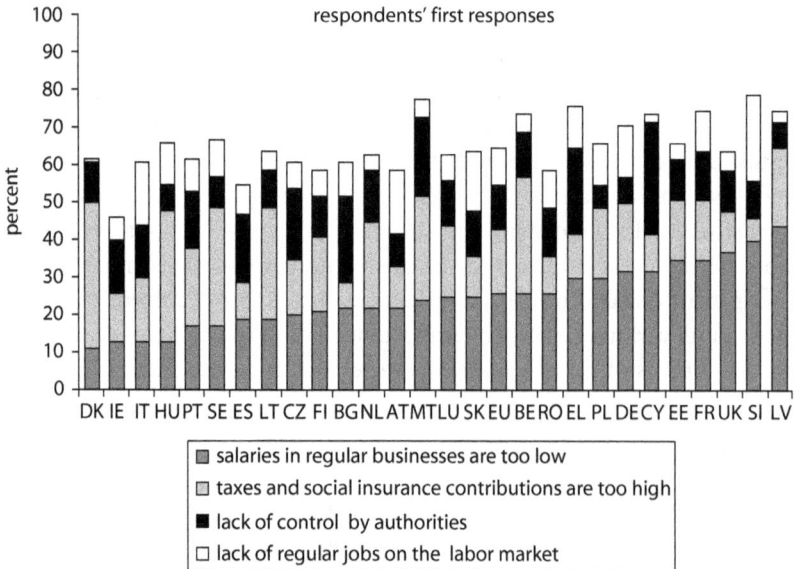

Source: Leibfritz 2011, for this volume, based on "Undeclared Work in the European Union", Eurobarometer survey, October 2007.

taxable sales to receive unrecorded cash. The Estonian Institute of Economic Research (Eesti Konjunktuurinstiituut) estimated that in 2008, 12 percent of employees received unreported wages (of which 6 percent received unreported wages on a regular basis and 6 percent only occasionally); the share of employees who received part of their wage undeclared declined from 16 percent in 2003 to 11 percent in 2006, before increasing again in 2007 to 14 percent. The decision not to report wages to the authorities appears to stem largely from employers, with employees having little influence on the decision (Staehr 2009). Some 31 percent of employees who received undeclared wages were satisfied with the situation, but 45 percent were not. Among those who were dissatisfied, 55 percent believed that they would lose their job if they did not accept this form of payment (Leibfritz 2011).

Although exact measurement of the extent of envelope wages paid is very difficult, Leibfritz (2011) cites the work of Williams (2008) who, in 10,671 face-to-face interviews in 11 central and eastern European countries, found that 10 percent of all employees received envelope wages, but with large differences across countries. In the Czech Republic only 3 percent of employees had received envelope wages in the previous 12 months, in Slovenia 5 percent, in Poland and Lithuania 11 percent, in Latvia 17 percent, and in Romania 23 percent. In Romania, employees received about 70 percent of their wages in this manner, while in the other countries the share of the undeclared wage as a percentage of total wage was much smaller.[1]

Another indication that taxation in general plays a prominent role in the economic considerations of firms comes from enterprise surveys. The World Bank enterprise surveys reveal that on average, 45 percent of firms in the EU's new member states and Croatia cited tax rates as a major obstacle to doing business in 2009 (figure 3.2). The results indicate that those respondents perceived tax rates to be high and a greater obstacle to doing business than regulations and administrative procedures. Tax administration (24 percent) and competition from informal enterprises (23 percent) were also considered obstacles, but licensing (14 percent), labor regulations (14 percent), and trade regulations (8 percent) figured less prominently as obstacles to doing business from firms' perspective.

The public finance literature suggests that taxes should be imposed in a manner that is least distorting to the economy. The wrong mix of tax instruments can reduce growth by distorting the choices of firms and households, including creating incentives to shift the demand and

Figure 3.2   Firms in the EU New Member States and Croatia Considered Tax Rates the Main Obstacle to Doing Business
percentage

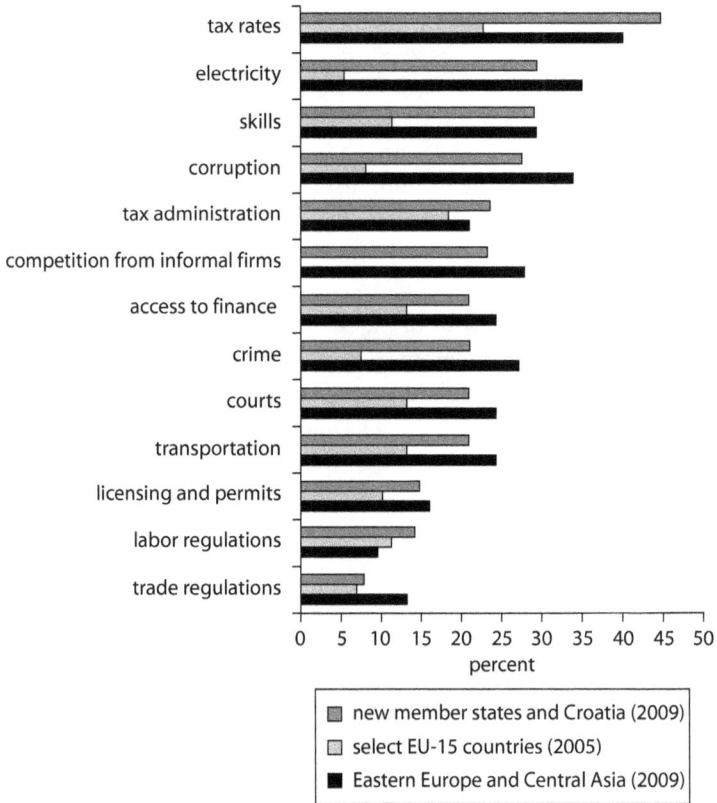

Source: Authors, based on World Bank 2012.
Note: The bars represent the percentage of firms that identify the respective issue as a main obstacle to doing business. Averages are unweighted. Selected EU-15 countries are Germany, Greece, Ireland, Portugal, and Spain.

supply of labor to the unregulated and untaxed market. Even among tax specialists, views differ about the significance of taxes for growth and employment. That depends, of course, not only on the level and structure of taxation but on many other, partly interrelated factors, such as the stage of economic development, institutional efficiency, cultural factors, and—last but not least—whether people feel that tax revenue is spent in a productive or an unproductive way. Those critical factors are taken up in chapter 4.

   In addition to its macroeconomic effects through aggregate growth and employment, taxation also affects undeclared work more directly at the micro level. As mentioned, relatively higher labor taxes can cause employers to pause before offering regulated employment (the labor demand effect), or they can encourage workers to work informally (the labor supply effect). When taxes on earnings from work are high relative to those on other forms of income, firms and workers may be forced into a trade-off between compliance and survival and may collude to evade taxes to cope with market competition. That situation can give rise to firms' declaring only part of salaries and paying envelope wages, thus reducing the effective tax on labor. In that case, observed formal sector employment does not decline, but government revenues are lower. A combination of high taxes on labor income and low taxes on other forms of income (capital income) can induce individuals to transform labor income into capital income to reduce their tax burden. The tax treatment of families (individual taxation or joint taxation, the granting of family allowances, and so on) may encourage secondary earners to work informally if additional formal income is taxed at a high marginal rate. Where the effective tax burden is lower for the self-employed than for dependent workers (because actual tax rates are lower, because of a lower tax base or a greater margin to underdeclared income), workers may shift—voluntarily or coerced by employers—from dependent employment to self-employment.

Special provisions, such as in-work benefits (employment tax credits) can reduce the effective labor tax rate and encourage formal employment, as discussed in chapter 5. However, as those benefits are generally withdrawn at higher incomes, they raise the marginal effective tax rate, which creates disincentives to increase work efforts and encourages underdeclaration of wages so as to receive full benefits.

The extent to which taxation results in undeclared work also depends on the effectiveness of tax administration. An effective tax administration is crucial for reducing undeclared work and tax evasion in general. If tax collectors have a reputation for being unprofessional and services for taxpayers are poor, individuals are more tempted to evade taxes or bribe government officials. Bribes impose a "corruption tax" on business, which is collected by corrupt individuals at the cost of the general public. The vulnerability to corruption also depends on the level of taxes, the complexity of the system, how much discretion is left to tax collectors, their salaries, and the internal control system of the tax administration. As will be discussed in chapters 4 and 5, tackling these issues can be key to improving compliance.

The impact of taxes on undeclared work also depends on factors that are not directly related to tax policies and tax administration. If other

obstacles to formal sector activity remain in place, reforms to the tax system and tax administration aimed at increasing formal employment and
reducing tax evasion may not be effective. Such obstacles can be income-
dependent social benefits, which create high effective marginal tax rates
and encourage workers to underdeclare wages. Furthermore, unfavorable
conditions for doing business, such as high barriers to market entry by new
firms and high administrative and compliance costs for existing firms, a
strict labor code, and a high minimum wage relative to market wages, can
reduce the creation of regular jobs. All are structural factors that are
addressed in later sections. This section examines how the taxation in the
EU's new member states can create strong structural incentives for firms
and households to turn to the informal labor market.

No consensus exists among economists about the effect of the overall
tax level on economic performance. A number of studies have found a
negative effect of higher tax levels on growth and employment (for
example, Tanzi and Schuknecht 1996; Leibfritz, Thornton, and Bibbee
1997; Daveri and Tabellini 2000), whereas others have failed to find a
strong link (for example, Agell, Lindh, and Ohlsson 1997). Based on comparisons with and between high-income countries, and considering their
lower per capita incomes and less-experienced tax administrations, Mitra
and Stern (2002) suggested that transition countries should aim at tax
revenue-to-GDP ratios in the range of 22 percent to 31 percent. According
to the Mitra and Stern benchmark, only Slovakia, Romania, and Lithuania
have "appropriate" tax levels, and the tax burdens in all of the other EU
new member countries are "too high." Estonia and Latvia straddle the
border between "appropriate" and "too high."

Leibfritz (2011) shows that if the trend line of an international comparison of tax-to-GDP ratios relative to GDP per capita (in purchasing
power parities) is used as a benchmark (see figure 3.3), the range of
"appropriate" or "desirable" tax levels for the EU new member countries
is a more generous 30 percent to 35 percent—that is, four to eight percentage points higher than suggested by Mitra and Stern. According to
this benchmark, among the EU new members, Estonia is a "low-tax country." In the years immediately prior to the global financial crisis, the Czech
Republic, Latvia, Lithuania, Poland, Romania, and Slovakia appeared as
"medium-tax countries." By contrast, Hungary and Slovenia appear as
"high-tax countries."

This type of benchmarking does not, of course, capture important differences in countries' preferences, which play an important part in determining

Figure 3.3   The Relationship between the Ratio of Tax to GDP and per Capita Incomes: An International Comparison

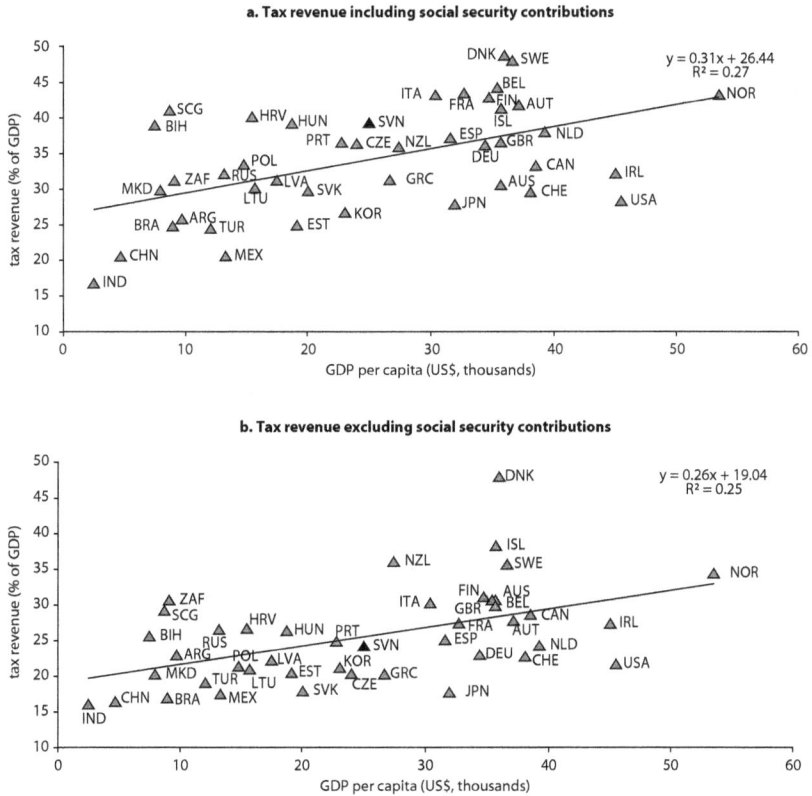

a. Tax revenue including social security contributions

$$y = 0.31x + 26.44$$
$$R^2 = 0.27$$

b. Tax revenue excluding social security contributions

$$y = 0.26x + 19.04$$
$$R^2 = 0.25$$

Source: Leibfritz 2010.

Note: Figures are for 2006 or 2007; 2004 for Argentina, Montenegro, and Serbia. GDP per capita based on current purchasing power parities.

the extent of taxation and how firms and households react to taxation (taken up in chapter 4). However, that some of the new members of the EU collect relatively high tax revenues despite widespread undeclared work suggests that firms and households that operate mainly in regulated markets have to carry a particularly large tax burden. That can make the option of working informally or semi-informally even more attractive for the firms and households who can take it. Tax incidence is, however, spread more evenly if the formal sector succeeds in shifting part of the tax burden to the informal sector by increasing output prices—which are purchased by informal firms or consumers who work informally—and by lowering the prices of inputs from informal firms.

The analysis of overall tax levels is only a very crude proxy for the possible effects of taxes on incentives to conceal activities because tax distortions are felt at the micro level. The tax mix is more important. Tax instruments differ with respect to their economic and distributional effects and their administrative costs. These differences present trade-offs between sometimes-competing government objectives, which have to be considered when designing the tax system. The new members of the EU rely to a large extent on indirect taxes and labor taxes, whereas capital is relatively lightly taxed. That tax mix aims explicitly to foster economic growth by shifting the tax mix away from capital income to less-distorting taxes, notably taxes on consumption. However, high labor taxes are mainly driven by the comprehensive social protection systems in place in all of the countries. Most of the benefits that those systems pay are structured to mimic market-based insurance and for that reason are intended to be financed mainly by earnings-dependent contributions from labor. Corporations are relatively lightly taxed to attract business investment, particularly foreign direct investment, to accelerate economic growth.

Leibfritz (2011) illustrates the relative bias toward consumption and labor taxes in the EU's new member countries with implicit tax rates, calculated by relating tax revenues to their corresponding tax bases (tables 3.1, 3.2, and 3.3. In Hungary and Slovenia which, as we have said, were benchmarked as relatively "high tax," the implicit tax rates are high

Table 3.1   Implicit Tax Rate on Consumption
percent

	1995–99	*2000–04*	*2005–07 (ranking)*
Hungary	28.6	26.4	26.4 (1)
Bulgaria	—	20.2	25.1 (2)
Slovenia	24.2	23.7	23.8 (3)
Estonia	19.6	19.9	23.3 (4)
Czech Republic	20.2	19.8	21.6 (5)
Slovakia	23.8	20.5	21.0 (6)
Poland	19.9	17.9	20.4 (7)
Latvia	19.4	18.1	20.0 (8)
Romania	15.9 (1999)	16.5	17.9 (9)
Lithuania	18.9	17.3	17.0 (10)
EU-25 average	21.3	21.1	22.0

Source: Authors.
Note: The implicit tax rate calculated by dividing consumption tax revenue by the macroeconomic tax base.

Table 3.2   Implicit Tax Rate on Labor
percent

	1995–99	2000–04	2005–07 (ranking)
Czech Republic	40.3	41.1	41.4 (1)
Hungary	42.9	40.2	39.5 (2)
Slovenia	37.5	37.6	37.3 (3)
Poland	36.1	32.9	34.1 (4)
Estonia	38.4	37.2	33.9 (5)
Lithuania	37.0	38.5	33.6 (6)
Latvia	36.8	36.9	32.4 (7)
Bulgaria	35.9 (1999)	35.5	31.7 (8)
Slovakia	38.3	36.1	31.4 (9)
Romania	37.6 (1999)	30.7	29.5 (10)
EU-25	35.9	35.4	34.8

Source: EU Commission.
Note: The implicit tax rate is calculated by dividing labor tax revenue by the macroeconomic tax base.

Table 3.3   Implicit Tax Rate on Capital
percent

	1995–99	2000–04	2005–07 (ranking)
Czech Republic	22.8	23.9	25.7 (1)
Slovenia	—	17.3	22.4 (2)
Poland	21.2	20.7	22.2 (2005–2006)(3)
Slovakia	30.1	21.6	18.4 (4)
Hungary	—	16.5	16.5 (2005–2006)(5)
Latvia	18.9	9.8	11.7 (6)
Lithuania	8.9	6.9	10.9 (7)
Estonia	10.9	6.6	8.9 (8)
EU-25 average	24.7	24.2	26.5

Source: Leibfritz 2010, for this volume, with data from EU Commission.
Note: The implicit tax rate is calculated by dividing capital tax revenue by the macroeconomic tax base.

on both consumption and labor. In Bulgaria, the Czech Republic, Poland, and Romania, which are "medium-tax countries," implicit tax rates differ significantly: the highest labor tax burden is in the Czech Republic and the lowest in Romania. Among the countries benchmarked as "low tax" (Estonia, Latvia, Lithuania, and Slovakia), the three Baltic countries have particularly low taxes on capital, whereas in Slovakia the tax burden is more evenly distributed across instruments.

According to Mitra and Stern (2002), the mix of tax instruments in the EU's new member countries is too biased toward indirect taxes and social insurance contributions, and the share of income taxes is too low. They suggest that a more balanced mix of taxation instruments—measured by share of total tax revenue—would be indirect taxes between 32 percent and 36 percent, income taxes between 27 percent and 29 percent, and social insurance contributions between 27 percent and 32 percent. Among the EU's new member countries, only Latvia and Lithuania have a tax mix close to this general guideline, although their share of indirect taxes is somewhat higher than suggested. In all other countries the shares of indirect taxes and social insurance contributions are too high, and the share of income tax is too low.

Quite apart from the general incentives created by the tax mix prevalent in most of the new EU members, labor taxes in these countries are relatively higher at lower earnings levels. A comparison with other EU, OECD, and neighboring countries shows that the tax wedge on labor at lower wage levels (33 percent of average wages) tends to be relatively high.[2] The tax wedge measures the difference between labor costs and the take-home pay of workers. It expresses the costs of social insurance contributions by employers and employees and the personal income tax of employees as a share of total labor costs. These taxes vary depending on family type and wage level. For a single person with no children who receives a gross wage 33 percent of the average wage, only a few EU-15 countries—including Sweden, Germany, Belgium, and Finland—charge higher taxes than most of the EU's new member states (figure 3.4).

Furthermore, labor taxation in the EU new member countries is not very progressive in structure. Although in most countries, labor taxes increase significantly with the wage level—for most of the EU-15 countries, by more than 10 percentage points between 33 percent and 100 percent of the average wage level—in the new member countries, labor taxes increase by less than 10 percentage points. A less-progressive structure is expected in countries with a higher tax wedge at lower wage levels, but the new member countries display especially low levels of progressivity.[3] All the new members except for Hungary and Slovenia, are below the trend line in a cross-county comparison (see figure 3.5). In particular, for singles without children, Bulgaria stands out with zero progressivity of labor taxes. This is important because low progressivity means that some room exists for lowering the tax wedge for low-wage earners in a fiscally neutral way by increasing progressivity.

But despite different degrees of progressivity, in most countries labor taxation is typically lower for low-wage earners.[4] The typical graph of the

Figure 3.4　Labor Taxation Is Higher for Low-Wage Earners in the EU New Member States

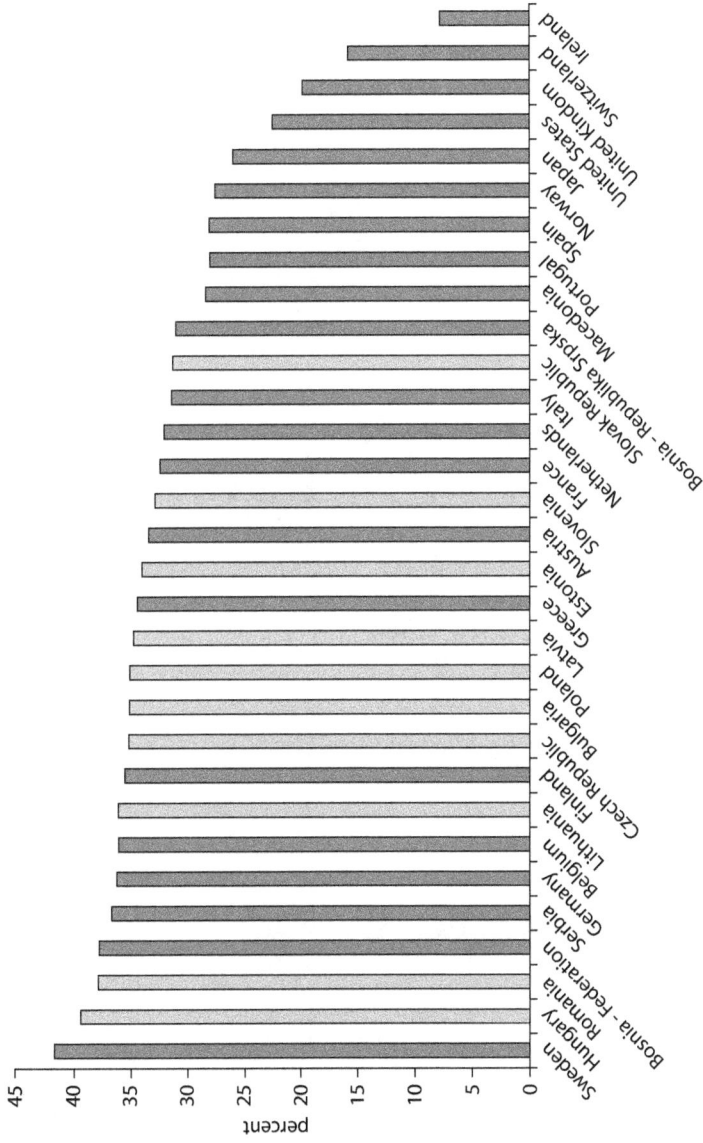

Source: Koettl and Weber 2012a, for this volume, based on OECD Tax and Benefit model.
Note: Columns represent the tax wedge for low-income earners (singles with no children at 33 percent of average wage) in 2008 (for Bosnia, Macedonia, and Serbia, 2009). Countries whose bars are light gray are the new member states.

Figure 3.5   In the New Member States, the Tax Wedge Tends Not to Be Very Progressive

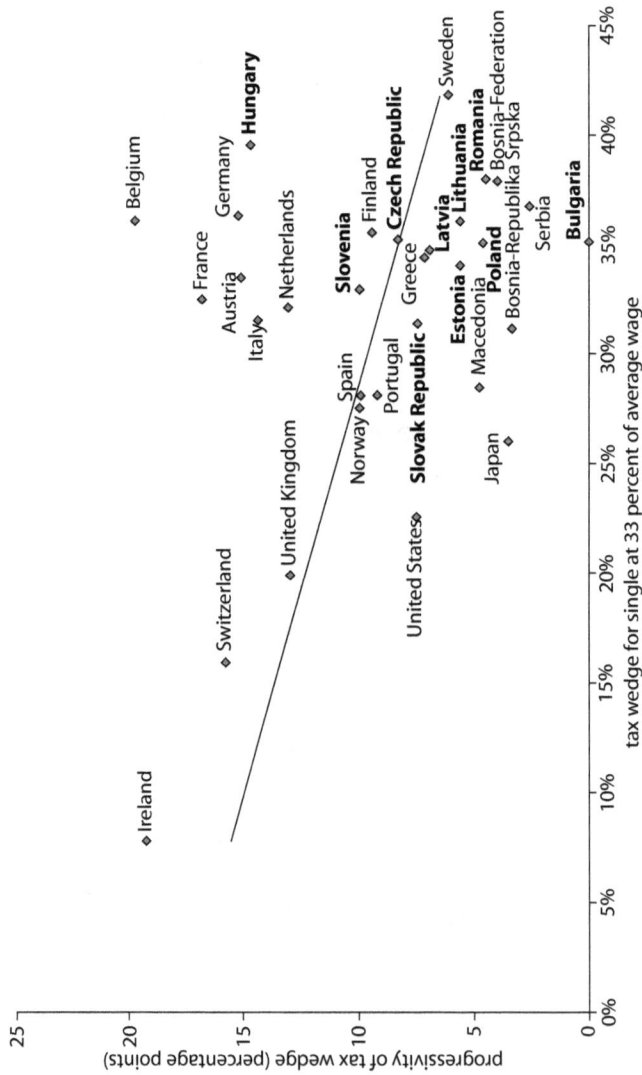

Source: Koettl and Weber 2012a, for this volume, based on OECD (2008).

Note: Data points represent the tax wedge for low-income earners (single person with no children at 33 percent of average wage; x-axis) in relation to a country's progressivity of the tax wedge (the percentage point increase of the tax wedge between 33 percent and 100 percent of the average wage; y-axis) in 2008 (for Bosnia, Macedonia, and Serbia, 2009). New member states in boldface.

tax wedge over the wage level for the EU new members is depicted in figure 3.6—in this case, for Estonia and Latvia. As can be seen, the tax wedge is lower for low-wage earners (around 26 percent for Estonia and Latvia) and starts to increase significantly from a certain wage level (around 20 percent of average wage) to levels of about 40 percent to 45 percent of total labor costs. What is interesting is that some countries display much lower tax wedges for low-wage earners, for example, Australia and the United Kingdom (see figure 3.6). Both have a tax wedge of 0 percent for low-wage earners, and only at levels above 20 percent of the average wage does the tax wedge increase significantly.

Furthermore, in the EU's new member countries the tax wedge tends to be high for a relatively large spectrum of low-wage earners. The wage level at which the tax wedge starts to increase significantly is relatively high. In many higher-income OECD countries, in contrast, the tax wedge is low for the lowest-wage earners but also tends to increase across the whole wage spectrum (see figure 3.7).

Putting the progressivity of taxes aside for a moment, taxing labor is generally considered less distorting to the economy than taxing capital. The reason is that labor is less mobile than capital, making it easier to tax, and a (pure) labor tax like the payroll tax does not affect capital formation. Greater capital mobility puts pressure on many countries—including the new members of the EU—to reduce corporate income tax rates to encourage investment, including foreign direct investment. This approach could help to formalize more transactions in a country if higher growth brings increased demand for formal labor. Furthermore, if the country succeeds in attracting foreign firms, tax collection may become easier, as those firms are more easily monitored and less likely to underdeclare income than the smaller domestic firms.

However, Leibfritz (2011) warns that shifting too much of the tax burden from capital to labor can be counterproductive. If the loss of revenue from lowering capital taxation has to be compensated by higher taxes on labor, the capital intensity of production tends to increase, and a country with an abundant labor force will then find it harder to exploit its comparative advantage in the production of labor-intensive goods and services. As a result, demand for formal labor inputs to production can fall, while demand for informal work remains high. Especially since production in the informal economy is more labor intensive than in the formal economy, lower labor taxation could lead to more formalization. Inordinately low capital taxation opens a gap between labor and capital taxation that can strongly encourage firms and households to evade labor

Figure 3.6   In Estonia and Latvia, the Tax Wedge for Low-Wage Earners Is Higher than in Australia or the United Kingdom

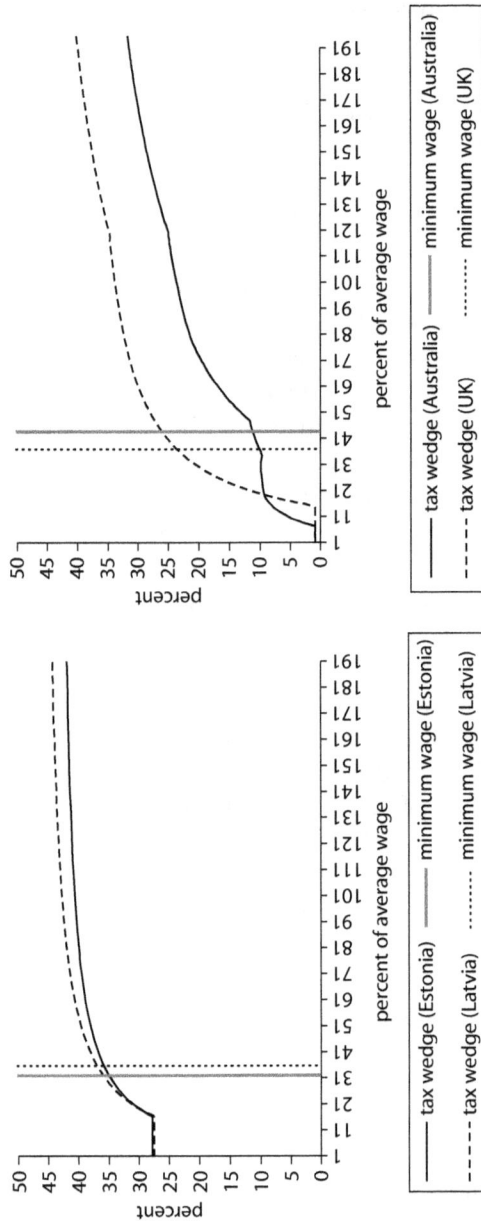

Source: Koettl and Weber 2012a, for this volume, based on OECD 2008.
Note: Graphs show the tax wedge for single person with no children.

Figure 3.7 In the New Member States, the Tax Wedge for the Lowest-Wage Earners Tends to Be High, and the Wage Level at Which It Increases Significantly Is Relatively High

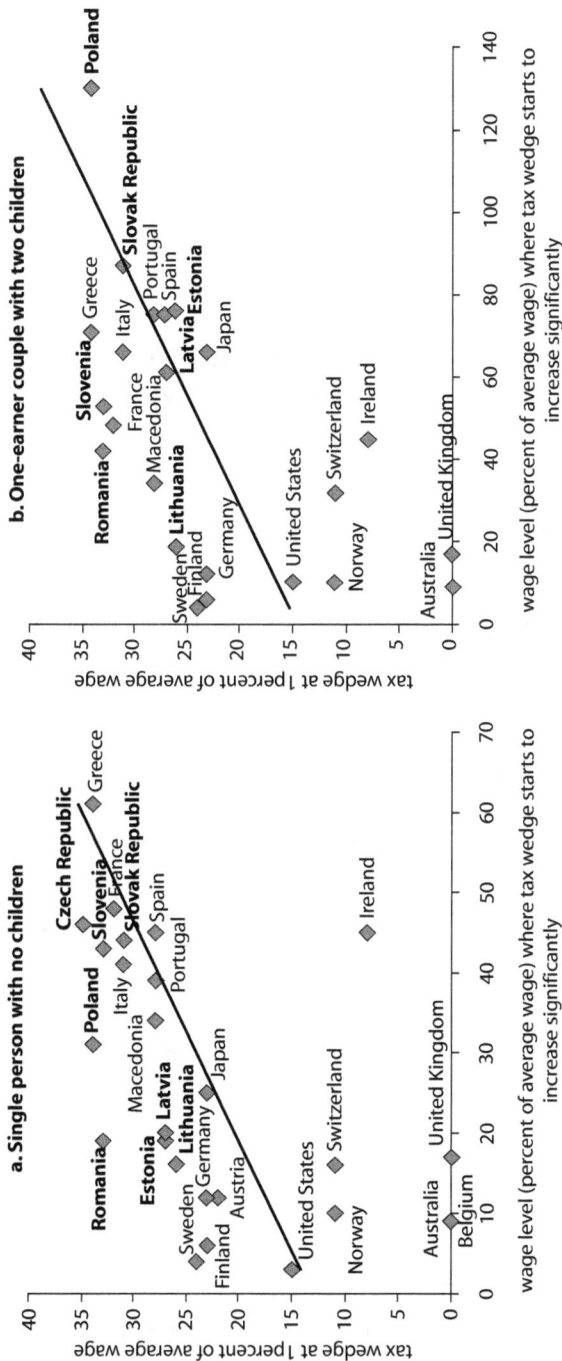

a. Single person with no children

b. One-earner couple with two children

Source: Koettl and Weber 2012a, for this volume, based on OECD 2008.

Note: The scatter plot depicts the wage level where the tax wedge starts to increase (x-axis) versus the tax wedge at 1 percent of average wages (y-axis). Hungary, the Netherlands, and Serbia feature falling tax wedges at low wage levels and are not depicted; nor is Bulgaria, which has a flat tax wedge. Austria, Belgium, and Canada have partly negative tax wedges at low wage levels, especially for families, and are not included in panel b (Canada also in panel a). The new member states are in bold.

85

taxes by reporting labor income as capital income. A certain degree of capital taxation is optimal, notably in countries that are vulnerable to informality (Penalosa and Turnovsky 2004). However, in a general equilibrium model for Canada, Brou and Collins (2001) found that shifting the mix of direct taxes away from labor toward capital increases the size of the informal economy. Schneider and Neck (1993) found a similar result for Austria.

The optimal mix between labor and capital taxation also depends on enforcement capacity (Slemrod and Yitzhaki 2000). If a government's capacity to monitor business income is low, it is more likely that high labor taxes lead to underdeclaration of wages, independent of the level of profit taxation. If the government has greater capacity to detect business income, firms would have no incentive to underdeclare wages if the profit tax was higher than the labor tax. Wage costs are usually deductible expenses, so that would increase the overall tax burden of firms. However, in the new member states of the EU, taxes on profits are much lower than taxes on labor, creating an incentive for firms to underdeclare wages, independent of the capacity of the administration to detect overall business income.

From a purely macroeconomic perspective, the effects of taxing labor and taxing consumption are similar, as neither affects capital formation.[5] Croatia has gone the farthest toward consumption-based taxation, as it not only collects a relatively high share of its tax revenues from indirect taxes and social contributions, but also has transformed its personal income tax into a consumption-based tax by allowing deduction of interest income. The effects of labor and consumption taxes on demand for formal labor depend on wage flexibility, as discussed in detail in later sections. In countries where the wage bargaining power of workers is great enough to resist a tax-induced fall in the net real wage by claiming higher nominal wages, both the labor tax and the consumption tax are shifted back to firms; thus wage costs increase, and as a result, employment falls (depending on the elasticity of demand). By contrast, if real wages are allowed to fall as a result of a higher labor tax or a higher consumption tax, labor demand is not affected. However, workers tend to supply less labor formally (depending on the elasticity of supply) and may instead shift to informal work to preserve real earnings. Similarly, buyers of goods and services may respond to a higher consumption tax by shifting purchases to the informal markets to prevent a decline in their real disposable income.

Given these similarities between taxing labor and taxing consumption, many economists argue that lowering labor taxes and increasing consumption taxes accordingly has no major effect on the extent and character of employment, as real wages remain broadly constant (Jackman, Layard, and Nickell 1996). However, those arguments ignore the fact that a general consumption tax (like the value-added tax or VAT) has a broader base than a labor tax, as consumption is financed by labor and capital income, wealth, and government transfers. However, the effects on prices of such a shift are also different because labor taxation affects producer prices, while consumption taxation affects consumer prices.

Reducing employer contributions to social insurance and increasing VAT accordingly to make up the difference, therefore, can lead to a fall in export prices and an increase in import prices, increasing the international competitiveness of firms in the same way as depreciation of the currency. There may also be some nominal wage rigidity, so that lowering labor taxes and increasing consumption taxes may—at least for a time—reduce wage costs for employers. It is, therefore, not surprising that a number of studies have found that shifting the tax burden from labor onto consumption increases employment and growth, in particular if transfer recipients are not fully compensated for the tax-induced increase in prices (for example, Daveri and Tabellini 2000; EC 2006).

Thus getting the tax mix right matters. Shifting away from labor taxes to consumption taxes can help to reduce demand for informal labor, goods, and services. However, Leibfritz (2011) points out the caution with which this conclusion has to be taken, depending on country context. Although reducing labor taxes would make formal labor inputs less expensive and increase formal sector output, the increase in consumption taxes can also lower demand for formal sector output. For this reason, the net effect of such a shift in the tax mix on formal sector output (and the size of the informal sector) can be ambiguous and depends on particular country circumstances. To illustrate this concern, Brou and Collins's (2001) general equilibrium model for Canada showed that a shift in the tax mix from income taxes to sales taxes increased the size of the informal economy, as the negative effect of the higher sales tax on formal sector output was larger than the positive effect from lower income tax, so that the size of the formal sector shrank.

The Interaction of Labor Taxes with Social Protection: Does Formal Work Pay?

In addition to the tax wedge, the withdrawal of social benefits can substantially increase the opportunity costs of taking up formal work for individuals with low skills and earnings potential. Think of an informal worker who earns a certain level of informal wage.[6] If that person were to consider taking up a formal job, various implicit opportunity costs would become apparent. First, assuming that the value of the marginal labor product does not change because of formalization, the total labor cost of the informal worker has to be the same as for the formalized worker. For the informal worker, total labor costs are the informal wage. For the formalized worker, total labor costs are the net wage, plus the income tax and both the worker's and the employer's social insurance contributions—in other words, the net wage plus the entire tax wedge. If one compares the informal wage with the worker's potential formal net wage, the entire tax wedge enters as an opportunity cost of formal work for the informal worker.

Second, informal workers also face implicit opportunity costs because they might lose certain income-tested benefits—most important in a typical EU member state with a comprehensive social protection system, social assistance, housing benefits, in-work benefits, and family benefits—once they have a formal income on record. For example, if an informal worker receives a certain amount of social assistance, the benefit will be decreased or completely withdrawn if the worker formalizes and has an official income on record. Thus, the amount of the withdrawn benefit also enters as an opportunity cost of formal work.

For these reasons, both losses—the tax wedge and withdrawn benefits—have to be taken into account when considering the implicit opportunity costs of formalization. At the same time, informal workers also gain entitlements from formalizing: the future right to an old age pension and rights to disability insurance, workers compensation, health insurance, and unemployment insurance, as well as rights under employment protection legislation. Arguably, the most important of these potential gains are an old age pension and health insurance. With regard to old age pensions, however, as a relatively predictable loss, the inability to earn income because of old age is something individuals are better at managing than their likely need for health care, which is far more difficult to predict and whose cost can vary hugely. Low-wage earners in particular might tend to strongly discount the value of future pension benefits because their concerns are focused on short-term income and, in cases of poverty, on day-to-day consumption. Also, any means-tested, noncontributory "social pensions" for the elderly might further discount the value of participation in a contributory pension plan.

The implicit costs of formalization for informal workers are the minimum value of social security benefits and employment protection laws that they receive in return for formalization. The value of the rights that they gain from formalization must exceed their implicit opportunity costs from formalizing. The graphs in figure 3.8 depict this implicit cost to the informal worker as a share of informal income—what we call the "formalization tax rate," or FTR.[7] The FTR measures the difference between total informal income (the informal wage, social assistance, and the family and housing benefits that an individual is entitled to if the state does not observe her earnings) and formal net income (formal net wage, in-work benefits, social assistance, and family and housing benefits to which she is entitled according to her observed income from work) as a share of informal income. It is the share of informal income that an informal worker has to give up to formalize.

Consider the contrasting examples of Bulgaria and Romania on the one hand, and Australia and the United States on the other. These examples are selected because they best illustrate how social protection policy and the design of benefit eligibility criteria create high opportunity costs for formal work. For lower wage levels, the FTR in Bulgaria and Romania is higher than in Australia and the United States. In Bulgaria, the FTR for single persons with no children peaks at around 70 percent (around 60 percent for Romania), at earnings equivalent to about 10 percent of the average wage. That means that in Bulgaria, single persons with no children who earn less than the minimum wage in the informal sector have to give up from 50 percent to 70 percent of their income to formalize. By contrast, in Australia and the United States, the FTR peaks at a much lower fraction of the average wage—around 40 percent in Australia and 30 percent in the United States—and at a higher wage level of around 30 percent to 40 percent of average wages (in the case of the United States, the FTR continues to increase at higher wage levels but at a slow rate).

A more comprehensive comparison shows that in the EU's new member states the opportunity costs of formal work tend to peak at lower wage levels than in high-income OECD countries. Figure 3.9 reveals that both for singles and for one-earner couples with two children, the costs of formalization in the new member states generally tend to be highest for low-wage earners (less than 30 percent of average wage for singles). In some countries, such as Bulgaria, Hungary, and Romania, the FTR for singles is particularly high and peaks at around 70 percent. For families, the FTR tends to be lower and peak at somewhat higher wage levels.

Figure 3.8 For Low-Wage Earners, the Opportunity Costs of Formal Work Are Higher in Bulgaria and Romania than in Australia and the United States

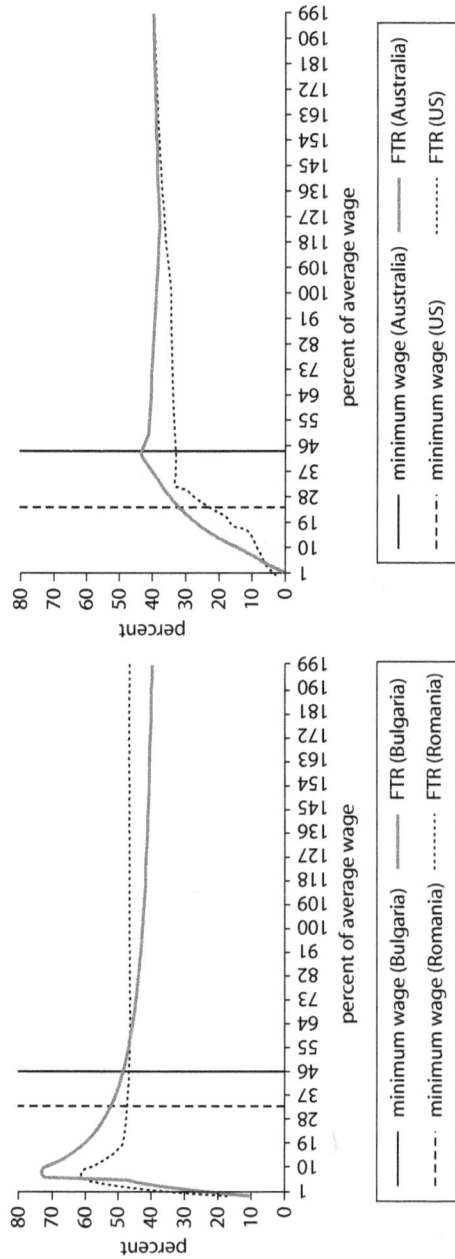

Source: Koettl and Weber 2012a, based on OECD 2008.

Note: FTR = formalization tax rate; graphs show the rate for a single person with no children.

Figure 3.9 In the EU New Member States, the Opportunity Costs of Formal Work Tend to Be Highest at Lower Wage Levels

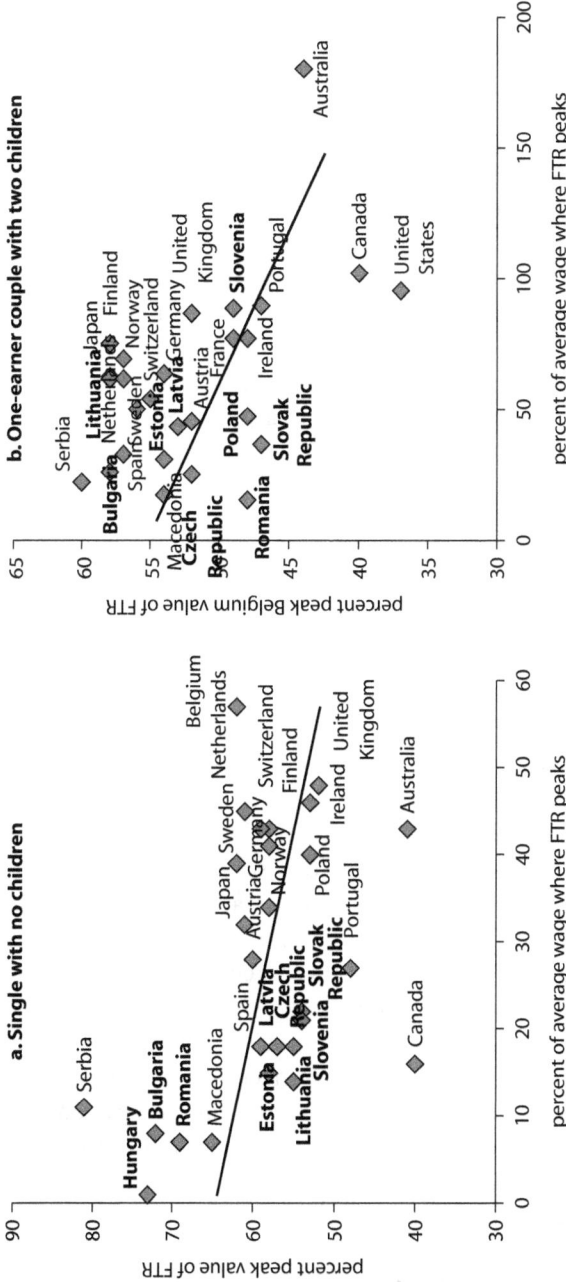

a. Single with no children

b. One-earner couple with two children

Source: Koettl and Weber 2012a, based on OECD 2008.

Note: The scatter plots depict the wage level where the formalization tax rate (FTR) peaks (x-axis) versus the peak value of the FTR (y-axis). Countries with a continuously and significantly increasing FTR were omitted. In countries where the FTR forms a plateau and increases only slightly with the wage level, the lowest wage level at which it stops increasing significantly was chosen as the peak. The new member states are in bold.

The main reasons for the high opportunity costs of formal work are (a) labor taxation, and (b) the sudden withdrawal of social assistance and family benefits at lower wage levels. Labor taxation has already been discussed above as theoretically one of the main obstacles to formal employment at lower wage levels. Also the design of income-tested benefits plays an important role. Social assistance is often paid out as an addition to earned gross income, to guarantee a minimum gross income. Any earned gross income is subtracted from social assistance that is paid out. That means that most formal jobs at low wage levels do not pay—the implicit value of social and employment protection that is gained from formalization would have to be enormously high. Even for higher-paid jobs, the net gain in income is not very high for the same reasons. For an informal worker, the sudden loss of social assistance due to even low levels of formal wages contributes to the implicit opportunity costs of formalization. A more gradual withdrawal of social assistance could decrease this disincentive. Income-tested family and housing benefits also contribute to the formalization tax rate if (prospective) formal income would exceed the threshold for eligibility.

The marginal effective tax rate (METR) also suggests that formal work does not pay at lower wage levels in many of the EU's member states. The METR measures, at a given wage level, how much of an additional euro earned in formal gross wages is taxed away, either as labor tax or in the form of withdrawn benefits. It is therefore an indication of how much it pays for workers to earn more gross income, either by increasing work hours or receiving higher wages.

In many countries, at low wage levels (less than 10 percent of average wages) every additional euro earned is subtracted from entitlements to social assistance; hence 100 percent of any additional euro earned is taxed away. For example, in the Czech Republic and Slovenia, every additional euro earned in formal income is 100 percent taxed away through withdrawal of social assistance at wage levels below 20 percent of the average wage (see figure 3.10). In other countries, such as Portugal and the United States, that is not the case. Structural incentives for formal work are better for low-wage earners in those countries: in Portugal, only 50 percent of every additional euro earned is taxed away, and in the United States the percentage is significantly less. In the United States, that is mainly achieved though so-called in-work benefits, that is, tax credits that subsidize work at low wage levels.

Overall, the new members of the EU tend to have high METRs— usually 100 percent—at low wage levels, although the METR tends to

Figure 3.10 For Low-Wage Earners, the METR Is 100 percent in the Czech Republic and Slovenia but Is Much Lower in Portugal and the United States

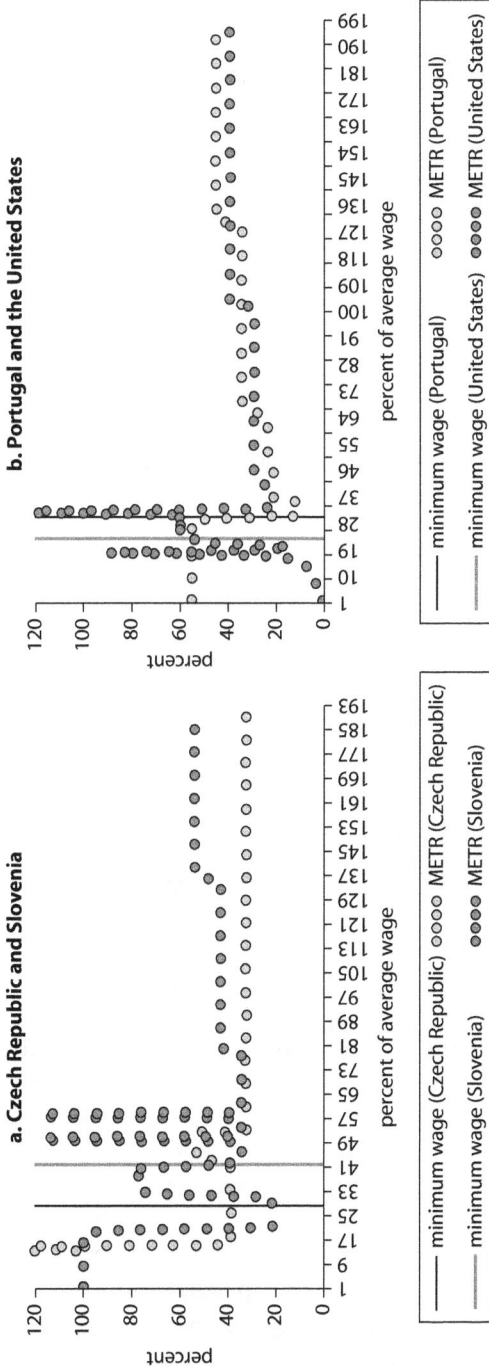

a. Czech Republic and Slovenia

percent of average wage

— minimum wage (Czech Republic) ○○○○ METR (Czech Republic)
— minimum wage (Slovenia) ●●●● METR (Slovenia)

b. Portugal and the United States

percent of average wage

— minimum wage (Portugal) ○○○○ METR (Portugal)
— minimum wage (United States) ●●●● METR (United States)

Source: Koettl and Weber (2012a), for this volume, based on OECD (2008).
Note: Graphs show the marginal effective tax rate for a single person with no children.

drop at lower wage levels faster than in high-income OECD countries (figure 3.11). A notable exception is Poland, which has the lowest METR at low wage levels of all countries. The reason is an apparent lack—at least according to the OECD tax and benefit model—of a comprehensive (federally administered) social assistance program. A locally administered social assistance program could exist that unfortunately is not captured by the OECD tax and benefit model. The same might also apply, for example, to countries such as Greece and Italy.

It is unlikely that the value that informal workers put on social insurance benefits and employment protection would exceed the high implicit costs of formalization. The analysis above shows that informal workers at low earnings levels have to give up significant amounts of their earnings to formalize, and it is unlikely that the rights they gain in return for formalization exceed those losses, particularly given the deterioration of the average replacement rates of mandated pension plans in the past 10 years in the EU's new member states. Besides employment protection, the most substantial advantages a worker gains from formalization are old age and disability pensions, health insurance, and unemployment insurance. Health insurance, which is arguably the most important social insurance entitlement with immediate—as opposed to future—benefits, can sometimes be obtained through a formally employed spouse or by registering as unemployed and might not enter into the value of formal benefits. The value of being vested in mandatory old age pensions could be further discounted by noncontributory social assistance or by alternative investments that a worker might deem superior. The design of income-tested benefits such as social assistance and family benefits can also discourage formal jobs, as formal income might easily lead to withdrawal of benefits.

But putting aside the problems in the incentive structure of the taxation and social protection system presented above, is there evidence that people perceive and react to the signals they receive? The graphs in each panel of figure 3.12 plot the observed rate of informality at different points of the earnings distribution and how it relates to the estimated tax wedge, FTR, and METR in six countries. Essentially the graphs show where in the synthetically represented incentive structure informal work is actually observed. In countries where the slope of the FTR is steepest at the lower end of the earnings distribution, the observed incidence of informal employment is highest. It is particularly pronounced in Bulgaria and Estonia but also observed in other countries.

Figure 3.11 In the New Member States, the METR Tends to Be High at Low Wage Levels but also to Drop Significantly at Lower Wage Levels than in High-Income OECD Countries

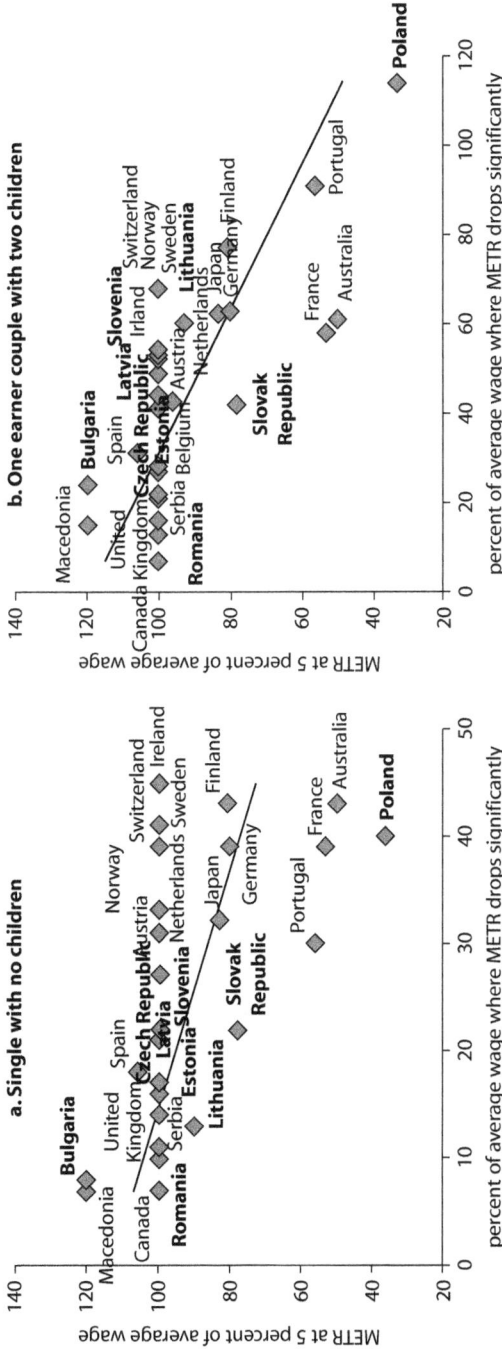

a. Single with no children

b. One earner couple with two children

Source: Koettl and Weber 2012a, for this volume, based on OECD 2008.

Note: The scatter plot depicts the wage level where the formalization tax rate (FTR) peaks (x-axis) versus the peak value of the FTR (y-axis). Countries with a continuously and significantly increasing FTR were omitted. In countries where the FTR forms a plateau and increases only slightly with the wage level, the lowest wage level at which the FTR stops to increase significantly was chosen as the peak. New member states are in bold.

Figure 3.12 Incidence of Informal Work and the Labor Tax and Social Protection Incentive Structure

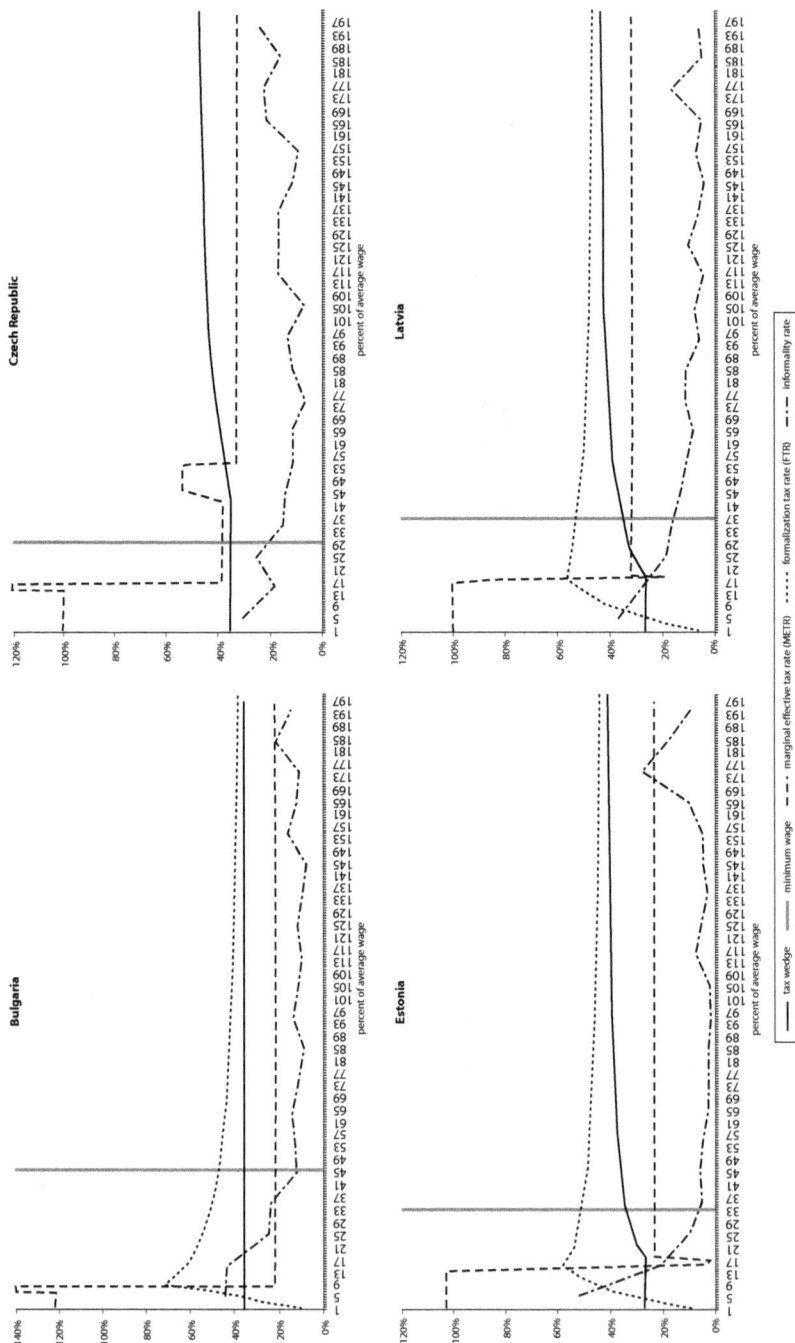

Figure 3.12 *(continued)*

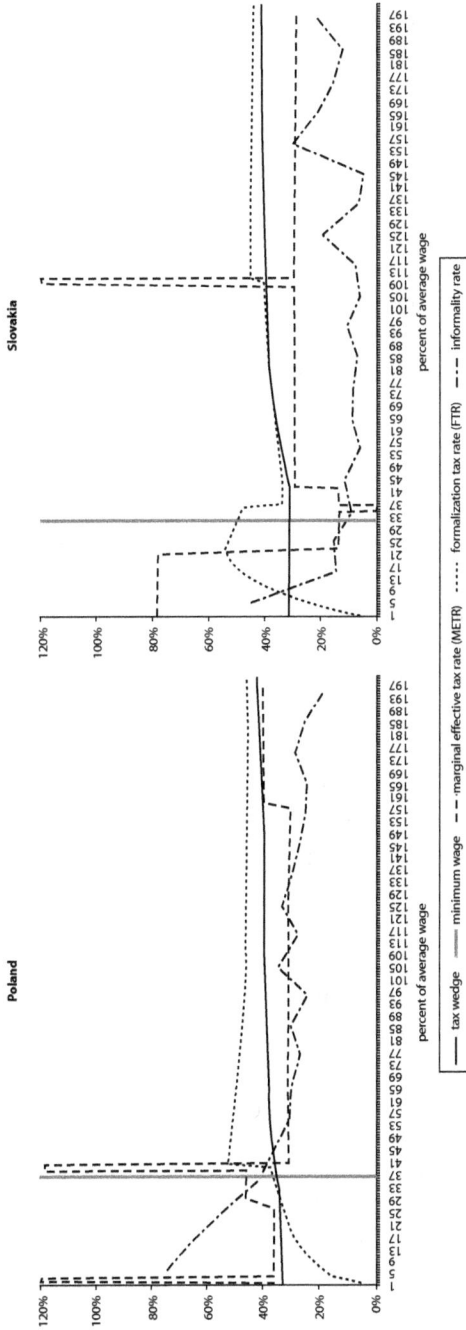

Poland

Slovakia

| tax wedge | minimum wage | marginal effective tax rate (METR) | formalization tax rate (FTR) | informality rate |

Source: Koettl and Weber 2012a, for this volume, based on OECD 2008.

Note: Figures show incentives structures for single earners with no dependent children. Figures in the appendix show the structure of incentives for a one-earner couple with two dependent children. Informality rates are by income group, independent of family structure.

To back up the graphical presentation in figure 3.12, regression analysis on microdata reported in table A.2 in the statistical appendix shows that the levels of both the FTR and METR have a strongly significant, positive correlation with the probability that a worker is engaged informally. In other words, greater individual disincentives to formal work (as measured by FTR and METR) correlate strongly with higher probabilities of being informal. Is this evidence that workers are responding to the incentives presented to them in the structure of taxation and social protection? Maybe, but causality cannot be established using cross-sectional data. In fact, causality could to some extent be reversed, at least in a country-by-country comparison: Because of high levels of informality, the government might have to increase taxes on the formal sector to raise sufficient revenues, hence increasing disincentives for formal work. Interestingly, the tax wedge yields a negative correlation with informality, indicating that the tax wedge is not sufficiently capturing disincentives to formal work. Although we would expect that a higher tax wedge is associated with higher informality, a closer investigation of the data reveals that the tax wedge is lowest with low-wage earners and strictly increases with income level. At the same time, the incidence of informality is highest among low-wage earners, which indeed suggests a negative correlation, as confirmed by the econometric analysis. In any case, readers should keep in mind that possibly much more than just the incentive structure of labor taxes and social protection is at play, as will be discussed in chapter 4.

With regard to reforming the design of social assistance, housing, and family benefits, the key is to keep the marginal effective tax rate in mind when designing benefit withdrawal. In other words, beneficiaries of social assistance, housing, and family benefits should gain from additional formal work—that is, any additional formal wage should also increase their net income, *including* benefits. If that is not the case, additional formal work does not pay, and beneficiaries will prefer to not work at all, or to work only informally, or will have a strong incentive to underreport their earnings. Arguably the role of social assistance in providing disincentives to formal work might be limited in most of the EU's new member states. Programs are usually tightly targeted to a small group of beneficiaries, so that coverage—even among the poorest—is very limited. In addition, targeted benefits are not particularly generous. Categorical benefits, such as family benefits, seem to play a much more important role.

To reform along these lines, withdrawal of benefits has to be phased as income increases, so that no sudden drops in net income occur. Eligibility criteria that restrict, for example, family benefits to those below a certain income threshold—often around 50 percent of average wage—result in very high METRs and a considerable drop in net income once the income threshold is crossed. The German Hartz IV reforms again offer a good example of how this can be avoided and how phased benefit withdrawal can be achieved.

Entitlements to free health insurance—if they exist—should be limited to the poor, and the entitlement should be based on a means test, not an income test. It is important that the poor have access to free health insurance, as sickness is a serious economic risk that can deepen poverty. Yet if free health insurance is easily accessible also by those who can afford to contribute to its cost, it decreases the value of formal work and increases incentives to work informally. It is therefore important to base decisions about who should have access to free health insurance on the means that a household has at its disposal, and not on formal income or formal employment status (such as registered unemployment, as is the case in some Balkan countries). This requires robust means-testing mechanisms, as opposed to income testing. It can be done by proxy-means testing—for example, looking at electricity consumption—or by frequent contacts between a social worker and the applicant.

Finally, it is worth pointing out that most of the reforms to social protection systems discussed above have significant fiscal costs. Given the current fiscal constraints, little fiscal space may be available to push through reforms. In particular, reforms that aim at making work pay at the low-wage end—wage subsidies, tax credits, and so on—can considerably reduce tax revenues, including social insurance contributions, or increase public expenditures. In this regard, however, the new members of the EU are in a favorable position as their tax systems are relatively nonprogressive. Making them more progressive could make future reforms along these lines fiscally neutral to a large extent.

Labor Market Regulations, Interventions, and Institutions

Turning to structural incentives that firms and people encounter in the labor market, this section presents the results of multicountry panel analysis by Fialová and Schneider (2011) and Hazans (2011b) that exploited variation in aggregate data across countries and over time. This approach is fraught with endogeneity problems that the contributing researchers have done their best to mitigate. That said, the results should be interpreted as cautious conditional correlations, rather than as presenting causal relationships.

In this section, it is helpful to distinguish among *regulations, interventions,* and *institutions.* The distinctions are important to understand how each can determine the extent of informal forms of work in a particular country's context. Regulations set the legal parameters of work, in the form of a minimum wage, restrictions on dismissal, or both. Interventions are deployed by the state to correct market failures, such as the inability of the private financial markets to viably insure the risk of unemployment (unemployment insurance) or to cope with uncertainties such as inflation (a publicly provided pension with income protection, or inflation-indexed bonds). Institutions are the condoned structures and agreed procedures by which interested actors exert their influence and make and carry out decisions. For the labor market, the best example is the space afforded in the legal codes of most middle-income countries—and certainly all the members of the EU—for collective bargaining through labor unions. This section presents evidence of how each of those influences the extent of informal work in its various guises.

Starting with minimum wages, the predictions of the simple two-sector labor pricing model presented in chapter 2 are clear-cut. A legislated minimum wage (or otherwise enforced nonmarket floor under wages) increases labor costs for firms and prevents them from offering formal employment to workers whose marginal productivity does not exceed the minimum. The effect will be stronger for workers with the lowest productivity, especially younger, less-experienced workers. Priced out of formal jobs, they will join those genuinely unemployed, take informal employment, or pretend to be job seeking while working informally.

Elaborations in the literature, however, reveal more ambiguity about the effect that a minimum wage could have on the extent of informal employment. A minimum wage might motivate workers to increase productivity, in the "efficient wages" framework (Rebitzer and Taylor 1995; Manning 1995), or persuade job seekers and some waiting outside the labor market to hold out for a formal job even if plenty of informal employment is on offer. To the extent that employers have to report to the tax authorities at least the portion of their wage bill equivalent to some multiple of the minimum wage, raising the minimum might in some circumstances force formalization at the margin of transactions and inputs to their production process.

All the new members of the EU have introduced legislated minimum wages. Although several older members do not have legally binding minimum wages, an effective minimum is secured through the collective bargaining process in Austria, Denmark, France, Germany, Italy, and

Sweden. Generally, legislated minimum wages in the EU's new members are considerably lower than the legislated or effective minimum wages in the older member states. Over the past decade, however, they have been on a clear upward trend (Fialová and Schneider 2009). Since 2000 the minimum wage, as a percentage of average wage, has risen fastest in Bulgaria and the Czech Republic (figure 3.13).

Measures of the minimum wage as a share of the average or median wage can, however, be deceptive, as argued by Maloney, Fajnzylber, and Ribiero (2001) and Cunningham (2007), and conceal the influence of wage regulation on labor market outcomes. Instead, graphical tools such as kernel density and cumulative distribution plots offer a more comprehensive way of measuring whether a minimum wage is binding on a large segment of workers. These tools also can be used to assess the impact of a minimum wage through "numeraire" effects (acting as a reference throughout the earnings distribution) and "lighthouse" effects (informing wage setting even in the unregulated part of the labor market).

Both graphical measures—kernel and cumulative density functions— for 12 EU members, including several of the new member states, are presented in figure 3.14 (extending over several pages). Both the formal and informal earnings distributions are plotted, and the informal distribution is presented using both the firm size criterion (employment in a firm of five or fewer workers) and the social insurance criterion (dependent workers only). The minimum wage is indicated by the vertical line, left of the origin. In the kernels, the impact of the minimum wage is seen in the shape (the steepness of the slope, spikes in the distribution) of the plots. In the cumulative density plots the influence of the minimum wage shows up mainly in "cliffs," or straight, vertical segments in the distribution.

The first notable feature among the panels in figure 3.14 is the similarity in shape between the earnings distribution of informal workers according to the two different criteria, firm size and social insurance contribution. Despite limitations in the available survey data, it is an encouraging corroboration of these proxies.

The second notable feature is the similarity in earnings distributions of formal and informal workers: only in Estonia, Slovenia, and Greece (although less significantly) do the shapes of the curves differ greatly. Plots for other middle- and upper-middle-income countries show more pronounced differences in the shapes of the distribution of informal and formal workers. The similarity may indicate less segmentation in most of the EU member labor markets.

Figure 3.13 Labor Market Regulations in Selected OECD and EU Countries

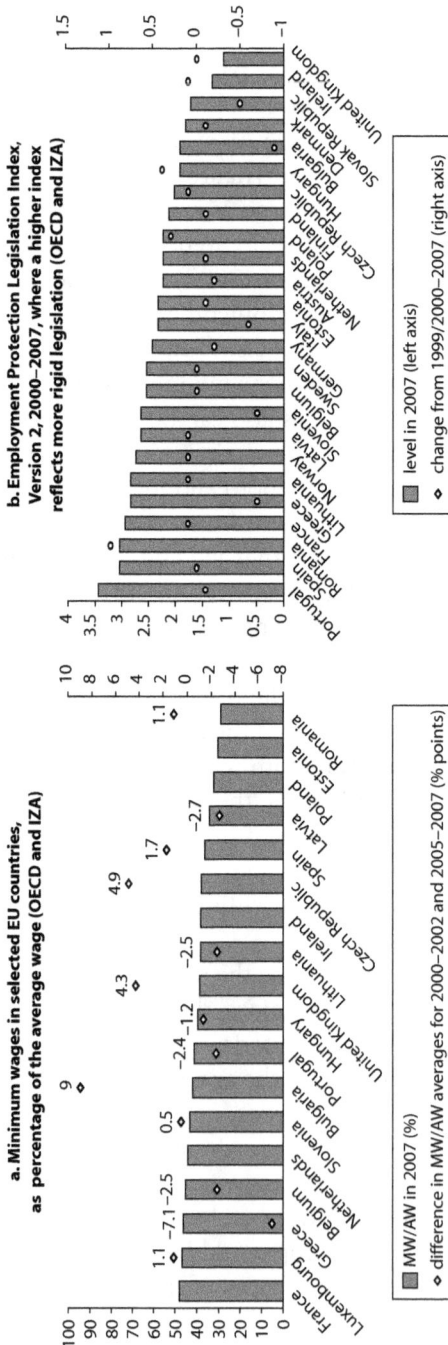

a. Minimum wages in selected EU countries, as percentage of the average wage (OECD and IZA)

- MW/AW in 2007 (%)
- ◇ difference in MW/AW averages for 2000–2002 and 2005–2007 (% points)

b. Employment Protection Legislation Index, Version 2, 2000–2007, where a higher index reflects more rigid legislation (OECD and IZA)

- level in 2007 (left axis)
- ◇ change from 1999/2000–2007 (right axis)

Source: Fialová and Schneider 2011, for this volume, with data from Lehmann and Muravyev 2010.

Figure 3.14 Kernel and Cumulative Density Functions of Workers Engaged Informally and Formally, by Hourly Earnings Reported in SILC 2008

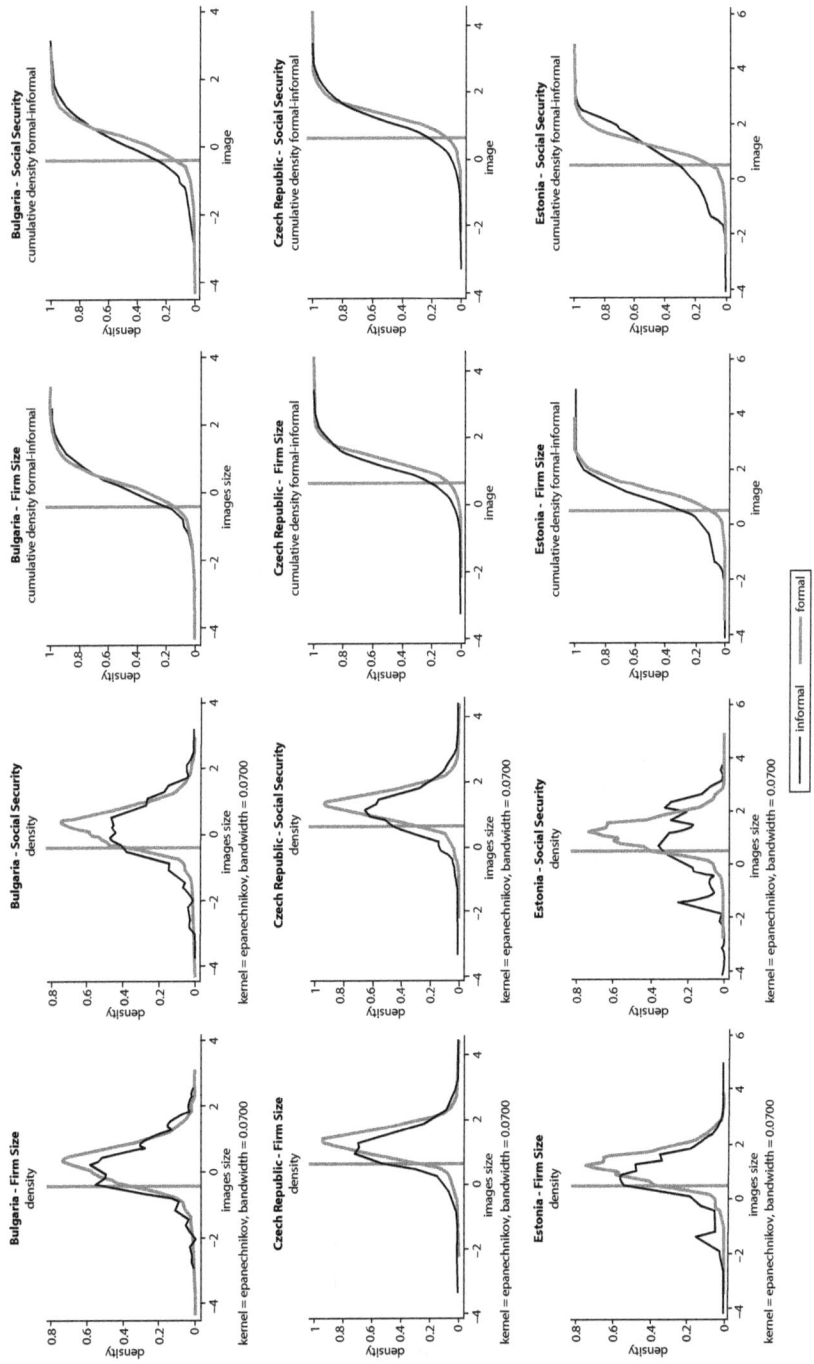

Figure 3.14 *(continued)*

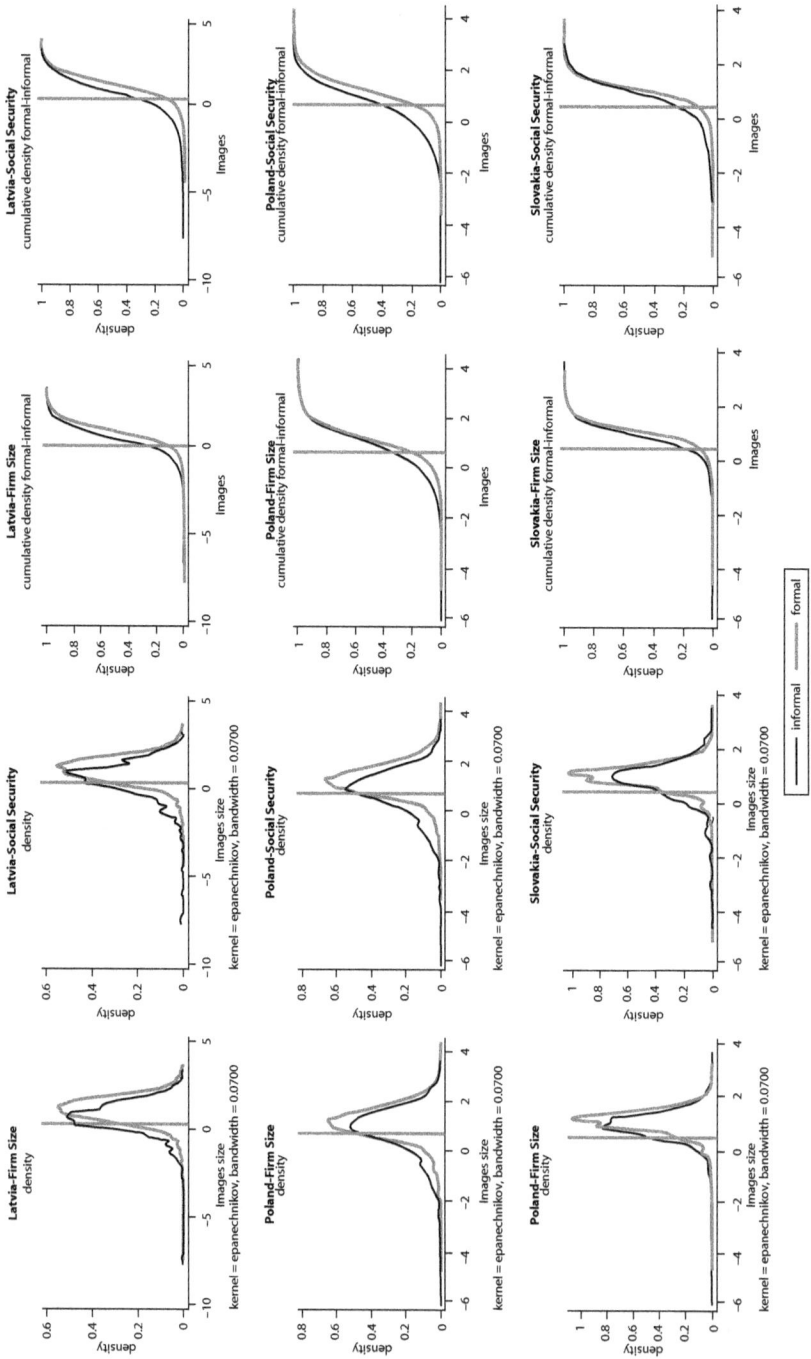

Latvia-Firm Size
density

Latvia-Social Security
density

Latvia-Firm Size
cumulative density formal-informal

Latvia-Social Security
cumulative density formal-informal

Poland-Firm Size
density

Poland-Social Security
density

Poland-Firm Size
cumulative density formal-informal

Poland-Social Security
cumulative density formal-informal

Poland-Firm Size
density

Slovakia-Social Security
density

Slovakia-Firm Size
cumulative density formal-informal

Slovakia-Social Security
cumulative density formal-informal

kernel = epanechnikov, bandwidth = 0.0700

informal   formal

Figure 3.14 *(continued)*

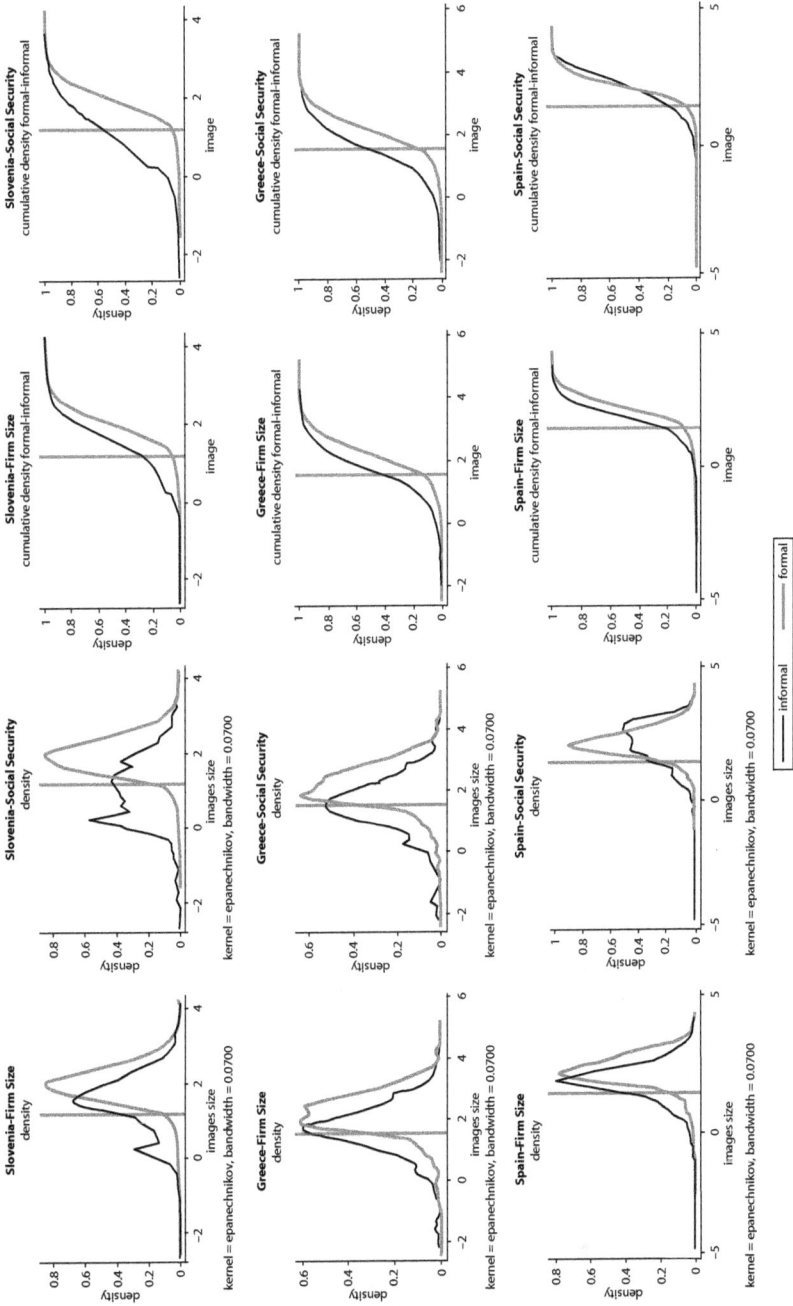

Figure 3.14 *(continued)*

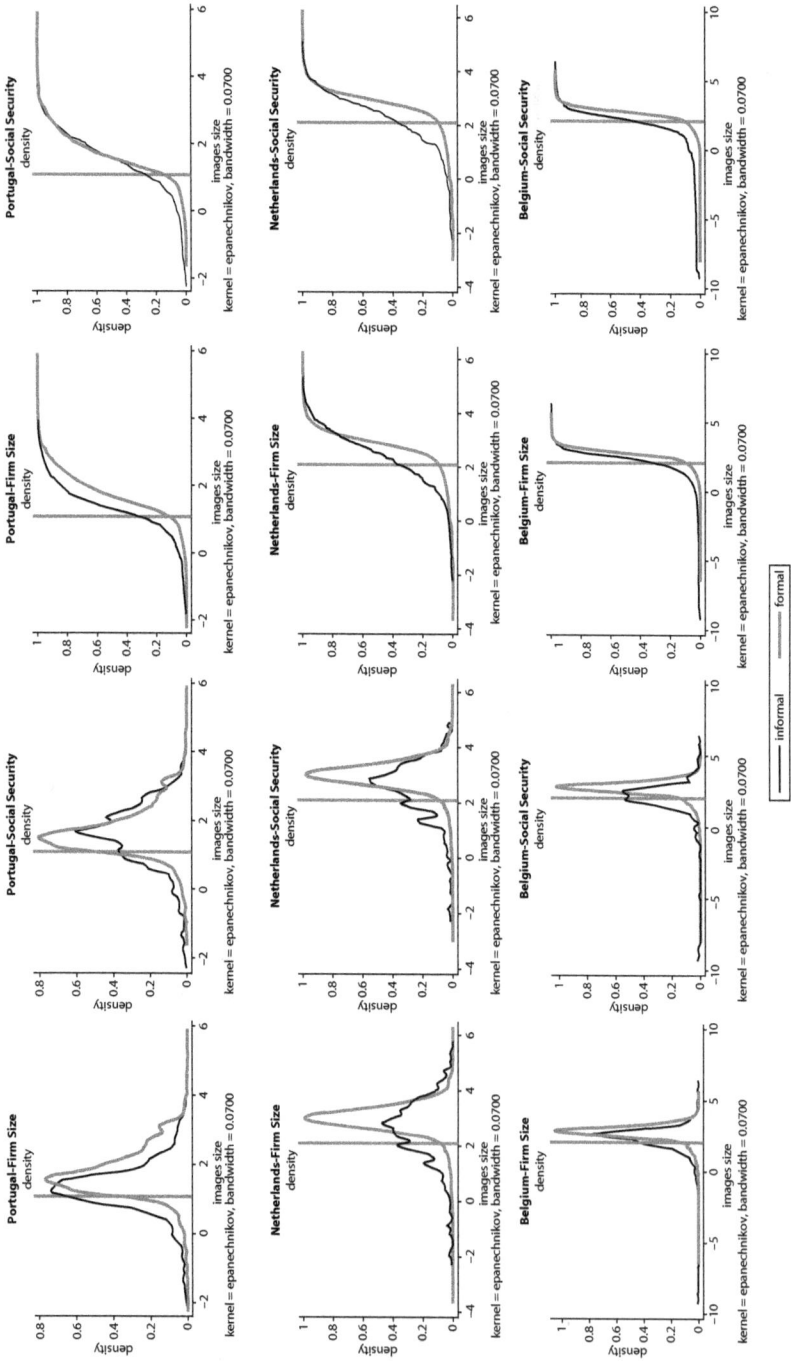

Source: Authors' calculations using Eurostat 2008.

Note: Firm-size: dependent and self-employed workers in firms with 5 or fewer workers are considered informal; social security: dependent workers not contributing to social insurance are considered informal.

The third feature worth noting is that although the minimum wage in most countries is influencing the shape the earnings distribution—most noticeably in the steepness of the curves for Poland, Slovakia, Slovenia, Greece, Spain, and Portugal—there is relatively little clumping or piling up (neither steep peaks in the kernels nor vertical segments in the cumulative density plots) at the minimum wage. That suggests that the distortions that are being introduced in the labor market by minimum wages, although present, are limited. Indeed, it is only in southern member countries (Greece, Spain, Portugal) and in the Netherlands that there is any noticeable clumping around the minimum. Intriguingly, however, it is the earnings distribution of informal workers that shows peaks at or closely around the minimum wage in those countries. That may be evidence of workers in small firms and those who do not contribute to social insurance using the minimum wage as a key reference point.

In a background paper prepared for this book, Fialová and Schneider (2011) looked at the determinants of informal economic activity using panel techniques on country-level data and found that the minimum wage is only weakly associated with the extent of informal production (Schneider, Buehn, and Montenegro 2010; measure of the shadow economy as a percentage of GDP); employment in small firms; the share of workers who do not contribute to social insurance; and the extent of self-employment. The minimum wage had no significant association when they restricted their sample only to EU members that also belong to the OECD (among them, four new members, the Czech Republic, Hungary, Poland, and Slovakia). That changes, however, when all new members are included. With the expanded sample, the level of the minimum wage has an unanticipated negative association with the extent of informal production as a share of GDP and the extent of employment in small firms, but has no significant association with any of the other proxy measures of informal employment. The result holds when their model is estimated using only the new member states. This unexpected reduction in the size of the shadow economy with an increase in the minimum wage could reflect the fiscal channel explained earlier, that is, a higher minimum wage forces firms and workers to declare a greater portion of their actual earnings.

A similar country-level econometric exercise by Hazans (2011b) used our preferred measures of the extent of informal work in the labor market—employment without a contract and informal self-employment—and shows that the minimum wage is differently related to informal work in different parts of the EU (see figure 3.15). In the southern and new member states, raising the minimum wage has the effect predicted in the

Figure 3.15 **Labor Regulations, Interventions, and Institutions on the Extent of Informal Work**

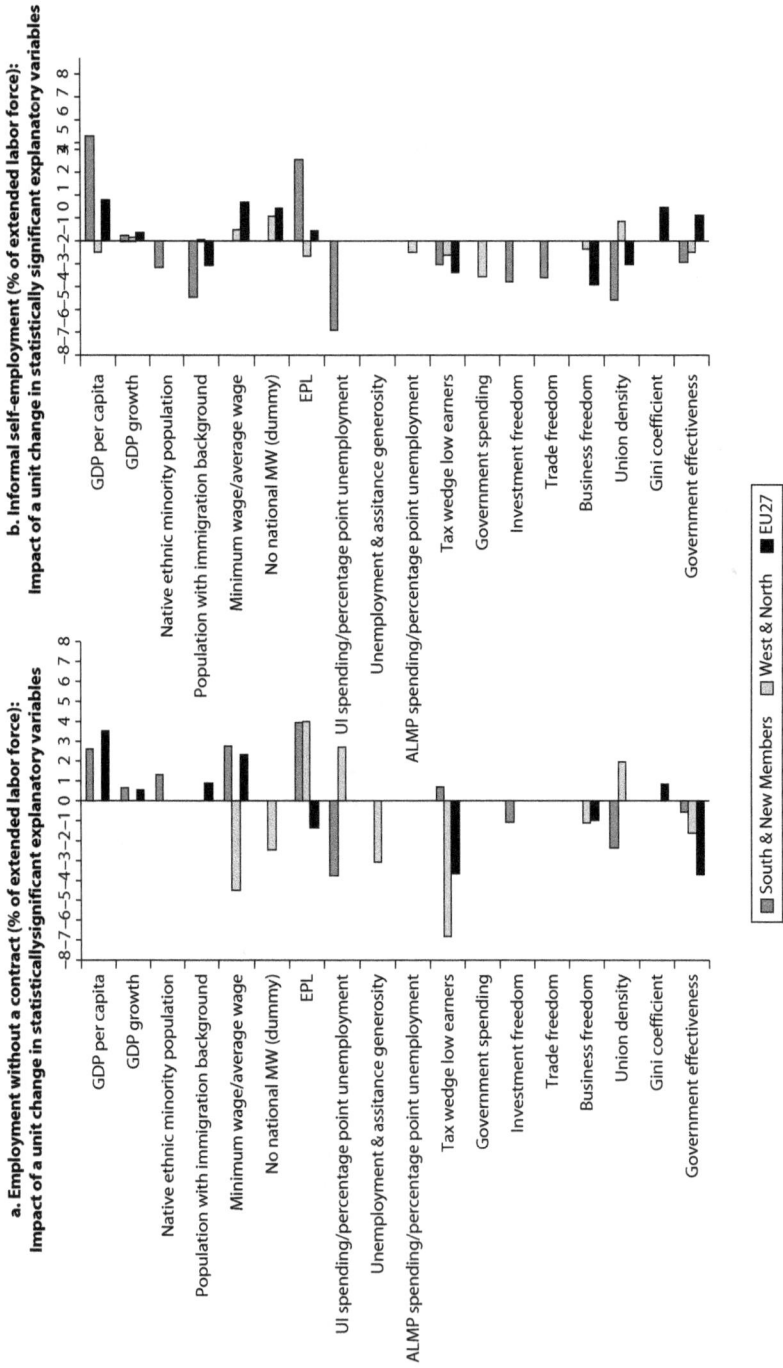

a. Employment without a contract (% of extended labor force):
Impact of a unit change in statistically significant explanatory variables

b. Informal self-employment (% of extended labor force):
Impact of a unit change in statistically significant explanatory variables

Legend: ■ South & New Members   □ West & North   ■ EU27

Source: Hazans 2011b, for this volume.
Note: See table A.3 in the statistical appendix for full results.

conventional models, increasing the share of workers without contracts in the labor force. However in the West and North, an increase in the minimum wage lowers the extent of employment without a contract. The motivational effect of the "efficiency wage" model may be at work in these countries, causing job seekers to wait for formal employment offers rather than take up informal work. An alternative explanation, where the minimum wage is more binding on informal work contracts, is that low-productivity workers are priced out of informal jobs. However, for both samples of EU member states, a higher minimum wage is associated with more extensive informal dependent employment and informal self-employment.

A second widespread form of labor market regulation, employment protection legislation or EPL, restricts employers' ability to dismiss workers and can reduce flows into, but also out of, unemployment. Strict EPL can slow new employment if restrictions on dismissing workers make employers wary of taking on someone new. The restrictions increase the attraction of using fixed-term contracts and past a certain threshold can cause employers to hire informally.

Using the OECD's (2004) measure of how strict employment protection is—and its application by Lehmann and Muravyev (2010) to non-OECD European countries—the most liberal (least restrictive on employers) conditions are found in Denmark, Hungary, Ireland, and Slovakia. France, Greece, Portugal, and Spain have the most restrictive regulation. Employment protection has relaxed noticeably in Austria, Greece, Italy, Portugal, and Slovakia. But over the same period, Hungary, Ireland, and Poland have tightened their employment protection laws. Fialová and Schneider (2011) note that although EPL in the EU's new member states is less than in the older members, some convergence has occurred, driven both by liberalization in parts of the West and also by growing restrictions among members in the East. Lithuania and Slovenia had the most restrictive legislation, although the latter has liberalized recently. Romania, in contrast, recently tightened its EPL and after Portugal and Spain, now has the most restrictive regulation.

Exploiting variations in the size of the shadow economy as a percentage of recorded GDP, as well as the four alternative measures of the extent of informal work across countries and over time, Fialová and Schneider (2011) showed that once a country's level of development has been taken into account, the strictness of EPL is the variable most consistently significant and robustly associated with the size the shadow economy and extent of informal work. Although this finding is consistent with earlier research on the impact of factor and product market regulation on firm and household decisions to transact "in the shadow" (Loayza, Oviedo, and Servén 2005), Fialová and Schneider's results are extraordinary for how consistently employment protection legislation is significantly related to an increasing scale of shadow production, the percentage of workers engaged in small firms, the share that fail to contribute to social insurance, and the extent of self-employment. The magnitude, direction, and significance of the estimated coefficients on the EPL index vary little across the new members and the older members of the EU. Hazans's (2011b) estimates of the impact of EPL on the extent of employment without a contract for the southern and new EU members are similarly significant and robust.

Labor market interventions—"active" labor market programs such as training and job search assistance, "passive" unemployment benefits and other forms of social insurance—predominantly financed from taxes on labor, are commonplace in EU member countries, including the new member states. The expected impact of imposing payroll taxes to finance social insurance on the incentives to informalize labor is relatively straightforward: all else equal, a higher tax wedge should increase the extent of informal work. But the expected impact of active and passive labor market programs is less so. By their intent, active programs that improve workers' human capital or eliminate some of the information asymmetries that delay or frustrate "matching" in the labor market should lower the extent of informal work. Active programs might also lower the search and training costs of firms and so indirectly subsidize the creation of formal jobs. Passive programs, such as unemployment benefits, can remove the urgency of finding a new job and thus also improve the quality of matches. However, the record of effectiveness of active programs is checkered at best, and if unemployment benefits are overgenerous or poorly designed, they can perversely lower people's motivation to look for and accept a job.

Belying easy answers, the two sets of panel estimation exercises conducted for the book show varying results, depending on the measure of informality and the EU member states included. Starting with active labor programs, Fialová and Schneider (2011) found that spending on those programs (as a percentage of GDP per percentage point of unemployment) significantly lowered the size of the shadow economy as a percentage of GDP, but only in the OECD members of Europe (including four new members). Spending on active programs also lowered the extent of informal employment when measured as the share of workers not making social insurance contributions, employment in small firms, and self-employment. But their results are vulnerable to changes in the sample of countries included, losing statistical significance. Hazans (2011b) found that spending on active programs significantly lowered the extent of informal self-employment, as well as unemployment and discouragement, both in western and northern Europe and in Europe at large; results for eastern and southern EU members are similar for unemployment but less conclusive with regard to informal employment.

Hazans (2011b) also found that the impact of passive interventions—unemployment insurance and the generosity of long-term social assistance benefits to the unemployed—varies across Europe. In the southern and new member states, spending on unemployment insurance benefits is at a relatively modest level but seems to help keep job seekers from having to accept informal forms of work. The same is true for the long-term social assistance to the unemployed, as long as its five-year average net replacement rate (including unemployment insurance benefits) does not exceed 55 percent. However, raising the replacement rate of long-term assistance (unlike unemployment insurance) also tends to increase the unemployment rate. In contrast, in western and northern European countries, higher spending on unemployment benefits (other things equal) increases informal dependent employment, as well as unemployment, and higher net replacement rates of social assistance benefits over five years seem to reduce the extent of informal work without increasing unemployment. Passive interventions such as unemployment insurance are designed to enable better matching of job seekers with employers offering jobs. It appears that in southern and new member states, unemployment insurance may perform this function without creating undue moral hazard in the form of informal work and unemployment. By contrast, in western and northern European countries, unemployment insurance might be encouraging—and even subsidizing—informal work.

The tax wedge on formal employment that is largely created by the financing structure of many of these interventions is expected to increase the size of the informal work force. And indeed among the southern and new member states Hazans (2011b) found the expected positive and highly significant association between the tax wedge and the share of workers without an employment contract. However, elsewhere in Europe the tax wedge shows a significant but unexpected effect on the size of the shadow economy and the extent of informal work. Fialová and Schneider (2011) and Hazans (2011b) found that in the older members of the EU, the size of the tax wedge is significantly associated with a lower share of employment in small firms, fewer workers who do not contribute to social insurance, a reduced rate of self-employment, and a smaller share of workers without an employment contract. This unexpected result shows a consistent regional pattern across several specifications: the significant, negative effect of labor taxes on all these measures of informal employment was found by Fialová and Schneider *only* in older members and by Hazans only in the western and northern members of the EU and when data from all European countries are pooled together. Both papers offer similar explanations for these counterintuitive results: not only is administrative capacity to enforce taxation likely to be greater in the older, higher-income EU countries in the West and the North, but a larger tax burden on labor may actually reflect the degree of credibility that the state enjoys in its role of providing public goods. These arguments are taken up in greater detail in chapter 4.

Koettl and Weber (2012b) offer an alternative explanation of the seemingly counterintuitive results on the tax wedge, as already discussed above. In their microeconometric analysis, they also found a negative correlation between the level of the tax wedge and informal employment. They argue that the tax wedge does not sufficiently capture disincentives for work, at least in microeconometric analysis. But they also argue that in the cross-country analysis, it might be more suitable to use the tax wedge not as measured at the average wage, but measured at lower wage levels because that is also the locus of informality in most countries, and using the tax wedge at higher wage levels could distort the analysis.

Finally, turning to institutions, although it is impossible to fully isolate institutions that have an impact on the labor market only from those that shape other social and economic interactions (and the background research for this book examined the impact of a wide range of institutional indicators), one institution in particular is directly relevant to the discussion in this section: collective bargaining, as proxied by the strength of labor unions. The impact of labor unions is to a large extent also captured in the previous discussion of minimum wages, employment protection legislation, and active and passive interventions. Both panel estimations conducted for this book used the share of unionized labor as a proxy for labor market institutions. Good arguments can be made why this exact measure may not fully capture the impact of collective bargaining and the power of unions—in many countries what unions succeed in negotiating for their members becomes binding for anybody in regulated employment, whether they are members or not.

Fialová and Schneider (2011) found that greater union density increases the size of the shadow economy, raises the share of workers in small firms, increases the share of noncontributing workers, and increases self-employment. These results are predicted by the conventional labor pricing models. However, their results vary greatly in impact and statistical significance and with changes to the sample of countries covered.

Hazans's (2011b) estimations are more stable and show a consistent pattern across the different regions of the EU. In the southern members and the new member states, the impact of unions is unexpected: greater union density lowers the share of workers without contracts and the extent of informal self-employment. In the western and northern member states, the impact is exactly opposite: greater union density increases the share of employment without a contract and self-employment, a result more consistent with the segmentation predicted in the conventional two-sector labor pricing models.

The importance of credible institutions may be reflected in these contrasting results. In the parts of the European Union where government's enforcement capacity is limited, where households and firms have fewer institutional channels to make their voices heard or to seek redress when the law is violated, labor unions (and indeed other nongovernment organized pressure groups) may be acting as default monitors and enforcers of the labor code. In contrast, where there are better-functioning structures to monitor and enforce regulations and plenty of other avenues for recourse when rules are broken or service providers fail to meet expectations, the role of unions can remain narrowly defined and their impact is likely to remain more along the lines that the textbook models predict. We will return to this line of reasoning in the last part of the book.

Notes

1. Another form of underreporting income is the "gratitude payment" for the services of some professions, notably medical doctors. In Hungary, Kornai (2000) interviewed medical staff and the general public and found that such cash-in-hand payments are deeply engrained in the medical system. Gratitude payments are most common for obstetrical services, heart operations, other difficult surgeries, and emergency house visits at night (for which about nine out of 10 people said that it is customary to give gratitude money).

2. In many countries, full-time work at 33 percent of the average wage is below the legal minimum wage. Nevertheless, the same tax wedge applies to someone receiving the average wage but working 33 percent of the time, although

there can be slight variations of the tax wedge for part-time workers when compared to full-time workers.

3. The assumed relationship is that tax systems need to raise a certain fixed amount of resources. Those that put higher taxes on lower wages have less need to increase taxes at higher wages and hence display less progressivity.

4. Exceptions are Hungary and the Netherlands, which have a social security contribution floor. Such a floor has to be paid independent of actual wages earned and therefore increases the tax wedge significantly at lower wage levels.

5. According to the theory of optimal taxation, both a consumption tax and a pure wage tax (such as social security contributions) are efficient, as they are intertemporally neutral; both the consumption tax and the pure wage tax do not tax interest income and therefore, in contrast to income taxation, do not distort saving and investment decisions.

6. We only consider workers who are not registered at all; partially formal workers who underreport their wages are not considered.

7. The term "formalization tax rate" was introduced by Koettl and Weber (2012b) and is defined and discussed in more detail there.

References

Agell, J., T. Lindh, and H. Ohlsson. 1997. "Growth and the Public Sector: A Critical Review Essay." *European Journal of Political Economy* 13: 33–52.

Brou, D., and K. A. Collins. 2001. "Winning at Hide and Seek: The Tax Mix and the Informal Economy." *Canadian Tax Journal* 49 (6): 1539–62.

Cunningham, Wendy. 2007. *Minimum Wages and Social Policy: Lessons from Developing Countries*. Washington, DC: World Bank.

Daveri, F., and G. Tabellini. 2000. "Unemployment, Growth and Taxation in Industrial Countries." *Economic Policy* 15: 47–104.

EC (European Commission). 2006. "Macroeconomic Effects of a Shift from Direct to Indirect Taxation: A Simulation for 15 EU Member Countries." Note presented at the OECD Working Party No. 2, November, Brussels.

———. 2007. "Undeclared Work in the European Economy." Special Eurobarometer 284/ Wave 67.3—TNS Opinion and Social, October, Brussels.

Eurostat. 2008. "EU-SILC—European Union Statistics on Income and Living Conditions." Luxembourg: Eurostat. http://www.eui.eu/Research/Library/ ResearchGuides/Economics/ Statistics/DataPortal/EU-SILC.aspx.

Fialová, K., and O. Schneider. 2009. "Labour Market Institutions and Their Effect on Labour Market Performance in the New EU Member Countries." *Eastern European Economics* 47 (3): 57–83.

————. 2011. "Labor Institutions and Their Impact on Shadow Economies in Europe." Background paper for "In from the Shadow: Integrating Europe's Informal Labor." Policy Research Working Paper 5913, World Bank, Washington, DC.

Hazans, M. 2011b. "What Explains the Prevalence of Informal Employment in European Countries: The Role of Labor Institutions, Governance, Immigrants, and Growth." Background paper for "In from the Shadow: Integrating Europe's Informal Labor." Policy Research Working Paper 5917, World Bank, Washington, DC.

Jackman, R., R. Layard, and S. J. Nickell. 1996. "Combating Unemployment: Is Flexibility Enough?" CEP discussion paper 293. Centre for Economic Performance, London School of Economics and Political Science, London, UK.

Koettl, J., and M. Weber. 2012a. "Disincentives for Formal Work in OECD and Eastern European Countries. A Descriptive and Empirical Analysis of the Tax Wedge, the Marginal Effective Tax Rate, and the Formalization Tax Rate." Policy Research Working Paper, forthcoming, World Bank, Washington, DC.

Koettl, J., and M. Weber. 2012b. "Does Formal work say? The Role of Labor Taxation and Social Benefit Design in the EU Member States." *Research in Labor Economics* 34:167–204.

Kornai, J. 2000. "Hidden in an Envelope: Gratitude Payments to Medical Doctors in Hungary." In *Festschrift in Honour of George Soros.* Budapest: CEU Press.

Lehmann, H., and A. Muravyev. 2010. "Labor Market Institutions and Labor Market Performance: What Can We Learn from Transition Countries?" Working Paper 714, Dipartimento Scienze Economiche, Universita' di Bologna.

Leibfritz, W., J. Thornton, and A. Bibbee. 1997. "Taxation and Economic Performance." OECD Economics Department Working Paper Nr. 176, Paris.

Leibfritz, W. 2011. "Undeclared Economic Activity in Central and Eastern Europe: How Taxes Contribute and How Countries Respond to the Problem." Background paper for "In from the Shadow: Integrating Europe's Informal Labor." Policy Research Working Paper 5923, World Bank, Washington, DC.

Loayza, Norman V., Ana María Oviedo, and Luis Servén. 2005. "The Impact of Regulation on Growth and Informality." Policy Research Working Paper Series 3623, World Bank, Washington, DC.

Maloney, William F., Pable Fajnzylber, and Eduardo Ribeiro. 2001. "Firm Entry and Exit, Labor Demand, and Trade Reform: Evidence from Chile and Colombia." Policy Research Working Paper Series 2659, World Bank, Washington, DC.

Manning, A. 1995. "How Do We Know that Real Wages Are Too High?" *Quarterly Journal of Economics* 110 (4): 1111–25.

Mitra P., and N. Stern. 2002. "Tax Systems in Transition." Policy Research Working Paper 2947, World Bank, Washington, DC.

OECD (Organization for Economic Cooperation and Development). 2004. *2004 OECD Employment Outlook*. Paris: OECD.

———. 2008. Benefits and Wages database, 2008. www.oecd.org/els/social/work-incentives.

Penalosa, C., and S. Turnovsky. 2004. "Second-Bet Optimal Taxation of Capital and Labor in a Developing Economy." Working Papers UWEC-2004-05-P, University of Washington, Department of Economics, revised April 2004.

Rebitzer, J. B., and L. J. Taylor. 1995. "The Consequences of Minimum Wage Laws: Some New Theoretical Ideas." *Journal of Public Economics* 56: 245–55

Schneider, F., and R. Neck. 1993. "The Development of the Shadow Economy under Changing Tax Systems and Structures: Some Theoretical and Empirical Results for Austria. *Finanzarchiv* 50 (3): 344–69.

Slemrod, J., and S. Yitzhaki. 2000. "Tax Avoidance, Evasion and Administration." National Bureau of Economic Research Working Paper No. 7473, Cambridge.

Staehr, K. 2009. "Estimates of Employment and Welfare Effects of Personal Labor Income Taxation in a Flat-Tax Country: The Case of Estonia." Chap. 7 in *Microfoundations of Economic Success: Lessons from Estonia*, ed. David Mayes. Riga: Edward Elgar.

Tanzi, V., and L. Schuknecht. 1996. "Reforming Government in Industrial Countries." *Finance and Development*, September, 2–5.

Williams, C. 2008. "Illegitimate Wage Practises in Eastern Europe: The Case of 'Envelope Wages.'" *JEEMS—Journal for East European Management Studies* 13 (3): 253–70.

World Bank, 2012. Enterprize Surveys Online data base. Available at http://www.enterprisesurveys.org. Last accessed May 25, 2012.

CHAPTER 4

Good Governance, Institutional Credibility, and Tax Morale

Forces other than the incentives created by taxation, factor market regulation, and social protection policies are at play in shaping the circumstances and choices of households and firms, governance, institutional credibility, and tax morale. Enforcement of regulations matters considerably, because it creates a powerful deterrent. Although compliance with regulations varies significantly across countries and is often quite low, it seldom falls to a level as low as predicted by the standard economic models of deterrence and punishment. Hence, enforcement alone cannot account for observed levels of compliance. With regard to tax compliance, the real puzzle is therefore why people pay taxes to the relatively great extent that they do, not why they evade them. The social norm of compliance, or "tax morale," may help to explain why people willingly conform. If taxpayers think they are in a better position to monitor and control politicians, their willingness to pay taxes increases. That, in turn, increases their confidence in the tax compliance of others, which positively reinforces tax morale. A higher degree of satisfaction with a country's democratic institutions also has a statistically significant, positive effect on tax morale.

Governance, Institutions, and the Shadow Economy

In the early 1990s the literature on informal employment and the shadow economy focused on the important topic of measurement. In the later part of the decade the focus shifted to the question of "exit" or "exclusion," where it has remained for many years. In their report on Latin America, Perry et al. (2007) prominently pointed out that the exit-or-exclusion question was a false dichotomy. The motivations and circumstances that lead people to transact in a heterogeneous informal sector offering goods and services that permeate far beyond housekeeping and petty trade—even taking the form of noncontracted employment in large businesses and public sector agencies—are self-evidently diverse. As discussed in chapter 2, exit and exclusion can have essentially the same implications and consequences. But the debate produced a large body of evidence that suggests that forces other than the incentives created by taxation, factor market regulation, and social protection policies are at play in shaping the circumstances and choices of households and firms. Perry et al. (2007) demonstrated that with evidence of a relationship between the size of the shadow economy and measures of governance and institutional credibility and with reference to a new emphasis in the literature on tax morale.

Figure 4.1 updates the evidence presented in Perry et al. (2007) with the internationally comparable measures of the shadow economy produced by Schneider, Buehn, and Montenegro (2010) for this volume, plotted against the World Bank's World Governance Indicators (WGI).[1] Across a broad selection of countries, the estimated size of the shadow economy as a share of GDP is inversely related to government effectiveness, control of corruption, the rule of law, and regulatory quality. Figure 4.2 shows how changes in these measures of governance and institutional quality have been accompanied by changes in the size of the shadow economy. The plots show the path of change from 2000 to 2007, as the countries that joined the EU in 2004 and 2007 (and others who aspire to membership in the future) made significant strides in strengthening governance and increasing the credibility of their institutions. Notably, in all four plots the relationship takes a downward-sloping shape: as government effectiveness, control of corruption, the rule of law, and regulatory quality were improved over the period 2000 to 2007, the shadow economy shrank. A part of this pattern reflects income and development, without a doubt, but only a part.

Figure 4.1 The Size of the Shadow Economy Is Inversely Related to Measures of Good Governance and Institutional Credibility

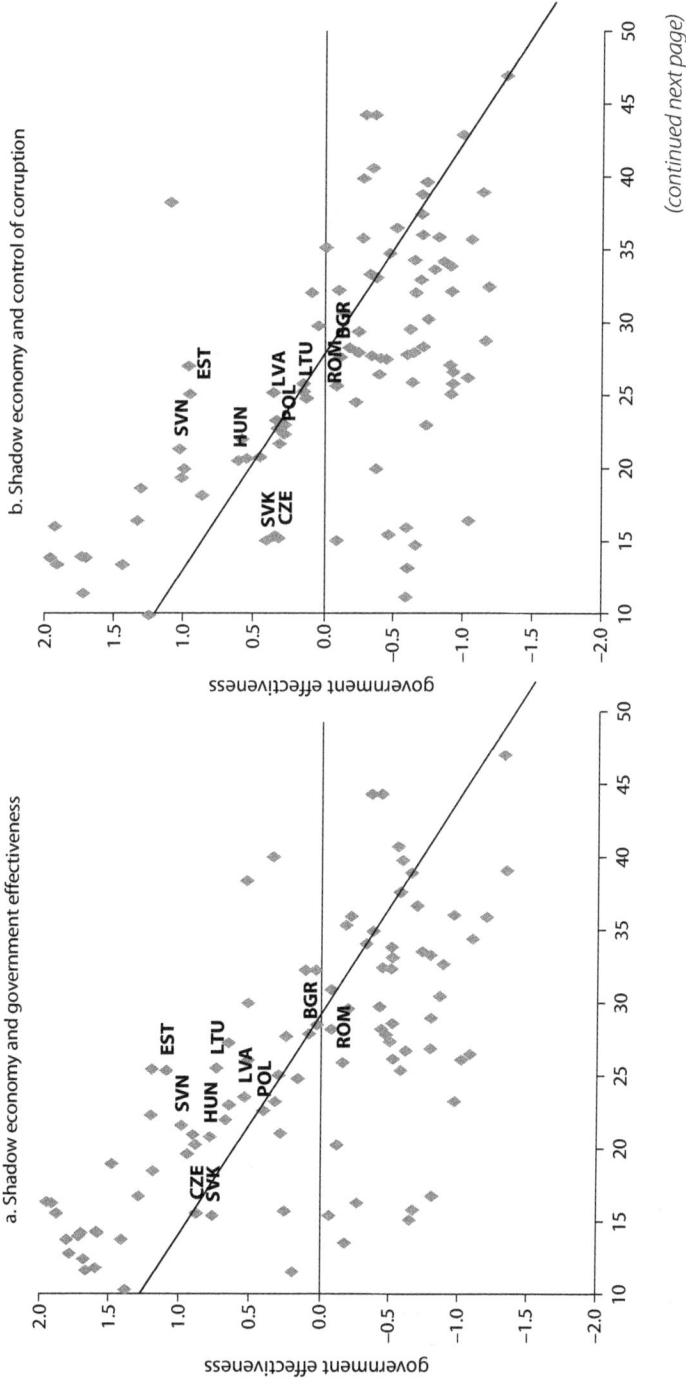

a. Shadow economy and government effectiveness

b. Shadow economy and control of corruption

(continued next page)

Figure 4.1 *(continued)*

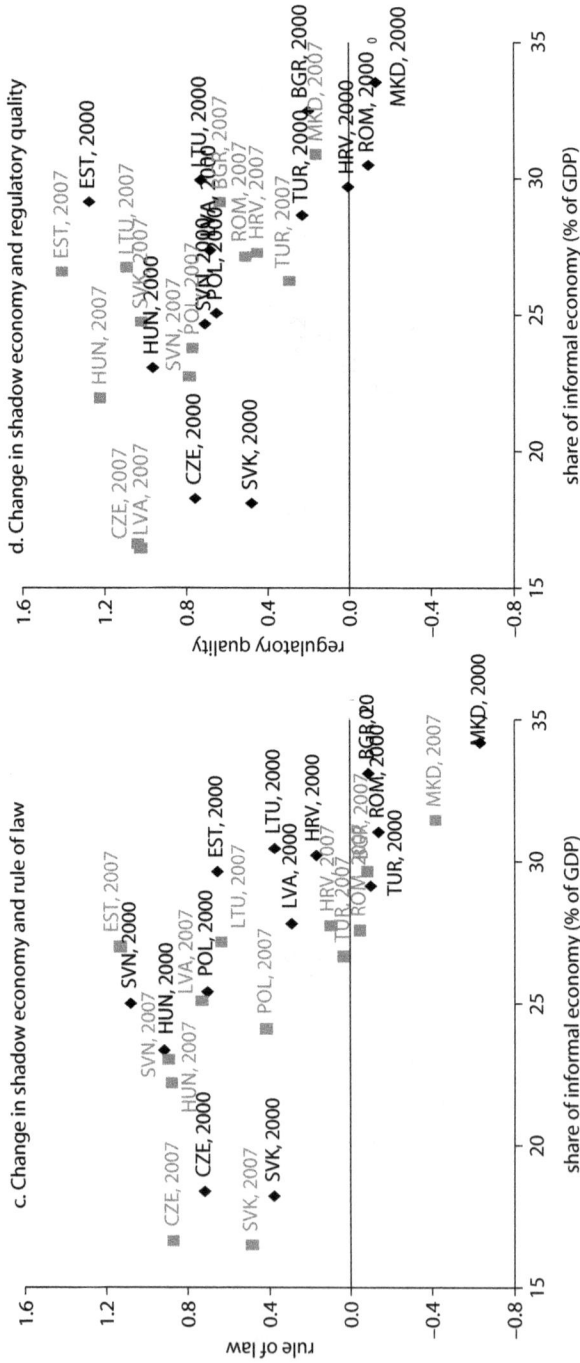

c. Change in shadow economy and rule of law

d. Change in shadow economy and regulatory quality

Source: Authors' calculations using Schneider, Buehn, and Montenegro 2010; and Kaufmann, Kraay, and Mastruzzi 2007.
Note: The x axis indicates the size of the shadow economy as calculated by Schneider, Buehn, and Montenegro 2010; the y axis indicates several world governance indicators as standardized by Kaufmann, Kraay, and Mastruzzi 2007.

Figure 4.2 As the EU's New Member Countries Improved Governance and the Credibility of Their Institutions from 2000 to 2007, the Shadow Economy Shrank

a. Change in shadow economy and government effectiveness

b. Change in shadow economy and control of corruption

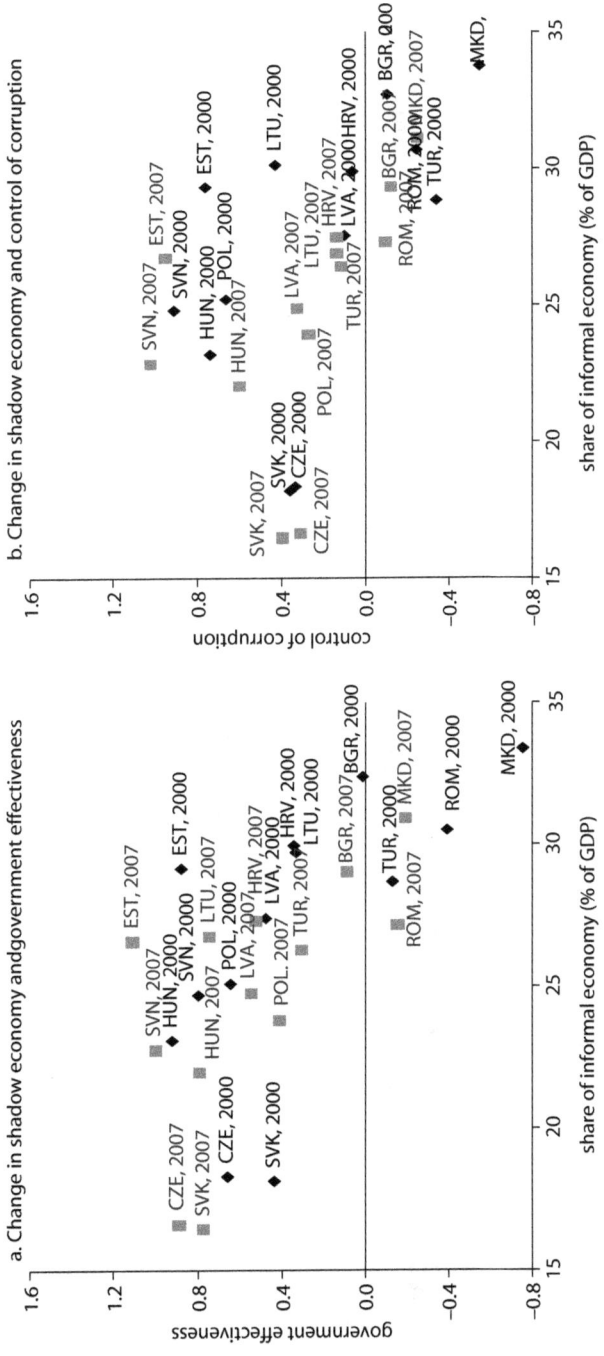

(continued next page)

Figure 4.2 *(continued)*

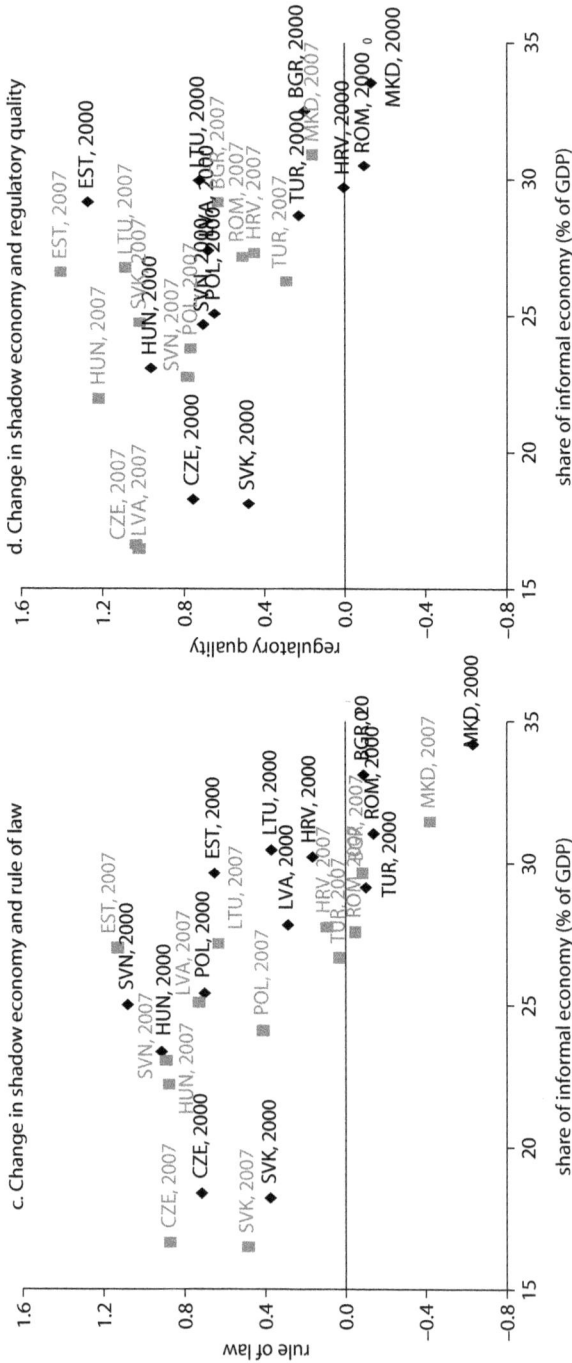

c. Change in shadow economy and rule of law

d. Change in shadow economy and regulatory quality

Source: Authors' calculations using Schneider, Buehn, and Montenegro 2010; and Kaufmann, Kraay, and Mastruzzi 2007.
Note: The x axis indicates the size of the shadow economy as calculated by Schneider, Buehn, and Montenegro 2010; the y axis indicates several world governance indicators as standardized by Kaufmann, Kraay, and Mastruzzi 2007.

Earlier in the book, where evidence from Hazans's (2011b) estimation of the drivers of informal employment was presented, the counterintuitive impact of taxation and the influence of labor unions alluded to the importance of governance and the credibility of institutions as shown in figures 4.1 and 4.2. Referring back to those results, one of the WGIs, government effectiveness, and similar measures of regulatory quality and the strength of property rights, provided by the Heritage Foundation, are shown to lower the extent of informal work and to be highly statistically significant, even after a country's level of development and structural incentives are accounted for. These variables are consistently significant and robust to changes in specification, estimation techniques, and the sample of countries included (see table A4 in the appendix).

Hazans's (2011b) estimations also reveal a close association between the extent of informal employment and a country's level of income inequality, as measured by the Gini coefficient. However, whereas other researchers have argued that the prevalence of informal work contributes to greater inequality, Hazans uses lagged variables and causality tests to show that the causal relationship may in fact run in the opposite direction: higher levels of inequality drive up the share of informal work. That result may further underscore the importance of institutional quality and credibility. If people interpret high levels of inequality as the state's falling short in its duty to provide public goods and correct market failures, it can erode their tax morale, as will be discussed in this chapter.

The Real Puzzle of Tax Compliance: Why People Pay Taxes, Not Why They Evade

In the first of two background papers for the book, Torgler (2011a) cites Adams's (1993) use of an inscription over the entrance to the United States Internal Revenue Service building: "Taxes are what we pay for a civilized society." An essential question for policy makers, Torgler points out, is the extent to which individuals are willing to pay that price. In answer to the question, a growing literature is fast converging on an important conclusion: the traditional cost-benefit approach that economists have taken to examine tax compliance is inadequate as a framework to understand why people pay taxes. Rather, the basic economic model of individual choice must be expanded by introducing aspects of behavior and motivation, which fall under the general rubric of behavioral economics.[2]

The basic theoretical framework used in nearly all research on tax compliance begins with Becker's (1968) crime and punishment model, first applied to tax compliance by Allingham and Sandmo (1972). In the model, a rational individual is viewed as maximizing the expected utility of a tax evasion gamble by weighing the benefits of successful cheating against the risk of detection and punishment. The individual pays taxes because he is afraid of getting caught and penalized if he does not report all income. The obvious policy implication here is that enforcement matters because enforcement can affect the financial considerations that motivate—at least in part—an individual's compliance choices: enforcement creates deterrence. However, this approach also concludes that an individual pays taxes because—and only because—of the economic consequences of detection and punishment. Thus governments can encourage greater tax compliance by increasing deterrence through more audits and steeper penalties.

However, it is now apparent from a growing body of evidence that the compliance we actually observe cannot be explained entirely by purely financial considerations, especially those determined by enforcement. Taxpayer audits are a central feature of the voluntary compliance system in all countries, largely because more frequent audits are thought to reduce tax evasion. But the percentage of individual income tax returns that are subject to a thorough tax audit is small in most countries, typically less than 1 percent of all returns. Similarly, sanctions are mild. The penalty even for fraudulent evasion seldom exceeds more than the amount of unpaid taxes, and those penalties are infrequently imposed. Civil penalties on nonfraudulent evasion are even milder.

In such circumstances, a purely probabilistic simulation of the evasion gamble suggests that most rational individuals should either underreport income or overclaim deductions not subject to independent verification, inasmuch as it is unlikely that their cheating will be detected and penalized (Alm, Martinez-Vazquez, and Torgler 2010). Even in the least compliant countries, however, evasion never rises to levels predicted by the conventional model. In fact, substantial numbers of individuals apparently pay all (or most) of their taxes all (or most) of the time, regardless of the financial incentives from the enforcement regime. The basic model of individual compliance behavior therefore implies that rational individuals (especially those whose incomes are not subject to third-party sources of information) should report virtually no income. But although compliance varies significantly across countries and tax regimes and is often quite low, it seldom falls to a level predicted by the standard model. Thus enforcement alone cannot account for observed levels of compliance. The real puzzle of tax compliance behavior is why people pay taxes, not why they evade them (Kirchler 2007; Slemrod 1992; Torgler 2007a).

What is behind the puzzle of tax compliance? The social norm of compliance, or tax morale, may help to explain why people willingly conform. If tax morale is a key determinant in enhancing compliance, then a variety of policies other than enforcement will help to reduce tax fraud. Improving knowledge about the causes and consequences of tax morale could lead to stronger tax policy through stronger voluntary compliance.

A number of empirical studies show a simple but strong inverse relationship between tax morale[3] and the size of the shadow economy in high-income, transition, and developing countries (Alm and Torgler 2006; Alm, Martinez-Vazquez, and Torgler 2006; Torgler 2001, 2005a report negative correlations with Pearson r values between –0.51 and –0.66). A simple linear regression suggests that a decrease of tax morale by one unit increases the size of the shadow economy as a percentage of GDP by roughly 20 percentage points. Moreover, tax morale can explain more than 30 percent of the total variance in the size the economy across countries. The relationship is confirmed in multivariate studies that indicate that tax morale has a very strong impact on the size of the shadow economy using cross-sectional and panel approaches (see Torgler and Schneider 2007a, 2009). In an extensive review of tax compliance in OECD countries, Feld and Schneider (2010) found that when compared to the impact of tax morale, the quantitative impact of deterrence is far less important.

Institutional Credibility: The Key to Building and Maintaining Tax Morale

Tax specialists are learning that reducing tax evasion is not simply a matter of applying stiffer penalties or increasing the frequency of audits. An effective monitoring and enforcement structure is necessary, of course, but not sufficient. Indeed, extreme penalties can backfire, particularly where institutions are weak, by creating a setting in which bribery and corruption are more prevalent and where the end result may be lower tax compliance and a general loss of trust. Designing effective policies for reducing tax evasion requires an understanding of the behavioral aspects of the tax compliance decision. If individual attitudes toward compliance are a function of social and cultural norms, measures to enhance those norms are an essential complement to the usual enforcement instruments.

Social norms of compliance are molded by a country's institutions. In representative democracies, taxation and public finance matters are agreed through those institutions. Governments require a degree of consent from the populace in the area of taxation and government activities (Bird, Martinez-Vazquez, and Torgler 2008). A key driver of evasion in Latin America is that most countries for many years lacked "an (implicit) social contract between governments and the general populace" (Lledo, Schneider, and Moore 2003). State legitimacy rests to a considerable extent on citizens' "quasi-voluntary compliance" (Levi 1988). Taxes are considered the price paid for government services, and for that reason taxpayers are sensitive to the way the government uses tax revenues. That is, taxpayers perceive their relationship with the state not only as a relationship of coercion and obligation but, more importantly, as one of exchange. Individuals will feel cheated if taxes are not spent efficiently. Inversely, if citizens believe their interests and preferences are properly represented in political institutions and that they receive an adequate supply of public goods, their identification with the state increases, and so too their willingness to contribute.

An inefficient state where corruption is rampant will lower citizens' trust in authority and their incentive to cooperate and contribute. A more legitimate state increases citizens' willingness to contribute. A growing number of studies show that state legitimacy and credibility can increase taxpayers' positive attitudes and commitment to the tax system, with an accompanying positive effect on tax compliance (Smith 1992). Hayoz and Hug (2007, p. 10) stress, "The state being considered as a part of the community and not as the hostile other or 'they' can reasonably expect to secure tax compliance." This is also true of governance and citizen participation in managing the rules of the game. Under socialist rule, in many parts of central and eastern Europe, there was little or no citizen participation, and a culture of distrust of state power developed that under the market-led system manifested itself as a deeply ingrained culture of tax evasion.

A succession of studies show that the more people are involved in establishing rules, the stronger is their sense of obligation to live by those rules (Kidder and McEwen 1989; Cialdini 1989; McEwen and Maiman 1986; Lempert 1972). Most fundamentally, giving individuals the chance to vote on setting the rules increases their tax compliance. Voting and public discussions prior to votes create a sense of civic duty, as taxpayers become aware of the importance of contributing to the creating and sustaining of public goods. Voting possibilities also provide their own utility. Citizens value the right to participate because it produces a so-called procedural utility (Alm, Jackson, and McKee 1993; Feld and Tyran 2002; Torgler and Schaltegger 2005).

In contrast, institutional instability, lack of transparency, and weakness in the rule of law undermine the willingness of citizens to be active in the formal economy. A sustainable tax system is based on taxation that is generally seen as fair and government that is considered responsive. That is achieved when people see a strong connection between tax payments and the supply of public goods (Bird, Martinez-Vasquez, and Torgler 2006). But in places where political elites, staff in the public administration, and legislators wield too much discretionary power, where institutions are neither credible nor working well, and where formal channels of accountability and recourse are missing or weak, citizens quickly lose their trust in the authority and credibility of the state.

For these reasons, in countries where corruption is systemic and government budgets lack transparency and accountability, people begin to feel justified in evading taxes, and it can quickly become an accepted social norm. Citizens who pay taxes will feel cheated if they believe that corruption is widespread, that their tax money is not spent well, that they cannot hold their government accountable for results, and that they are not protected by the rule of law. The greatest danger arises when a critical mass of tax avoiders and evaders forms that pushes society past the tipping point referred to in chapter 2, raising the marginal cost of compliance to such an extent that compliance becomes unviable. Empirical evidence from natural and lab-type experiments has shown time and again that the more widespread the knowledge that others are not paying their taxes, the more noncompliance increases (Torgler 2011a; 2011b). As Bergman (2002) puts it, "Nobody likes to pay taxes, but what they dislike even more is feeling like a sucker, knowing they are the only one paying taxes."

Tax Morale in Europe

A growing empirical literature documents the nature of tax morale in Europe (reviewed in considerable detail in Torgler 2011a and 2011b for this volume) and how it has changed in recent years. Alm and Torgler (2006) combined data from a large number of European countries and in their analysis distinguish between behavioral norms in southern and in northern European countries. Their results show that people from northern Europe have higher levels of tax morale than people from southern Europe. A person from a southern European country is 1.3 percentage points less likely to state that tax evasion is never justified. Similarly, Weck (1983), Weck, Pommerehne, and Frey (1984), and Frey and Weck-Hannemann (1984) used cross-country survey results to develop a "tax immorality" index for various countries. They showed that southern European countries have higher tax immorality than most other countries. Reflecting on those findings, Kirchgässner (1999) points out that in the northern European countries, state and religious authority were historically held by a single entity, in contrast to the majority of countries in southern Europe. Offenses against the state were therefore also religious offenses and consequently a sin. Of course, such country-level observations have to be considered with care, as tax morale can vary widely even in different areas within countries. Torgler and Schneider (2007b), looking at Switzerland, Spain, and Belgium, observed that cultural and regional differences within a country affect tax morale significantly.

At the household level, Frey and Torgler (2007) examined tax morale in a large set of formerly socialist and western European countries using microdata covering more than 32,000 observations.[4] With the governance indicators developed by Kaufmann, Kraay, and Mastruzzi (2004), they found that all the institutional variables have a statistically significant, positive effect on tax morale. The strongest quantitative effects, however, were observed for voice and accountability, political stability, and regulatory quality. An improvement in the voice and accountability scale by one unit increases tax morale (that is, the probability of stating that tax evasion is never justified) by 7.5 percentage points. The importance of greater voice and accountability and lower corruption to tax morale is also confirmed by Torgler (2011b), who found further significant impact on the size of the shadow economy: improvements in voice and accountability and lower levels of corruption lower the size of the shadow economy as a percentage of GDP.

Frey and Torgler (2007) also explored the importance of trust between taxpayers and the state. If taxpayers think they are in a better position to monitor and control politicians, their willingness to pay taxes increases. A higher degree of satisfaction with a country's democratic institutions has a statistically significant, positive effect on tax morale. For example, an increase in trust in the justice system or in parliament by one unit raises the percentage of people who report the highest tax morale by more than three percentage points. Similarly, a one-unit increase in satisfaction with the way democracy is developing raises the proportion of people who say that tax evasion is never justified by 1.5 percentage points. Supporting analysis by Torgler and Schneider (2007a; 2009) shows that that improving governance, institutional quality, and tax morale lowers the incentives to evade taxes. The results are robust using more than 25 proxies of governance and institutional quality, testing for endogeneity, and running a broad variety of specifications.

If the credibility of institutions affects tax morale and the size of the shadow economy, it may be worthwhile to explore also its impact on tax performance. Recalling the conceptual framework presented in chapter 2, the level of tax performance may be related to the availability of "exit options." The more taxpayers believe that others work in the shadow economy, the lower not only the transaction costs but also the moral costs of behaving dishonestly and evading taxes by moving their own activities to the shadow economy. In this way, the potential intrinsic motivation to comply and contribute to public sector activities is crowded out. The relationship has been shown empirically by Bird, Martinez-Vasquez, and Torgler (2006) and can quickly spiral into a vicious cycle: if more people are transacting in the shadow economy, it reduces tax revenue and the resources available to maintain public goods or implement institutional reforms. That subsequently increases the returns to participation in the shadow economy (Dreher, Kotsogiannis, and McCorriston 2009).

Katsios (2006) documents such a downward spiral effect in Greece, where its inability to tax the shadow economy constrains the government's ability to create and maintain public goods. That erodes the state's credibility and increases distrust in government and formal institutions, which can lead to further deterioration of institutional conditions. Dreher and Schneider (2010, p. 6) state that "better institutional quality … increases the benefits entrepreneurs derive from operating in the official sector"; reduces the shadow economy; and "should thus reduce corruption and the size of the shadow economy alike." Once operations are transferred to the shadow economy, the entrepreneur can no longer benefit from the public goods available in the formal economy (Choi and Thum 2005). However, the value of those public goods will depend on the level of corruption, as the greater the level of corruption, the lower the tax effort, and hence the less resources available for public goods.

The importance of institutional strengthening to improving tax morale is clear in the empirical literature, and given the transformation of institutions in the 10 countries that joined the EU in 2004 and 2007, it is reasonable to expect an impact on tax morale and the extent of compliance. In the second background paper for this book, Torgler (2011b) examined how tax morale has changed in the new member states. In countries negotiating their accession to the European Union, the intention to accede acted as a catalyst for rapid tax reform shaped along "western" lines (Martinez-Vazquez and McNab 2000), with changes in tax systems carried out to bring them in line with the EU-15 (Owsiak 2007). Aspiring new members from central and eastern Europe enacted changes that simplified their tax systems, which contributed to an increase in tax compliance and reduction of tax compliance costs (Hayoz and Hug 2007). Preparing for accession to the EU promoted important institutional reforms, which may have slowed since the new member states joined. Respondents from some of the central and eastern European countries actually reported higher values of tax morale than certain western European countries in 1999 (Frey and Torgler 2007).

Following a period of rapid and measurable institutional strengthening leading up to accession, however, in seven out of the 10 countries that joined the EU in 2004 and 2007 a decay of tax morale occurred between 2000 and 2008. In the Czech Republic, Estonia, Latvia, Lithuania, Poland, Romania, and Slovakia, the decrease in tax morale between 2000 and 2008 is statistically significant (at the 1 percent or 5 percent level). In 1999, the Czech Republic, Poland, and Slovakia had a tax morale value above 2. In 2008 the values were below 2 but still substantially higher than in Estonia, Latvia, and Lithuania. Along with the three Baltic countries, Romania had the lowest levels of tax morale in 2008. Hungary had the highest tax morale value, followed by Bulgaria, Slovenia, Slovakia, and the Czech Republic. Hungary and Slovenia experienced a statistically significant increase in tax morale. Although governance and institutional quality improved substantially throughout the 1990s, in the decade following progress appears to have slowed (table 4.1).

What are the forces that have shaped tax morale in the 10 new members of the EU? Table A5 in the appendix presents Torgler's (2011b) estimation results, using ordered probits regressions and the scaled dependent variable tax morale. The usual control variables show that older people and women exhibit higher tax morale. Education and regularly following the news affect tax morale positively; but having stronger political interest lowers tax morale. Married people have the highest tax morale, and church attendance is also correlated with higher tax morale. These results are consistent with the existing tax morale

Table 4.1   In Some of the EU's New Member Countries, Tax Morale Has Deteriorated since 1999

	Tax morale 1999	Tax morale 2008	Prob > |z|	N
Bulgaria	2.316	2.391	0.397	2441
Czech Republic	2.209	1.923	0.000	3660
Estonia	1.563	1.259	0.000	2468
Hungary	2.252	2.536	0.000	2482
Latvia	2.113	1.561	0.000	2474
Lithuania	1.433	1.546	0.044	2370
Poland	2.228	1.809	0.000	2548
Romania	1.97	1.775	0.001	2514
Slovakia	2.181	1.925	0.000	2780
Slovenia	2.122	2.265	0.017	2359

Source: Torgler 2011b, for this volume, using European Values Survey 2011.

Box 4.1

Changing Social Norms: German Reunification and Tax Morale

Tax morale is not exogenous, nor does it remain stable over time. Unexpected events and planed changes in political and economic systems can have a substantial impact on tax morale and compliance, and subsequently on the extent of the shadow economy. Scholars believe that a process of social learning is at work in determining social norms that shape tax morale.

A dramatic illustration of this social learning process was observed in the reunification of East and West Germany. Germany today has the 14th-smallest estimated shadow economy in the OECD (16 percent of GDP). In the EU, it has the sixth-lowest share of the labor force in dependent employment without a contract (1.7 percent) and the 17th-lowest share in informal self-employment (10.3 percent).

German reunification offers a quasi-natural experiment that provides valuable insights into how tax morale changes when societies are integrated in a new institutional environment. Feld, Torgler, and Dong (2008) analyzed the differences in tax morale between people in East and West Germany and the convergence of tax morale between 1990 and 1999. German reunification provides particularly valuable insights because many common factors that can determine tax morale (language, similar education systems, and a shared cultural and political history prior to the separation) can be controlled for. The researchers examined how taxpayers adapted to a new legal environment that sends signals about how they should behave and how others behave.

(continued next page)

Box 4.1 *(continued)*

In a short space of time, East German citizens were taken out of one system and thrust into another. After the Iron Curtain fell, former citizens of the German Democratic Republic (GDR) were exposed to West German structures of social welfare and taxation, along with the whole set of formal and informal social rules and the benefits and obligations that they afforded. Although penalties, enforcement, and deterrence were commonplace in the old GDR, black markets and the shadow economy were nevertheless ubiquitous. All GDR citizens could readily observe that their fellow citizens engaged regularly in the shadow economy. Getting around the rules not only was a socially acceptable norm but also was essential to meet even mundane daily needs. After unification, East German taxpayers were confronted with new laws and new deterrence levels. They could observe new social norms and the tax morale of the West German taxpayers and adjust their behavior accordingly.

Feld, Torgler, and Dong's (2008) findings indicate that although the levels of tax morale of respondents to the European Values Survey from the East and the West varied significantly in 1990, by 1999 they had converged. The 1999 levels of tax morale did not differ significantly between the two regions, whether in simple descriptive analysis, in nonparametric tests, or in a differentiated multivariate analysis. Within just nine years after unification, tax morale strongly converged, in particular because of a significant increase in the level of tax morale in the East. Interestingly, older individuals in the East, who were exposed to the GDR regime for a longer time, were less likely to change their social norms. As Kasper and Streit (1999) argue, the East Germans had to unlearn the social norms of their old institutional environment and learn new ones, requiring both time and practice.

The researchers argue that a key mechanism in this process is "conditional compliance," that is, individuals pay their taxes conditionally on the pro-social behavior they observe in others around them. People are more willing to pay their taxes if they perceive others to be honest. Although their prior institutional circumstances required them to be consummate evaders, East Germans were integrating into a society with high levels of tax morale. The extent to which others contribute triggers cooperation and systematically influences the willingness to contribute. Relying on survey evidence from 30 European countries, Frey and Torgler (2007) showed that if taxpayers believe tax evasion is common, their tax morale decreases. In contrast, if they believe that others are honest, their tax morale increases.

Source: Torgler 2011a.

literature (Torgler 2007b). The independent variables of interest are trust in government, trust in the justice system, governance quality, and trust in the European Union. All four factors are statistically significant and have a positive effect on tax morale. However, the estimated coefficient on the variable trust in the European Union is only statistically significant at the 10 percent level. The quantitative effects of these variables on tax morale are quite similar: around 1.5 percentage points for a unit increase in a four-point scale in the three trust variables; and 0.7 percentage points for a unit increase in the 10-point scale variable governance quality.

Several researchers have pointed out that the prospect of membership in the EU worked as a catalyst for rapid institutional reforms for the eventual new member countries—including reform of taxation and the institutions that affect tax morale. Preparation for membership "is widely credited with having brought about an alignment of the ten post-communist countries' systems of governance, economies and legal structures with the West European member states, and the EU's *acquis communautaire*" (Epstein and Sedelmeier 2008, p. 796). The external incentive of EU accession enabled the political and social consensus necessary for remarkable reform achievements in the 1990s. However, after accession was achieved, the political difficulties of sustaining the momentum of institutional reforms reasserted themselves. The changes in tax morale in the 10 new members are consistent with this observation.

For that reason, Torgler (2011b) argues that there is still much to be done to improve not only the quality of governance generally, but that of tax administrations specifically. The empirical findings in table A5 indicate that increasing individuals' trust in the government, and in the justice system in particular, has a significant positive influence on tax morale. These results are consistent with earlier findings on what drives tax morale in central and eastern European countries (Torgler 2003a). Improving citizens' trust in the legal system has also been found to raise tax morale significantly in a wider range of cultural contexts, from India to Canada and Japan (Torgler 2004).

Notes

1. Readers should note that two of the WGI are used in some of the specifications in the Multiple Indicator Multiple Causes (MIMIC) estimation of the shadow economy: government effectiveness and regulatory quality. However,

when they are included, their relative importance is low, and their omission makes little or no significant difference in the final estimates.

2. Behavioral economics can be broadly defined as an approach that uses methods and evidence from other social sciences to inform the analysis of individual and group decision making in the face of constraints.

3. Tax morale is most widely measured using responses to the World Values Survey (and European Values Survey) question, "Please tell me for each of the following statements whether you think it can always be justified, never be justified, or something in between: ... Cheating on tax if you have the chance." The question leads to a 10-scale index of tax morale with the two extreme points *never justified* and *always justified*.

4. Central and eastern European countries included are Belarus, Bulgaria, Croatia, the Czech Republic, Estonia, Greece, Hungary, Latvia, Lithuania, Poland, Romania, Russia, Slovakia, and Ukraine. Western European countries included Austria, Belgium, Great Britain, Denmark, Finland, France, Germany, Iceland, Ireland, Italy, Malta, Netherlands, North Ireland, Portugal, Spain, and Sweden.

References

Adams, C. 1993. *For Good and Evil: The Impact of Taxes on the Course of Civilization.* London: Madison Books.

Allingham, M. G., and A. Sandmo. 1972. "Income Tax Evasion: A Theoretical Analysis." *Journal of Public Economics* 1: 323–38.

Alm, J., B. R. Jackson, and M. McKee. 1993. "Fiscal Exchange, Collective Decision Institutions, and Tax Compliance." *Journal of Economic Behavior and Organization* 22: 285–303.

Alm J., J. Martinez-Vazquez, and B. Torgler. 2006. "Russian Attitudes toward Paying Taxes—before, during, and after the Transition." *International Journal of Social Economics* 33 (12): 832–57.

———, eds. 2010. *Developing Alternative Frameworks for Explaining Tax Compliance.* London: Routledge.

Alm, J., and B. Togler. 2006. "Culture Difference and Tax Morale in Europe and the United States." *Journal of Economic Psychology* 27 (2): 224–46.

Becker, G. S. 1968. "Crime and Punishment: An Economic Approach." *Journal of Political Economy* 76: 169–217.

Bergman, M. 2002. "Who Pays for Social Policy? A Study on Taxes and Trust" *Journal of Social Policy* 31 (2): 289–305.

Bird, R., J. Martinez-Vazquez, and B. Torgler. 2006. "Societal Institutions and Tax Effort in Developing Countries." In *The Challenges of Tax Reform in the Global*

Economy, ed. J. Alm, J. Martinez-Vazquez, and M. Rider. 283–338. New York: Springer.

Bird, R. M., J. Martinez-Vazquez, and B. Torgler. 2008. "Tax Effort in Developing Countries and High Income Countries: The Impact of Corruption, Voice and Accountability." *Economic Analysis and Policy* 38: 55–71.

Choi, J. P., and M. Thum. 2005. "Corruption and the Shadow Economy." *International Economic Review* 46: 817–36.

Cialdini, R. B. 1989. "Social Motivations to Comply: Norms, Values and Principles." In *Taxpayer Compliance*, vol. 2, ed. J. A. Roth and J. T. Scholz. 200–27. Philadelphia: University of Pennsylvania Press.

Dreher, A., and F. Schneider. 2010. "Corruption and the Shadow Economy: An Empirical Analysis." *Public Choice* 144 (1, July): 215–38.

Dreher, A., C. Kotsogiannis, and S. McCorriston. 2009. "How Do Institutions Affect Corruption and the Shadow Economy?" *International Tax and Public Finance* 16: 773–96.

Epstein, R., and U. Sedelmeier. 2008. "Beyond Conditionality: International Institutions in Postcommunist Europe after Enlargement." *Journal of European Public Policy* 15 (6): 795–805.

European Values Survey. 2011. *European Values Study 1981–2008*. Longitudinal Data File. GESIS Data Archive, Cologne, Germany, ZA4804 Data File Version 2.0.0 (2011-12-30) DOI:10.4232/1.11005.

Feld, L., and F. Schneider. 2010. "Survey on the Shadow Economy and Undeclared Earnings in OECD Countries." *German Economic Review* 11 (2): 109–49.

Feld, L. P., B. Torgler, and B. Dong. 2008. "Coming Closer? Tax Morale, Deterrence and Social Learning after German Unification." CREMA Working Paper Series, 2008–09, Center for Research in Economics, Management and the Arts, Basel, Switzerland.

Feld, L. P., and J.-R. Tyran. 2002. "Tax Evasion and Voting: An Experimental Analysis." *KYKLOS* 55: 197–222.

Frey, B. S., and B. Torgler. 2007. "Tax Morale and Conditional Cooperation." *Journal of Comparative Economics* 35: 136–59.

Frey, B. S., and H. Weck-Hannemann. 1984. "The Hidden Economy as an 'Unobserved' Variable." *European Economic Review* 26: 33–53.

Hayoz, N., and S. Hug, eds. 2007. *Tax Evasion, Trust, and State Capacities. How Good Is Tax Morale in Central and Eastern Europe?* Bern: Peter Lang.

Hazans, M. 2011b. "What Explains Prevalence of Informal Employment in European Countries: The Role of Labor Institutions, Governance, Immigrants, and Growth." Background paper for "In from the Shadow: Integrating Europe's Informal Labor." Policy Research Working Paper 5917, World Bank, Washington, DC.

Kasper, W., and M. E. Streit. 1999. *Institutional Economics. Social Order and Public Policy.* Cheltenham, UK: Edward Elgar.

Katsios, S. 2006. "The Shadow Economy and Corruption in Greece." *South-Eastern Europe Journal of Economics* 1: 61–80.

Kaufmann, D., A. Kraay, and M. Mastruzzi. 2004. "Governance Matters III: Governance Indicators for 1996–2002." *World Bank Economic Review* 18: 253–87.

———. 2007. "Worldwide Governance Indicators: Worldwide Ratings of Country Performances on Six Governance Dimensions from 1996 to Present." World Bank, Washington, DC.

Kidder, R., and C. McEwen. 1989. "Taxpaying Behavior in Social Context: A Tentative Typology of Tax Compliance and Noncompliance." In *Taxpayer Compliance*, vol. 2, ed. J. A. Roth and J. T. Scholz. 46–75. Philadelphia: University of Pennsylvania Press.

Kirchgässner, G. 1999. "Schattenwirtschaft und Moral: Anmerkungen aus ökonomischer Perspektive." In *Der Sozialstaat zwischen "Markt" und "Hedonismus"?* Hrsg. S. Lamnek and J. Luedtke. 425–45. Opladen: Westdeutscher Verlag.

Kirchler, E. 2007. *The Economic Psychology of Tax Behaviour.* Cambridge: Cambridge University Press.

Lempert, R. O. 1972. "Norm-Making in Social Exchange: A Contract Law Model." *Law and Society Review* 1: 1–32.

Levi, M. 1988. *Rules and Revenue.* Berkeley: University of California Press.

Lledo, V., A. Schneider, and M. Moore. 2003. "Pro-poor Tax Reform in Latin America: A Critical Survey and Policy Recommendations." Institute of Development Studies, University of Sussex, March.

Martinez-Vazquez, J., and R. M. McNab. 2000. "The Tax Reform Experiment in Transition Countries." *National Tax Journal* 53: 273–98.

McEwen, C. A., and R. J. Maiman. 1986. "In Search of Legitimacy: Toward an Empirical Response Analysis." *Law and Policy* 8: 257–73.

Owsiak, S. 2007. "Taxes in Post-Communist Countries—Old and New Challenges." In *Tax Evasion, Trust, and State Capacities. How Good Is Tax Morale in Central and Eastern Europe?* ed. N. Hayoz and S. Hug. 187–225. Bern: Peter Lang.

Perry, Guillermo E., William F. Maloney, Omar S. Arias, Pablo Fajnzylber, Andrew D. Mason, and Jaime Saavedra-Chanduvi. 2007. *Informality: Exit and Exclusion.* Washington, DC: World Bank.

Schneider, F., A. Buehn, and C. Montenegro. 2010. "Shadow Economies All over the World: New Estimates for 162 Countries from 1999 to 2007." Background paper for "In from the Shadow: Integrating Europe's Informal Labor." Policy Research Working Paper 5356, World Bank, Washington, DC.

Slemrod, J., ed. 1992. *Why People Pay Taxes. Tax Compliance and Enforcement.* 193–218. Ann Arbor: University of Michigan Press.

Smith, K. W. 1992. "Reciprocity and Fairness: Positive Incentives for Tax Compliance." In *Why People Pay Taxes. Tax Compliance and Enforcement,* ed. J. Slemrod. 223–58. Ann Arbor: University of Michigan Press.

Torgler, B. 2001. "Is 'Tax Evasion Never Justifiable?'" *Journal of Public Finance and Public Choice.* 19: 143–68.

———. 2003. "Tax Morale in Transition Countries." *Post-Communist Economies* 15: 357–81.

———. 2004. "Tax Morale in Asian Countries." *Journal of Asian Economics* 15: 237–66.

———. 2005. "Tax Morale in Latin America." *Public Choice* 122: 133–57.

———. 2007a. *Tax Compliance and Tax Morale: A Theoretical and Empirical Analysis.* Cheltenham, UK: Edward Elgar.

———. 2007b. "Tax Morale in Central and Eastern European Countries." In *Tax Evasion, Trust and State Capacities. How Good Is Tax Morale in Central and Eastern Europe?* ed. Nicolas Hayoz and Simon Hug. 155–86. Bern: Peter Lang.

———. 2011a. "Tax Morale and Compliance: Review of Evidence and Case Studies for Europe." Background paper for "In from the Shadow: Integrating Europe's Informal Labor." Policy Research Working Paper 5922, World Bank, Washington, DC.

———. 2011b. "Tax Morale, Eastern Europe and European Enlargement." Background paper for "In from the Shadow: Integrating Europe's Informal Labor." Policy Research Working Paper 5911, World Bank, Washington, DC.

Torgler, B., M. Schaffner, and A. Macintyre. 2010. "Tax Compliance, Tax Morale, and Governance Quality." In *Developing Alternative Frameworks for Explaining Tax Compliance,* ed. J. Alm, J. Martinez-Vazquez, and B. Torgler. 56–73. London: Routledge.

Torgler, B., and C. A. Schaltegger. 2005. "Tax Amnesties and Political Participation." *Public Finance Review* 33: 403–31.

Torgler, B., and F. Schneider. 2007a. "Shadow Economy, Tax Morale, Governance and Institutional Quality: A Panel Analysis." IZA Discussion Papers 2563, Institute for the Study of Labor (IZA), Bonn, Germany.

———. 2007b. "What Shapes Attitudes toward Paying Taxes? Evidence from Multicultural European Countries." *Social Science Quarterly* 88: 443–70.

———. 2009. "The Impact of Tax Morale and Institutional Quality on the Shadow Economy." *Journal of Economic Psychology* 30: 228–45.

Weck, H. 1983. "Schattenwirtschaft: Eine Möglichkeit zur Einschränkung der öffentlichen Verwaltung? Eine ökonomische Analyse." *Finanzwissenschaftliche Schriften* 22. Bern: Lang.

Weck, H., W. W. Pommerehne, and B. S. Frey. 1984. *Schattenwirtschaft*. München: Franz Vahlen.

Williams, C. 2008. "Illegitimate Wage Practices in Eastern Europe: The Case of 'Envelope wages.'" *Journal for East European Management Studies* 13 (3): 65–83.

CHAPTER 5

Policies to Bring Work In from the Shadow

The new member states of the EU have undertaken many structural and administrative reforms with the objective of increasing revenues and encouraging economic growth. Despite the reforms, it is still relatively difficult to pay taxes. Giving the tax administration agency the responsibility to collect and audit not only taxes, but also social insurance contributions, can offer substantial benefits from synergy effects and help to reduce undeclared and underdeclared work. In addition, further policy reforms to improve the structure of taxation, to make social protection incentives work better for low-wage earners, and to optimize labor market regulations, interventions, and institutions, are necessary to bring work in from the shadow economy. But structural reforms might not be sufficient. To make genuine progress, the new member states also have to enhance tax morale by improving governance, accountability, transparency, with the ultimate goal of building citizens' trust into their government.

This book focuses on the objective of policy makers to bring as much economic activity in from the shadow economy as they can. Deriving specific policy guidance from a multicountry study of 10 countries at various levels of economic and institutional development is impossible. From the conceptual framework and empirical evidence presented in the book thus far, a set of general policy suggestions can be formulated that are relevant for all the EU new member states and indeed for other upper-middle-income and high-income countries in other regions.

Improving the Structure of Taxation

Notwithstanding the importance of institutional credibility to raising and maintaining tax morale, documented in chapter 4, the tax mix and structures of taxation can clearly make a difference to the incentives of firms and households. As we argued earlier, although an incentive-compatible and effective tax administration may be a necessary condition for reducing tax evasion and informal work, it is not sufficient. That said, reforms to the structure and administration of taxation are still important for policy makers to consider. As in many other areas of government, the new member states of the EU have undertaken structural and administrative reforms to taxation with the objective of increasing revenues and encouraging economic growth. This section summarizes some of the reforms, drawing on case studies from the region to formulate implications for policy.

Effective tax administration requires a high quality and a sufficient quantity of staff and an efficient allocation of human resources across all functions, especially auditing. However, as discussed previously, relying only on stronger enforcement can have an ambiguous effect: although it forces some firms into compliance, others may drop out of the market or go underground. For that reason, in addition to the objective of raising revenue, a tax administration agency should also consider its service function for taxpayers, enabling them to meet their obligations to comply with the tax code without undue difficulty and at minimum transaction costs. The task of a tax administration agency is easier if the tax burden is relatively light, the system is relatively simple, and the withholding of taxes at the source of income is widely practiced. Tax compliance costs vary considerably among the new member countries. The time spent by the typical firm on tax compliance is least in Estonia, which also has a good ranking worldwide (among the 181 countries included). By contrast, the Czech Republic has the highest compliance costs among the EU new member countries and also ranks poorly in the wider context (figure 5.1).

The effectiveness of collecting social insurance contributions—which make up the bulk of the tax wedge on labor—varies considerably in the region. Table 5.1 compares the implicit "productivity" of social insurance contributions, calculated as the ratio between the revenue yield (as a

Figure 5.1   Ease of Paying Taxes: Time Spent on Tax Compliance

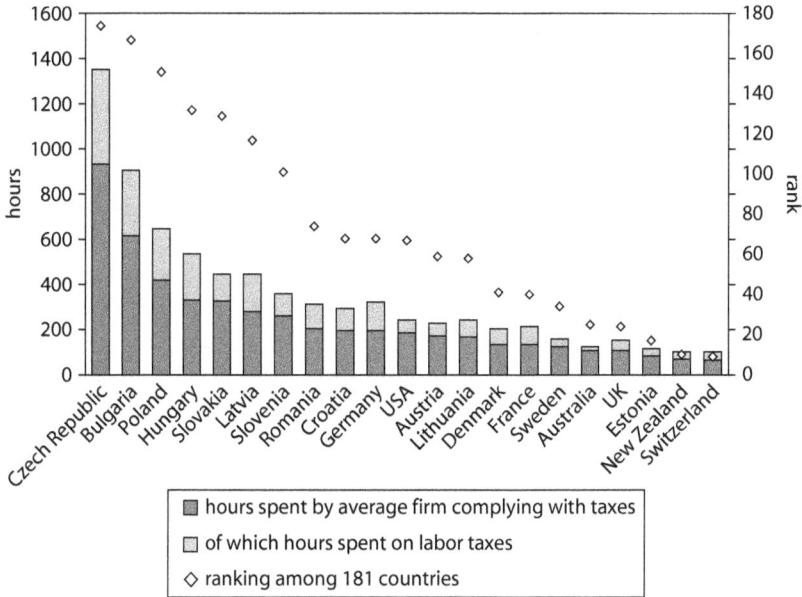

- ■ hours spent by average firm complying with taxes
- □ of which hours spent on labor taxes
- ◇ ranking among 181 countries

Source: Leibfritz 2011.

Table 5.1   Productivity of Social Insurance Contributions, 2008

Country	Revenue (% of GDP) (1)	Total social security rate (%) (2)	Implicit productivity: (1) divided by (2)
Estonia	12.6	33.0	0.38
Slovenia	14.3	38.2	0.37
Czech Republic	16.2	45.0	0.36
Poland	11.4	37.7	0.30
Hungary	13.9	50.5	0.28
Lithuania	9.3	34.0	0.27
Latvia	8.8	33.1	0.27
Slovakia	12.1	48.6	0.25
Bulgaria	8.1	34.4	0.24
Romania	10.3	52.0	0.20

Source: Leibfritz 2011, for this volume.
Note: The total social contribution rate is the sum of employer and employee contribution rates to public insurances for old age pensions, sickness, work injury, and unemployment.

percentage of GDP) and the combined contribution rate (percentage). This indicator is only a crude proxy for the effectiveness of collecting social insurance contributions, which is also affected by the design of social insurance, such as income ceilings, and most important, by the extent of undeclared work. In Estonia, one percentage point of the contribution rate yields 0.38 percent of GDP as revenue, whereas in Romania it yields only 0.20 percent of GDP. Estonia receives higher revenues than Romania, although Romania's statutory contribution rate is 19 percentage points higher, and it receives a revenue amount similar to Slovakia's, although that country has a contribution rate that is more than 15 percentage points higher.

Giving the tax administration agency the responsibility to collect and audit not only taxes but also social insurance contributions can offer substantial benefits from synergy effects and can help to reduce undeclared and underdeclared work. It can reduce administrative costs for both taxpayers and the administration and reduce evasion and fraud through better cross-checking and auditing. Bulgaria, Croatia, Estonia, Hungary, Latvia, Romania, and Slovenia all have integrated tax and social insurance contribution collection and auditing. Elsewhere, Australia, Canada, Ireland, Italy, New Zealand, Norway, Sweden, the United Kingdom, and the United States have integrated collection of tax and social insurance contributions. But in the Czech Republic, Lithuania, Poland, and Slovakia, social insurance contributions are still collected separately by independent social insurance institutions. Slovakia and the Czech Republic are planning to introduce integrated collection systems soon, and the integration of revenue collection in these two countries is supported by the World Bank. In Bulgaria, a Revenue Administration Reform project, also supported by the World Bank, appears to have led to increased compliance.

Turning to the structure of taxation, one of the most visible and fundamental components of tax reforms in the EU's new member countries was the introduction of flat taxes, which were designed with the explicit objectives of encouraging enterprise and investment and simplifying the tax system to promote greater participation. Are flat personal income taxes reducing undeclared work in the shadow economy? More than half of the new member states of the EU have implemented flat income taxes (table 5.2).

The key to appreciating the impact of the structural reforms is to keep in mind that the new flat tax was part of a bundle of measures. The transition from a progressive to a flat personal income tax was accompanied, in most cases, by a reduction of the corporate income tax rate, which implied a general reduction of income taxation. In some cases, the reduction of tax rates was also accompanied by a broadening of the tax base. The expected compliance outcome is in fact theoretically ambiguous. On the one hand, Staehr (2009) argues

Table 5.2   Flat Taxes on Personal Income

Country	Tax rate in 2009 (%)	Year of flat tax introduction
Estonia	21	1994
Lithuania	15	1994
Latvia	25	1995
Slovakia	19	2004
Romania	16	2005
Czech Republic	15/23	2008
Bulgaria	10	2008

Source: Leibfritz 2011, for this volume.

that because the labor supply elasticity of high earners is low relative to that of low-income earners, a tax reform that shifts the tax burden from higher- to lower-income earners—as is generally the case with a revenue-neutral flat tax reform—could actually reduce participation in the formal labor market. On the other hand, because the introduction of the flat tax was not revenue neutral in most cases and the elimination of the progressive rate schedule was accompanied by an increase in the personal basic allowance, its effect on the labor market and on tax compliance could be positive, depending on country-specific circumstances.

Several studies have examined the impact of flat tax reforms on undeclared income. Peter (2008) found that the transition countries that adopted the flat personal income tax saw a significant decline in tax evasion after reforms. In Russia, which introduced a flat personal income tax in 2001, Ivanova, Keen, and Klemm (2005) found that, although compliance increased substantially with reform, that might be explained by accompanying improvements in administration and enforcement. Gorodnichenko, Martinez-Vasquez, and Peter (2007) confirmed that after the introduction of the flat tax in Russia, evasion declined, and they argue that because more compliance cannot be explained by changes in enforcement, less evasion is a result of the new incentive structure of the flat tax.

Given the wide range of factors other than taxation that are associated with undeclared work, as discussed in chapter 3, a flat tax is probably not a "magic bullet" for reducing informal work. However, if a flat tax reform is part of a package that increases the effectiveness of tax collection and improves the general regulatory framework for business, a good chance exists that undeclared work could decline. Leibfritz (2011) for this volume offers three case studies of structural tax reform from

Estonia (box 5.1), Slovakia (box 5.2), and the Czech Republic (box 5.3). The common ingredient of success in those country cases seems to be greater transparency, simplification, and ease of compliance, rather than the new flat tax rate structure, per se.

Another measure widely deployed to encourage greater compliance and reduce informal undeclared work is the establishment of special taxation plans and protocols. With the objective of easing the burden of taxes and other regulations, governments sometimes offer special schemes—such as presumptive taxation—for the self-employed. Such measures can encourage entrepreneurship, reduce compliance costs for

Box 5.1

Estonia's Tax Reform

In 2004, undeclared work in Estonia was only 7.3 percent of GDP, down from 10 percent in 2001 and the lowest among the EU new member countries (Leibfritz 2011). Independent estimates show that Estonia achieved a marked drop in the prevalence of unreported employment from 1998 to 2002 (from 19.5 percent to 9.6 percent), while in Latvia and in Lithuania it increased (from 16.3 percent to 22.5 percent, and from 7.2 percent to 11.7 percent, respectively) (Meriküll and Staehr 2008). According to surveys by the Estonian Institute of Economic Research, the share of employees who regularly or occasionally receive envelope wages declined from 16 percent in 2003 to 12 percent in 2008. Many point to Estonia's tax reforms as the secret of its success.

Estonia established a tax system that is simpler and more transparent than those in most other eastern new member states. It was the first European country to introduce a flat tax rate structure (in 1994), eliminating the progressive income tax schedule and applying the same rate (originally 26 percent) to personal and corporate income. From 2005, the flat tax was gradually reduced to 21 percent, and at the same time the personal basic exemption was more than doubled in nominal terms—a measure that greatly mitigated the impact of the flat tax on lower-income households. In 2000, retained profits became fully tax exempt, and since then only distributed profits are taxed.

But despite high economic growth in the aftermath of the reform, the tax rate reductions did not lead to a Laffer curve effect. Revenues from the personal

(continued next page)

Box 5.1 *(continued)*

income tax and the corporate income tax declined from around 8 percent and 2 percent of GDP in the second half of the 1990s, to around 6 percent and 1.6 percent of GDP in 2004–08. Although the tax reform did not lead to higher revenues, it enhanced simplicity, transparency, and compliance and is generally supported by the population and most political parties (OECD 2009). Most of the flat tax revenue is raised from higher income groups with relatively low labor supply elasticities, so that the adverse effect of this tax on employment is relatively small. Some observers argue that because the elasticity of labor supply is higher for low- and middle-income earners, reductions of the flat tax rate and the doubling of the basic allowance have increased the incentives for formal employment and thus contributed to reducing informal work, notably among middle- and lower-income earners.

In 2009, Estonia continued to simplify the tax system by extending the standard VAT rate to more goods and services, which previously were taxed at the reduced rate. Furthermore, the reduced VAT rate was increased from 5 percent to 9 percent. The reduction of the overall tax burden may also have contributed to combating undeclared work by reducing incentives to evade tax (direct effect) and contributing to higher growth and employment (indirect effect). During 2000–07, the overall tax burden (as measured by tax revenue as a percentage of GDP) averaged around 31 percent of GDP, down from more than 36 percent in 1995. The reduction of the overall tax burden was the result of lower labor taxes (four percentage points of GDP), and to a lesser degree lower capital taxation (by around one percentage point of GDP), while taxes on consumption remained broadly constant.

Together with Slovakia, Estonia has the lowest labor tax wedge among the EU new member countries. But low-income earners, who are most vulnerable to undeclared work, face a somewhat higher labor tax wedge than the OECD average, although it is lower than the EU-15 average and lower than in most other new member countries. Social insurance contributions are the largest component of the labor tax wedge. The government carried out reforms to social protection designed to tighten the link between contributions and benefits, including increasing the element of individual savings in the pension system and reforming unemployment insurance. Furthermore, individuals (including the self-employed) receive public health insurance only if a minimum amount of social insurance contributions (the "social tax") has been paid. Exceptions are granted to pensioners,

(continued next page)

Box 5.1 *(continued)*

pregnant women, those under 19 years old, students, and dependent spouses of contributors.

The Estonian Tax and Customs Board (EMTA) is among the most modern tax collection agencies in the EU, with simplified tax administration structures and pervasive use of e-government. Estonia's rates of electronic filing (personal income tax, 85 percent in 2007; corporate income tax, 88 percent; and VAT, 90 percent) are not only the highest among the new member countries but among the highest in the world. As a result, Estonia belongs to a group of countries with relatively low costs of tax compliance, as measured by the time spent preparing, filing, and paying taxes. EMTA collects all general taxes, custom duties, and (since 1999) social security contributions. The modernization of tax collection allowed EMTA to shift resources to areas that help ensure better compliance.

An important measure taken to improve tax compliance was to ensure that public procurement is only carried out with firms who do not have any tax arrears.

EMTA works closely with the Estonian Labor Inspectorate to exchange risk analysis and conduct joint operations, as well as cooperating with the Citizenship and Migration Board. EMTA applies a so-called client-based approach by raising awareness of tax compliance, using risk analysis to identify potential tax evaders, and contacting firms and individuals. For example, it sends notice letters to potential payers and receivers of envelope wages, which according to EMTA increased tax revenues by 59 million krooni.

Despite much progress to modernize the tax system and tax administration, some features of the Estonian tax and benefit system continue to make it vulnerable to tax evasion and avoidance. The fact that social insurance contributions are (with a few exceptions) only paid by the employer reinforces the perception of workers that those contributions are general taxes on business rather than premiums for risk-pooling arrangements. Currently, evasion is often initiated by the employer as a means to reduce labor costs. It has been argued that if employer contributions are transformed into employee contributions, workers would become more aware of the relatively high labor tax wedge and would attempt to evade it; the relatively high amount of evasion by the self-employed, who directly pay their contributions, is taken as a prime example. However, in contrast to those of the self-employed, the contributions of employees are, like those of employers, withheld at the source, and any concealment of earnings requires that employers and employees collude. The pressure to evade contributions would therefore

(continued next page)

Box 5.1 *(continued)*

probably decline with a shift in statutory responsibility for contributions, as social insurance coverage is more in the interest of employees than of employers.

The tax treatment of dependent workers and self-employed workers also is uneven. Although the self-employed have to pay personal income tax and social insurance contributions at the same rates as dependent workers, they have more opportunities to underdeclare income, and they also benefit from generous deductions for operating costs. Furthermore, in contrast to social insurance contributions for employees, a ceiling limits the income of the self-employed that is subject to contributions, but it only benefits high-income earners (making more than 15 times the minimum wage). If the self-employed are organized as corporate firms, they also benefit from the lower capital taxation vis-à-vis labor taxation. For example, some medical doctors are organized as corporate entrepreneurs and pay their income out as dividends rather than as wages, thus avoiding the higher labor taxes. The gap between capital and labor taxation also encourages managers of firms to transform part of their wage into capital income and distribute it as dividends. According to estimates by EMTA, the revenue lost from firms' paying dividends instead of salaries amounted to 193 million krooni (0.1 percent of GDP) in 2007. The Estonian financial newspaper *Äripäev* (June 31, 2009) reported that Estonia's top lawyers earn most of their income as dividends and pay social insurance contributions only on 10 percent to 20 percent of their income.

Source: Leibfritz 2011, for this volume.

taxpayers, help the tax administration collect revenue from the hard-to-tax sectors, and ease the transition from informal to formal work, thus bringing more people into the tax net and under social insurance coverage. However, as Leibfritz (2011) cautions, special simplified tax schemes for the self-employed come with benefits but also risks. They can encourage individuals to avoid or evade taxes by shifting their work into the preferential status, for example, from dependent employment into self-employment or bogus self-employment. Furthermore, even an indirect subsidy to small firms—in the form of presumptive taxation—might encourage an inefficient firm structure with too many small firms. The gains of simplified tax schemes must therefore be weighed against the risks.

Box 5.2

The Slovak Republic's Tax Reform

According to the Slovak Statistical Office, undeclared work in Slovakia was responsible for 13 percent to 15 percent of GDP in 2000 and has declined only moderately in recent years. According to the IMD World Competitiveness report, tax evasion hampers business activity less in Slovakia than in most of its neighbors, with the exception of the Czech Republic (Leibfritz 2011). Slovakia has been successful in broad regulatory and business-friendly reforms that have improved the investment climate and encouraged enterprise. In 2004, under the slogan "Making work pay," Slovakia implemented a fundamental reform of its taxation, in tandem with reforms to social benefits and the labor market, aimed at promoting growth and employment by increasing investment and incentives to work. The main tax measures were the introduction of a flat personal income tax and the unification of its rate with those of the corporate income tax and the VAT at 19 percent.

Prior to the reform, the personal income tax had a progressive rate structure ranging from 10 percent to 38 percent; the corporate income tax had a standard rate of 25 percent, with 15 percent and 18 percent reduced rates; and the VAT had a standard rate of 20 percent and a reduced rate of 14 percent. The flat personal income tax includes a basic personal exemption, which is linked to the subsistence level, is reduced gradually at higher incomes, and is phased out if the tax base is equal to or greater than 100 times the subsistence level. The average tax rate increases with rising income, thus making the income tax slightly progressive. However, as social insurance contributions are subject to an income ceiling, the overall tax on labor becomes regressive at higher income levels. Furthermore, the tax bases of the personal and the corporate income tax were broadened by eliminating or reducing exemptions and deductions. Excises on mineral oil, beer, and tobacco were increased, and the tax on the transfer and assignment of real estate was abolished in 2005.

As in Estonia, the flat tax reform in Slovakia did not lead to a Laffer curve increase in revenues, but rather to lower revenue as a percentage of GDP. Overall, the tax reform was designed to be revenue neutral. In the four years after the reform, revenue from personal income taxes (as a percentage of GDP) was 0.8 percentage points lower than in the four years before, but the revenue from the corporate income tax was 0.2 percentage points higher. Revenue from the

(continued next page)

Box 5.2 *(continued)*

VAT and excises increased by 0.3 and 0.4 percentage points. Total tax revenue declined by almost three percentage points of GDP. Two-thirds of the decline was caused by lower revenue from social insurance, and one-third by lower general taxes. But because government expenditures declined even faster (as a percentage of GDP) than revenues, Slovakia was able to reduce its general government budget deficit from more than 7 percent of GDP between 2000 and 2003, to less than 3 percent between 2004 and 2007, and that also helped the country meet the criteria for joining the euro zone in 2009.

The tax reform reduced taxes on income and shifted more of the tax burden onto consumption, which increased incentives to work and to save (Brook and Leibfritz 2005). Although it was not solely attributable to the tax reform, between 2004 and 2008 Slovakia achieved an average annual growth of 8 percent, the highest of the new EU member countries. Employment increased by almost 3 percent per year, while unemployment declined from around 18 percent in 2004 to less than 10 percent in 2008.

The flat tax made it easier for taxpayers to comply and thus helped reduce undeclared work, but the size of that effect remains unclear. The labor tax wedge declined for low-income earners as a result of an increase in the personal income exemption, which left minimum wages free of personal income tax. The tax wedge also declined for high-income earners because of the elimination of the progressive rate structure. Average wage earners, married workers with children, and nonworking spouses benefited from the refundable child benefit, while the tax wedge for single earners remained broadly constant.

In 2005, part of social insurance contributions for old age pensions was redirected to mandatory individual worker savings accounts. Because workers have property rights over the savings, that portion of contributions is no longer considered in OECD statistics as labor taxes. The incentive effect of this measure, however, is unclear. Because the forced saving did not reduce labor costs, it had no positive effect on labor demand. A positive effect from higher labor supply would only result if workers perceived the savings part of their social insurance contribution as wholly owned rather than as a tax.

Overall the tax reform of 2004 made the tax system simpler and more transparent. Together with other changes, it also led to a decline in the overall tax burden, including the tax on labor. The tax reform and the tightening of social benefits should, in principle, have led to a marginal decline in informal work, the

(continued next page)

Box 5.2 *(continued)*

more so as economic growth was high and employment increased until 2007. But undeclared work appears to have declined only marginally since the reform, suggesting that other factors are also at play. Indeed, many low-skilled workers remain unemployed, often for a long duration, and in particular in the less-developed eastern regions. Those workers tend to be low-skilled, which reduces their productivity below the minimum wage, and they therefore have difficulty finding a regular job. They are also reluctant to leave their region to find a job elsewhere and, as a result, tend to resort to informal work.

Although structural factors other than taxation can still explain a large part of informal employment in Slovakia, some undeclared work may still—despite the tax reform—be related to taxation. Although there is a ceiling on the income subject to social insurance contributions (but not for social health insurance) the labor tax below three, and now four times the average wage is regressive. Second, the significant step upward of the income tax (19 percent) just after the minimum wage may encourage workers to underdeclare wages. Another problem arises because self-employed workers benefit from a lower base of social insurance contributions, so that their labor tax wedge is lower than if they worked as employees. That could be encouraging bogus self-employment.

The government responded to these problems by introducing a general employment tax credit in 2009, which reduces the effective labor tax on lower incomes. To finance this measure, the government discussed eliminating (or raising) the income ceilings and perhaps including capital income in the base for social insurance contributions. The latter measure would also help discourage people from declaring labor income as capital income, although it would weaken the link between contributions and benefits.

Although tax reforms have made Slovakia's tax system simpler and easier to manage, the system of tax collection has not kept pace. It is still relatively cumbersome for taxpayers to comply. The average firm needs 325 hours per year to comply with business taxes, whereas in Estonia only 81 hours are needed. The government is currently working with the World Bank to reform tax collection and unify the collection of general taxes and social insurance contributions, as is already done in Bulgaria, Estonia, Hungary, Latvia, Romania, and Slovenia.

Source: Leibfritz 2011, for this volume.

Box 5.3

The Czech Republic's Tax Reform

Like Estonia, among the eastern new member countries the Czech Republic appears to have succeeded in containing undeclared work. According to the Czech Statistical Office, undeclared work in the Czech Republic was 9 percent to 10 percent of GDP in 2006/07, the second-lowest after Estonia, and has not changed in recent years. According to business surveys for the IMD World Competitiveness report 2010 (reported in Leibfritz 2011, for this volume), in the Czech Republic tax evasion is less important than in any of the other EU new member countries. That success is not just a reflection of tax policy. The Czech Republic has a highly skilled workforce and moderate wage regulation. Hanousek and Palda (2008) found that in the Czech Republic between 1995 and 2006 the percentage of tax evaders rose, leveled off, and then declined, thanks to structural changes and better macroeconomic conditions.

Underdeclaration of work is widespread among the self-employed, the registered unemployed, and even workers with formal jobs. It is more common among low-skilled workers than higher-skilled workers, although tax evasion among the latter is significant. Horáková and Kux (2003) found that undeclared work is most widespread among the self-employed, those in small enterprises, low-skilled workers, and workers with secondary jobs. In 2007 about 40 percent of all workers in the construction sector worked as self-employed, and more than 150,000 of those self-employed workers in the construction sector could, in principle, perform their contracted work also as dependent employees. Between one-eighth and one-fourth of all self-employment in the Czech Republic is bogus self-employment, known as *švarcsystém*.

Although the statutory labor tax rates (personal income tax and social insurance contributions) are the same for employees and the self-employed, the latter benefit from a lower tax base. In 2006, the base for social insurance contributions for the self-employed was 50 percent of profits (up from 40 percent in 2004 and 45 percent in 2005). It is also easier for the self-employed to underdeclare earnings by deducting personal expenses as business expenses or by failing to declare sales. As a result, many of the self-employed simply declare the minimum wage, which is required to receive social insurance coverage. According to model calculations by Prusa et al. (2009), the self-employed in the Czech Republic have a particularly

(continued next page)

Box 5.3 *(continued)*

low effective tax burden; in 2005, the calculated unit tax cost (comprising all labor taxes) for the self-employed was only around 23 percent, while for workers in corporations it was around 41 percent. The ratio between the unit tax costs of the self-employed and those of the dependent employed is thus only around 56 percent, the lowest among the 19 EU countries that were considered in the study. In Hungary this ratio is 64 percent, and in Slovakia it is around 66 percent. In comparison, Denmark has one of the most balanced tax treatments of income from self-employment and dependent employment, with a ratio between the unit tax costs of around 92 percent.

The introduction of a flat personal income tax in 2008 replaced a progressive tax schedule with four tax brackets (of 12 percent, 19 percent, 25 percent, and 32 percent), with a uniform tax rate of 15 percent. However, because social insurance contributions are now included in the personal income tax base, the tax rate, as calculated on a conventional base (that is, excluding social insurance contributions), is 23 percent. Tax credits (including the basic tax credit) and allowances for working low-income groups were increased. A ceiling on the income base for social insurance contributions was established, at four times the average salary, and the ceiling for the self-employed will be raised to the same level. The corporate income tax rate was gradually lowered from 24 percent in 2007 to 19 percent in 2010, and at the same time the tax base was expanded. The reduced VAT rate was raised from 5 percent to 9 percent.

Although it is too early to assess, the government hopes that the changes will reduce evasion. Yet the system of tax collection in the Czech Republic remains cumbersome. A typical firm needs 930 hours per year to comply with the tax laws. That is the heaviest compliance burden among the new EU member countries and puts the Czech Republic among the lowest rankings internationally. With technical support from the World Bank, the government will unify the collection of general taxes, custom duties, and social insurance contributions, in the hope of considerably easing tax compliance.

Source: Leibfritz 2011, for this volume.

As shown in chapter 1, the share of self-employed in the labor force varies considerably across Europe and among the new EU member countries. Self-employment is highest in Romania, Poland, and Bulgaria and lowest in Estonia and Slovakia. In several countries the share of self-employed declined between 1995 and 2007 (notably in Hungary, Latvia,

Lithuania, and Poland), whereas in a few others it has increased (notably in Slovakia and to a smaller degree in Estonia).

In Hungary, entrepreneurs or contract workers with annual gross revenue below a certain amount can choose a scheme known as the "simplified entrepreneurs' tax" (EVA). Under EVA, entrepreneurs are not required to record their expenses but pay a flat income tax rate of 25 percent. Paying EVA eliminates all other income tax or other levies on their business activity besides social insurance contributions, which are allowed to be paid only on the minimum wage, independent of actual income (although higher payments to social insurance are also allowed). Those choosing EVA must add VAT (usually 20 percent) to their invoices, but they neither make VAT payments to the tax office, nor can they claim tax credits on their inputs. A similar scheme for cultural workers acting as employees—the "EKHO" scheme—provides a simplified and favorable tax treatment.

For individuals who are taxed under the EVA and EKHO schemes, labor tax wedges are significantly lower than for employees. The difference is particularly large for higher-income earners: the labor tax wedge for high-income earners in the EVA is less than 20 percent, compared with more than 60 percent for normal (dependent) employees with the same income (Leibfritz 2008). The main reason for the lower tax wedge is that the income tax rate is flat, and social insurance contributions are allowed to be based on the minimum wage. In contrast, for employees the personal income tax is progressive, and social insurance contributions are proportional to income and—for the employer contribution—without any cap. So although the special schemes provide an incentive to move from untaxed to taxed employment, they also create incentives to shift activity from dependent employment into self-employment to qualify for the special treatment. Furthermore, as taxpayers in these schemes cannot claim VAT credits on their inputs they have no incentive to ask for an invoice from their suppliers. With a tax base defined as "VAT-increased revenues," these individuals may also underdeclare revenues by not giving a receipt to their clients.

In Poland, unincorporated small and medium enterprises (SMEs) and the self-employed can choose either to be taxed at the uniform 19 percent tax rate (general taxation scheme) or to pay a lump-sum tax (presumptive tax scheme) in which the tax turnover (registered revenues) and the tax rate vary according to the nature of the business. The lump-sum tax is in most cases below the corporate income tax (CIT) and personal income tax (PIT) rates of 19 percent on capital income. In the general regime, firms can deduct wage costs as expenses, which increases the incentive to declare their employees. But that is not the case in the presumptive tax regime, which makes underreporting labor relatively more attractive. Self-employed individuals (own-account workers or sole traders) are entitled to a flat tax rate of 19 percent on their declared income, compared to the progressive rate structure applicable to labor income of dependent employees. Furthermore, as it is difficult for the tax authorities to assess actual earnings, the self-employed may pay only a minimum social insurance contribution (based on the minimum wage, which corresponds to 60 percent of the average wage). In 2005, the social insurance base of the newly self-employed was reduced for the first 24 months to 30 percent of the minimum wage. As a result of all these measures, the self-employed tend to have a much lower tax wedge than regular employees. Some anecdotal evidence indicates that firms are encouraging their dependent employees to report themselves as self-employed to reduce taxes. To reduce the incentive for fictitious self-employment, the government has tightened the eligibility criteria, and it has also reduced the tax wedge for employees (OECD 2008b).

Another special scheme that leads to tax avoidance and evasion is the social insurance scheme for farmers (KRUS), to which farmers pay a flat rate contribution, so that their labor tax burden is significantly less than for nonfarm workers and the self-employed. It encourages people to hold small plots of land so as to classify as farmers, even if they are not actively working as farmers (Leibfritz 2011). It also increases informal work in rural areas and creates disincentives to move out of farming into more productive sectors.

Although it is intuitively easy to understand the incentives that special tax schemes create to report bogus self-employment, the phenomenon does not seem to be captured in the survey data. Assuming that self-employed people have relatively greater autonomy in organizing their work day, Hazans (2011a) used responses to the ESS to try to detect nominally self-employed people who are in fact dependent employees (figure 5.2). People who reported being self-employed also reported very high levels of autonomy in how they decide to organize their work every day. Across Europe, the reported autonomy of the self-employed is significantly greater than that of dependent employees, formal and informal. Of course, the ESS data are not conclusive proof that the concern about bogus self-employment is overstated.

Figure 5.2   The Informally Self-Employed Report More Autonomy in How They Organize Their Time

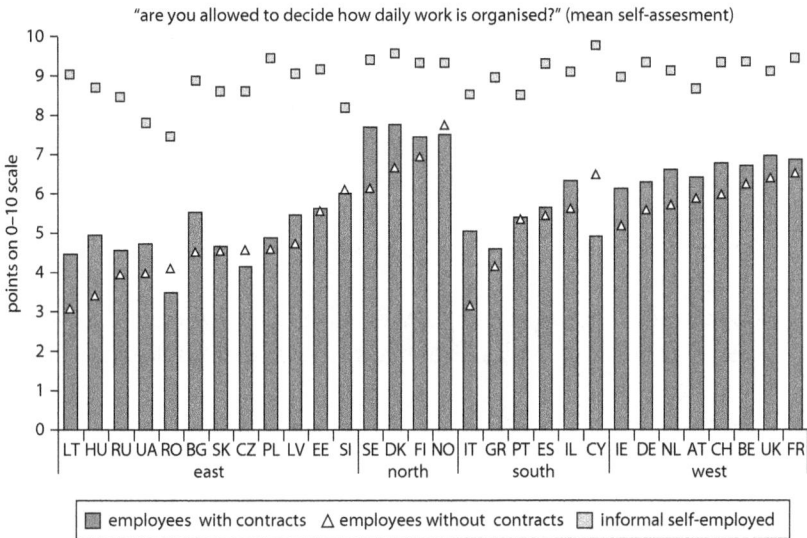

"are you allowed to decide how daily work is organised?" (mean self-assesment)

points on 0–10 scale

LT HU RU UA RO BG SK CZ PL LV EE SI | SE DK FI NO | IT GR PT ES IL CY | IE DE NL AT CH BE UK FR
east   north   south   west

■ employees with contracts   △ employees without contracts   ▢ informal self-employed

Source: Hazans 2011a, for this volume.

Drawing on case studies of structural reforms of taxation, in his background paper for the book Leibfritz (2011) proposes the following general guidelines for improving incentives to formalize work:

- *Shift the relative weights of instruments in the tax mix away from taxing labor earnings to less-distorting and more easily enforced taxes.* The already-high taxes on consumption constrain the extent to which a shift away from labor taxes can be made up with more intensive use of VAT. Given the tax instruments currently deployed, a more promising shift is to a progressive tax on real estate.
- *Lower the rates of effective marginal taxes by smoothing the rate structure.* The ultimate smoothing would come about with the introduction of a flat rate structure. However, it can also be achieved by introducing intermediate rates where current effective marginal rates spike, increasing incentives to evade. Another important way to smooth the spikes is by introducing a more gradual withdrawal of income-targeted social assistance (discussed in greater detail below).
- *Simplify the tax structure by removing minor taxes and minimizing exemptions and loopholes.* Not only would that reduce compliance costs for

firms and households, but it could also broaden the base of the more effective tax instruments.

- *Minimize the pure-tax component of mandatory social insurance plans by tying benefits closely to contributions and shifting the financing of social insurance plans with a primarily redistributive objective to general taxation.* Given the existing, formidable deficits between benefits payments and contributions in most social insurance plans in the region, and the projected decline in the size of the labor force, closer alignment between benefits and contributions will very likely require a reconsideration of what benefits should continue to be offered by state-organized social insurance plans.
- *Integrate collection and auditing of taxes and social insurance contributions* to reap the benefits of administrative synergies and enable cross-checking and verification.
- *Automate administrative processes and interactions between the tax authorities and taxpayers,* taking advantage of e-filing and other Internet-based procedures to lower transactions costs and increase the effectives of monitoring.

Better Social Protection Incentives: Making Formal Work Pay for Low Earners

Chapter 3 examined the incentives created for firms and workers from the interaction of labor taxation and noncontributory forms of social protection. We showed with a synthetic representation of those incentives—the formalization tax rate and the effective marginal tax rate—how the most common social protection structures in the EU's new member countries create a powerful impetus for informal employment and even for inactivity. The chapter demonstrated those disincentives to formal work, presented actual observed rates of informal employment at critical inflection points in the incentive structure, and showed the strong association between work disincentives and informal employment, noting also that labor taxation and the design of social benefits are but two pieces in the large puzzle of informality and inactivity.

The synthetic representation of social protection incentives highlights how, for lower-wage earners in particular, the value of the social insurance coverage and employment protection that come with formal employment would at times have to be enormously high to offset the opportunity costs. That leads to the conclusion that formal (part-time) jobs at low wage levels—so-called mini-jobs and midi-jobs—may not in fact be an economically viable option for low-productivity job seekers in many countries. From that observation arises another instance of how the exit and exclusion explanations for undeclared labor can amount to the same thing: if the interaction of labor taxation and entitlement to social assistance benefits makes formal mini- and midi-jobs unviable to a substantial segment of the European working-age population, and in effect penalizes them if they take up formal employment and social insurance coverage, informality (and inactivity) is not only a deliberate choice of exit but also a matter of exclusion.

The literature repeatedly identifies two main policy levers to make formal work pay: to decrease labor taxation at lower wage levels and to smooth incentives with regard to social assistance, housing, and family benefits. The results presented in chapter 3 seem to some extent contradictory. Panel estimations using country-level data show that a larger tax wedge actually reduces the share of informal workers. A possible explanation for this result might be that using a single indicator for the tax wedge per country—usually the tax wedge measured at average wage for a single individual with no children—does not sufficiently capture actual work disincentives. As the descriptive analysis has shown, the tax wedge varies considerably depending on family structure and income level. Another possible explanation is that the tax wedge may be reflecting confidence in the state in its role of creating and maintaining public goods. That idea is supported by the fact that the country-level result is only statistically significant in western and northern EU member countries (which are clearly driving the result for the EU-27 as a whole, as shown in figure 3.15). Set against the discussion in chapter 4, those are the countries where institutional credibility and tax morale are the highest in Europe (and in wider international rankings).

Regarding the tax wedge, current social protection financing structures in several countries discriminate against lower earners. For example, Hungary applies a minimum social insurance contribution at very low wage levels (less than 20 percent of average wage). Among the EU-15 countries, only the Netherlands uses the same approach. Among those waiting to be EU members, Serbia applies such a floor. A minimum contribution floor increases the tax burden considerably for those in low-paying, part-time jobs. In several EU and OECD countries—and also in other countries in the region, such as Bosnia and Herzegovina—no such floor exists, at least not above the minimum wage. For part-time work at the minimum wage, the floor is usually adjusted by the actual hours worked, so that the tax wedge is not acting regressively for workers with lower earnings.

Other options for reducing the tax burden on low-income earners include incentives linked to wage subsidies, social insurance contribution credits, or so-called in-work or employment-conditional benefits—cash benefits or refundable income tax credits conditional on formal employment. Germany has introduced a phased social insurance contribution schedule as part of the Hartz IV reforms that came into force early in the 2000s. Monthly wages less than €400 are not subject to social insurance contributions. For monthly incomes between €401 and €800, the contribution rate rises gradually to the full share. The drawback of these types of measures is that they can carry a stigma for workers who benefit. They also incur a fiscal cost. However, those costs have to be weighed against the benefits of having people who were working informally (or inactive) in formal jobs.

Another way of improving incentives is to channel credits and subsidies to workers via their personal income tax returns. In the United States, for example, various refundable ("non-wastable") tax credits (the "earned income credit" and the "making work pay" credit) are available to low-wage earners and their families. For a U.S. taxpayer with one child, 34 percent of earned income up to US$9,000 is refundable, which amounts to the equivalent of a cash benefit of about US$3,000. This refundable credit is phased out at incomes above US$16,000. Similar benefits are available for other family types and single persons earning low incomes.

With regard to reforming the design of social assistance, housing, and family benefits, the key is to keep the marginal effective tax rate in mind when designing benefit withdrawal. In other words, beneficiaries of social assistance, housing, and family benefits should gain from additional formal work—that is, any additional formal wage should increase their net income, *including* benefits. Otherwise, additional formal work does not pay, and beneficiaries will prefer not to work at all, to work informally, or to underreport earnings. The extent to which social assistance creates disincentives for formal work is probably limited in the EU's new member countries. Programs are usually tightly targeted to a small group of beneficiaries, so coverage, even among the poorest, is low. Categorical benefits—available regardless of income—such as family allowances are far more prevalent. Nevertheless targeted, "last resort" assistance has increased across the region, as part of countries' response to the recent economic crisis. To the extent that income-targeted forms of social assistance gain importance as a permanent feature of social protection systems in the region, policy makers should take these considerations into account.

To make formal work pay for the lowest earners receiving income-tested social assistance, the withdrawal of benefit has to occur gradually as income increases. Sudden drops in net income have to be avoided. Eligibility criteria that restrict, for example, family benefits to those below a certain income threshold—often around 50 percent of the average wage—result in very high marginal effective tax rates and a considerable drop in net income once the income eligibility threshold is crossed. The German Hartz IV reforms again offer a good example of how that can be avoided and how gradual benefit withdrawal can be achieved. However, although it is clearly good social protection policy, the impact of smoothing the marginal effective tax rate on its own should not be oversold. Empirical evidence of a positive reaction—formalization of more workers—to this type of reform is scarce.

Entitlement to free health care coverage—where it exists—can be a powerful incentive. Such entitlements would ideally be limited to poor households and be based on a means test, not an income test. It is important that poor people have access to free health care, as sickness is a serious economic risk that can further deepen poverty. Yet if free health insurance is easily accessible also by those who can afford to contribute to social health insurance, it can decrease the value of formal work and increase incentives to work informally. It is therefore important to base decisions about who should have access to free health insurance on the means that a household has at its disposal, and not on formal income or formal employment status (such as registered unemployment, as is the case in some countries). That requires robust means-testing mechanisms, as opposed to income testing. It can take the form of proxy-means testing—for example, looking at electricity consumption—or of frequent contacts between a social worker and households in vulnerable populations. Of course, shifting the finance structure for a defined but guaranteed package of health coverage—for low-frequency, high-cost health treatment, treatments with proven preventive value, and measures that contain the external costs of ill health, such as immunization—to general taxation obviates the issue and does away with the need for means testing.

Most of the reforms that make formal work pay have immediate fiscal costs. Given the current fiscal constraints on governments across the EU, little space may be available to push them through. In particular, wage subsidies, tax credits, and other such measures can considerably reduce tax revenues, including social insurance contributions, or increase public expenditures. In this regard, however, the EU new members are in a relatively favorable position. As shown in chapter 3, their tax systems are relatively nonprogressive. Making them more progressive could make future reforms along these lines fiscally neutral to a large extent.

With respect to social protection, the general guidance for policy makers that can be drawn from this discussion is summarized in the following:

- *Consider offsetting the burden of the tax wedge* with targeted wage subsidies for low-productivity jobs, social insurance credits, and in-work employment-conditional benefits.
- *Lower the opportunity costs of formal employment for people eligible for social assistance* by shifting to a gradual withdrawal of benefits, earned income tax credits, or both.

Labor Market Regulations, Interventions, and Institutions

The standard labor pricing models discussed in chapter 2 conclude that minimum wages increase labor costs for firms and prevent them from offering formal employment to workers the marginal value of whose labor does not exceed the imposed minimum. The results presented in chapter 3 paint a more nuanced picture. In country-level panel estimations on a sample restricted to the EU's new member states, the level of the minimum wage has an unanticipated negative impact on the scale of informal production and on the extent of employment in small firms. We infer from this unanticipated result that the minimum wage is acting as a lever of fiscal policy, containing the extent of informal employment and the size of the shadow economy by setting the minimum amount that firms have to declare.

When one uses a more precise measure of informal work—the share of the labor force in employment without a contract and informal self-employment—similar panel estimations reveal that in the southern members and in the new member countries of the EU, raising the minimum wage increases informal employment, as the classical model predicts. However in the western and northern member countries, the impact of an increase in the minimum wage is exactly the opposite: a higher minimum wage lowers the extent of employment without a contract. Our inference from this result is that the imposed minimum is acting as an "efficiency wage" that attracts workers into formal jobs. For a pooled sample of all EU countries, raising the minimum wage increases the extent of informal self-employment, which indicates that care has to be taken by policy makers to strike the right balance in what can sometimes be a trade-off between ensuring a socially suitable minimum level of earnings and encouraging offers of formal employment, even for the least productive workers.

The second area of labor market regulation examined in the empirical research for this book is employment protection legislation (EPL)—essentially, restrictions on dismissal that raise firing and hiring costs for firms. EPL is the most consistently significant and robust driver of the size of the shadow economy as a share of GDP and labor informality proxied by various measures. Although not examined explicitly in the papers commissioned for the book, the negative impact of EPL on the availability of formal employment has been found to be greater for younger job seekers.

With greater diversity and the rise of services, restrictions on dismissal once important for worker protection in the highly monopsonistic labor markets of economies with a dominant manufacturing sector may have outlived their utility. In the southern member countries of the EU, where EPL is the most restrictive, segmentation has emerged that restricts all but the most educated new entrants to the labor market to part-time and informal work. The need to loosen the constraints of EPL on the labor market lies at the core of Denmark's renowned "flexicurity" model of labor regulation that shifts protection away from jobs to people through intensive deployment of capacity-building and job search assistance.

Indeed, the results presented in chapter 3 indicate that spending on such "active" intervention measures seems to lower the extent of informal employment in OECD member countries and northern and western EU member countries. The lack of a measurable significant effect of spending on these programs in the (non-OECD) new member states may reflect an inappropriate program mix (for example, more training and less job search assistance), design problems, or mundane—but important—weaknesses in implementation of the interventions.

The impact of "passive" interventions—unemployment insurance—also varies across Europe. In the southern and new member states, spending on unemployment insurance benefits is at a relatively modest level, but it seems to help keep job seekers from having to accept informal forms of work. The same is true for long-term social assistance to the unemployed, as long as its five-year average net replacement rate (including unemployment insurance benefits) does not exceed 55 percent. However, raising the replacement rate of long-term assistance (unlike unemployment insurance) also tends to increase the unemployment rate. In contrast, in western and northern European countries, higher spending on unemployment benefits (other things being equal) increases informal dependent employment, as well as unemployment, whereas higher net replacement rates of social assistance benefits over five years seem to reduce the extent of informal work without increasing unemployment. Passive interventions such as unemployment insurance are designed to enable better matching of job seekers with employers offering jobs. It appears that in southern and new member states unemployment insurance may perform that function without creating undue moral hazard in the form of informal work and unemployment. By contrast, in western and northern European countries, unemployment insurance might be encouraging—and even subsidizing—informal work.

Turning to labor market institutions, the discussion and analysis have centered on collective bargaining and the role of labor unions. The conventional labor pricing model would lead one to expect stronger collective bargaining to enforce segmentation in the labor market and protect unionized insiders from wage arbitrage pressures from non-unionized outsiders. But yet again, the impact of unions on the extent of informal work differs between the northern and western members, and the southern and new members of the EU. In the southern and new member states, greater union density lowers the share of workers without contracts and the extent of self-employment. In the western and northern member states, the impact is exactly opposite—that predicted by the conventional models. We infer from this mixed result that, on one hand, where institutions that enable people to have greater voice and enforce accountability are still weak (or missing), labor unions are exercising that function. On the other hand, where people have plenty of well-trodden, well-established avenues to seek recourse, unions need not bear broad responsibility for voice and accountability and instead can focus on their core competence: securing the best deal for their members.

Drawing policy guidance for the labor market from cross-country analysis is a perilous task. Nevertheless, we venture the following points:

- *Maintain nonmarket minimum wages at a low level relative to average market wages for low-skill jobs.* When that is done, the minimum wage is more likely to serve the social function of guaranteeing a socially suitable minimum consumption ability from work, without choking off the creation of jobs, particularly for younger workers, those with less education, and those whose marginal product is low.

- *Adopt the "flexicurity" approach of protecting people rather than protecting jobs.* Although some level of labor market regulation is necessary to prevent abuses, employment protection legislation may do more damage to employment outcomes than good in competitive, internationally integrated economies. The less monopsonistic the labor market, and with global demand, the more important it is to provide income security in case of job loss and to enable workers to move between jobs.

- *Improve the incentive structure of income support programs for the unemployed to better match the risk of unemployment and implementation capacity.* This book has presented evidence that modest spending on unemployment insurance (say, within 0.1 percent of GDP per percentage point of unemployment, as in most of the new member states) may have a positive impact on outcomes. However, where unemployment benefits are relatively more generous, or where monitoring capacity is weak, the benefits of providing income support for the unemployed could be had, and perverse incentives (moral hazard) could be minimized, by introducing an individual savings element to unemployment insurance plans. Chile introduced a mixed system of unemployment insurance in 2001, in which individual saving accounts are underpinned with a risk-pooling safety net. Employers and workers are required to pay into accounts, and when workers leave or lose employment, they can draw on a specified portion their accumulated savings. Should a person's job search extend longer than five months, they receive a defined minimum unemployment benefit. In a mixed plan, the relative importance (weights) of individual savings and risk pooling can be adjusted to structural changes in the labor market that affect the rate of turnover and average search periods (that is, the relative frequency and size of the losses from unemployment).

Improving Governance, Institutional Credibility, and Tax Morale

The process of improving governance and increasing institutional credibility is long and difficult, as policy makers in all of the EU's new member countries can attest. Although gains are difficult to measure with precision, according to the best available and most widely recognized indexes, all of the EU new member states have made substantial progress in increasing government effectiveness, controlling corruption, strengthening the rule of law, and improving the quality of regulation. Yet despite that progress and the measurable impact it has had on improving tax morale and shrinking the size of the shadow economy, governments are eager to achieve more.

Much of the policy literature on how to improve and sustain tax morale suggests starting with a shift in how taxation is conducted. Feld and Frey (2002b) argue that tax morale rises when tax officials treat taxpayers with respect. The inverse is also true: tax morale falls when tax administrators treat taxpayers as suspicious and requiring coercion to pay taxes. Suspicion, control, and coercion on the part of the tax administration can crowd out people's intrinsic motivation to act as good citizens. If tax administrators start with a presumption of trust and good citizenship and establish transparent payment procedures, taxpayers are more likely to respond positively. Gambetta (1988) writes, "Trust appears to be a resource like no other; it is not depleted through use but rather through lack of use." Hence, the more that regulatory interactions are based on trust, the more likely it is that regulators will be able to nurture the development of reciprocal trust relationships. Feld and Frey (2002b) showed empirically that a change in treatment improves tax morale and compliance. A shift in the orientation of taxation was key in raising tax morale and compliance in Australia.

With reference to the recent wave of tax reforms in transition countries, Torgler (2011a) cites Owsiak (2007), who stresses that

> reforms under way ... should concentrate on measures enhancing citizen trust in law and on the removal of sources of tax-related abuse. The establishment of a legal framework that would render the tax system stable, transparent, simple, friendly to taxpayers, accompanied by concurrent implementation of a rational mechanism for allocating and controlling public spending, highlighting the relation between the taxes collected and the benefits gained by local communities, would ultimately determine whether society will welcome the development of tax-related civil behavioural patterns." (223)

Box 5.4

Building Trust and Better Service in Australia's Tax Administration

A strong increase of tax morale took place in Australia during the 1980s and 1990s. In the early 1980s, the government faced numerous complaints about the income tax system. The perception prevailed among the public that many people were not meeting their tax obligations, and it was clear that taxpayer compliance had eroded. An example that occurred during the late 1970s was the "bottom of the harbor" schemes, in which company profits were stripped before they could be taxed and the records conveniently lost. The more widespread the perception that others were not paying their share, the more noncompliance increased. As a consequence, taxation reform was a prominent issue to taxpayers during the mid-to-late 1980s. In the 1986/87 financial year, the Australian Taxation Office (ATO) shifted its orientation on taxation and introduced a self-assessment system that proved more cost-effective. Starting from a position of trust in the taxpayer nurtured voluntary compliance. Of course, if such a system is to be sustainable in the long term, a backup strategy must be in place to detect and penalize those who attempt to cheat the system, for example, postassessment audits and penalties for illegitimate returns.

During the 1980s demand was growing for public administration bodies to become more market focused, service oriented, open, and efficient (Hughes 1994; Job and Honaker 2003). In response, the ATO adopted a new organizational structure. Instead of focusing so much on compliance management, risk control, or structuring the application of enforcement discretion, the ATO expanded its focus to include better service, the customer experience, quality, and transparency (see Job and Honaker 2003). In fact, the ATO was among the first tax administrations in the world to implement a new client-based organizational structure, in which staff are assigned to units that focus on specific groups of customers, for example, salary and wage earners, small business income taxpayers, and large business income taxpayers. One of the advantages of a client-based structure is that it allows tax administrations to better match their enforcement and educational programs to the compliance patterns of particular groups (Verhorn and Brondolo 1999). If taxpayers see that the changes bring about better compliance levels among other taxpayers, it can influence their own tax morale. A client-focused approach is also likely to increase trust among taxpayers, who are more likely to feel that their needs are being considered in the regulatory process.

Source: Torgler 2011a, for this volume.

Evidence in the tax morale literature indicates that where citizens hold positive attitudes toward the tax authority and the tax system, tax morale and collection are significantly greater. Respectful and fair treatment of taxpayers induces respect for the tax system and leads to cooperation. In contrast, opacity, inefficiency, and unfairness in interactions between the tax administration and the taxpayers erode the intrinsic motivation to pay one's taxes.

Evidence from several countries also shows that instead of heavy focus on compliance management, risk control, and enforcement, better results are likely when the tax administration becomes more focused on service, customers, quality, transparency, and making the process of compliance as painless as possible. Where the tax administration tries to be honest, fair, informative, and helpful, acting as a service institution and thus treating taxpayers as partners and not inferiors in a hierarchical relationship, tax morale increases and taxpayers have stronger incentives to pay taxes honestly.

As suggested by the strong inverse relationship shown in figures 4.1 and 4.2, control and elimination of corruption are also critical to improving tax morale. In countries where corruption is systemic, the obligation of paying taxes quickly vanishes as a social norm. Corruption generally undermines the tax morale of citizens, who feel cheated if they perceive that the public finances are being squandered or used for ill gain. At the extreme, people can feel strongly entitled to evade taxes and the structures of the formal economy. Again, a good place to begin cleaning house is in the tax administration itself. In many formerly centrally planned economies, the tax administration still has a relatively higher degree of discretionary power over how tax liabilities are assessed and resources are collected, and that can create greater opportunities for corruption (Levin and Satarov 2000). Tanzi (2002) lists a number of telltale signs that corruption is likely to be a problem in a country's tax administration:

(a) if the tax laws are difficult to understand and interpret, so that taxpayers need a lot of assistance to comply;
(b) when paying taxes requires frequent contacts between taxpayers and tax administrators;
(c) where the wages of staff in the tax administration are low;
(d) where administrative procedures—such as the criteria for the selection of taxpayers for audits—lack transparency and are not closely monitored;

Box 5.5

Building Institutions and Tax Morale in Spain after Franco

With an estimated shadow economy of 22.5 percent of GDP in 2007, Spain is at
the higher end of the range for OECD countries (although it is still considerably
lower than Greece, which has the largest shadow economy at 27.5 percent of
GDP, among the older members of the EU). In 2009, Spain ranked 14th among EU
countries in the portion of workers in dependent employment without a contract
(5 percent), with about half as many as the United Kingdom (9.8 percent). However, Spain joins Portugal in fifth place in the share of the labor force in informal
self-employment (14.3 percent).

Fundamental changes in Spanish society during the more than 30 years since
the death of Francisco Franco and the transition to plural democracy offer an
opportunity to examine citizens' attitudes toward paying taxes and the ways in
which those attitudes are affected by changes in government institutions.
Martinez-Vazquez and Torgler (2009) used survey data from the World Values Survey (WVS) and the European Values Survey (EVS) to observe the evolution of tax
morale in Spain from 1981 to 2000. The evolution of tax morale in modern Spain
is particularly interesting because of the constitutional and political changes in
that country since 1975. The advent of a fully democratic state, deep reforms of
tax policy and tax administration, a significant push for decentralization, and its
accession the European Community are fundamental institutional changes that
are likely to have changed tax morale.

Tax morale was low at the end of Franco's regime, and tax evasion at the close
of the 1970s amounted to as much as 40 percent of tax receipts (Comin 2007).
Most Spaniards acknowledged widespread tax fraud. The tax system offered many
opportunities for avoidance and evasion, which were seized with enthusiasm particularly by the wealthy. Little political will existed to prosecute tax fraud. Indeed,
tax evasion was not even a criminal offense: if caught, evaders suffered only small
administrative sanctions. After Franco's death, the first democratic elections took
place in 1977, and a new social contract was drawn between all political forces in
the country in what became known as the Moncloa Pacts of 1977. The pacts set
the foundations for political reform, with a new constitution being approved in
1978. The pacts also set the blueprints for deep fiscal reform, including legislation
making tax evasion a crime. The goals of the Moncloa Pacts were to introduce
policy and institutional reforms in the public and private sectors that would bring
Spain into line with the systems of its European neighbors.

(continued next page)

Box 5.5 *(continued)*

Fiscal and other institutional reforms gained momentum in 1982. Profound tax reforms took place between 1983 and 1987. Spain's accession to the European Community in 1986 required, among other things, the introduction for the first time of the VAT. The personal income tax was overhauled with an emphasis on vertical equity and progressivity. Also important for the evolution of tax morale in the period, a major effort got under way to increase horizontal equity, to ensure that all citizens were meeting their obligations. The government modernized the tax administration apparatus. It expanded the territorial presence of the tax agency, computerized services, upgraded professional careers for tax officials, and created other instruments to increase voluntary taxpayer compliance and fight tax evasion.

From 1996, a second wave of tax reforms increased the relative importance of indirect over direct taxes. The government reduced its budget deficit and debt levels in order to join European Monetary Union. Economic realities had already forced many of Spain's European neighbors to emulate tax changes in the United States and elsewhere in the world by lowering rates, broadening tax bases, putting more emphasis on consumption taxes, and containing the costs associated with social insurance contributions. Tax rates on capital gains were reduced in 1996 and in 1998, and a new, more favorable tax regime for small and medium-size companies was enacted.

Martinez-Vazquez and Torgler (2009) show that from 1981 to 2000, Spain succeeded in designing general institutional reforms, including tax policy and tax administration reforms, that led to significant increases in tax morale. A key empirical result reported in their paper is the significant changes in tax morale over time, as reflected by the time effects estimated across the four time periods when the surveys were conducted. The time effects remain statistically significant in different specifications of the estimation. Tax morale increased steadily from 1981 to 1995 and then declined slightly, but nevertheless rose significantly through 1999/2000. The tax and other institutional reforms that started with the Moncloa Pacts and continued through the accession to the European Community helped boost Spanish citizens' tax morale.

Key to Spain's progress in increasing tax morale, compliance, and tax revenues were measures to increase not only progressivity, but the perceived fairness of taxation, or "horizontal equity." Taxpayers need to believe that compliance is an obligation of all citizens, even those with economic and political power.

Source: Torgler 2011a, for this volume.

(e) where tax administrators have discretion over the determination of tax liabilities, selection of audits, and litigations; and

(f) where acts of corruption on the part of tax administrators are either ignored, or when discovered penalized only mildly.

Hand in hand with control of corruption, the quality of institutions clearly matters to improving and sustaining high levels of tax morale. Torgler (2011a) presents a chain of logic that is both clear and intuitive. Good governance and a higher level of institutional quality allow people to express their social preferences with confidence by their involvement and participation in the political process. That enhances the identification of citizens with the state's institutions and can counteract inclinations to be noncompliant. Participation and identification therefore reduce free-rider problems. If citizens and authorities interact with a sense of collective responsibility under inspiring institutional structures, the system may be better governed and the policies more effective, as accountability promotes effectiveness through its impact on government behavior (Schaltegger and Torgler 2007).

Not surprisingly, many studies have found that a participatory political process is key to raising and sustaining tax morale. In a comparative study of European countries and the United States, Alm and Torgler (2006) found that the highest tax morale is observed in the United States and in Switzerland, two countries with very strong traditions of direct democracy. The possibility of taxpayers' voting on fiscal issues, and thereby being involved directly in the political decision-making process, enhances their sense of civic responsibility (Feld and Frey 2002a) and thus their tax morale. Because direct democracy helps to ensure that taxes are spent according to citizen preferences, the motivation to pay taxes may increase. Several studies have explored tax morale in Switzerland in depth, as the level of direct democracy varies substantially across the country's 26 cantons. Pommerehne and Weck-Hannemann (1996) found that tax evasion is lower in cantons with a higher degree of direct political control. Torgler (2005b) also found that a higher level of direct democracy leads to higher tax morale. Voting on tax issues has a positive effect on tax compliance (Alm, McClelland, and Schulze 1999; Feld and Tyran 2002; Torgler and Schaltegger 2005).

Moreover, studies of the link among local autonomy, tax morale, and tax compliance show that in smaller administrative structures of tax policy, citizens' preferences are able to be better served than where a uniform tax system is designed for a population with heterogeneous preferences (Torgler, Schneider, and Schaltegger 2007). More evidence from Switzerland shows that a higher level of local autonomy is correlated with higher tax morale and a smaller shadow economy. This outcome may be driven by the everyday interaction between taxpayers and local politicians and bureaucrats. Less distance between taxpayers and the tax administration and local government may induce trust and thus enhance tax morale. Politicians and members of the administration are better informed about the preferences of the local population. Furthermore, there is a politico-institutional aspect: if politicians are elected at the local level, they have an incentive to take the preferences of their constituency into account and thus to spend local tax revenues according to local preferences (see Frey and Eichenberger 1999). Although the findings in this strand of the literature may not be sufficient grounds to shift to a system of public services financed solely from local taxation, they provide a strong basis for greater transparency in the way public finances are managed and used and stronger accountability of decision makers to taxpayers—both of which can be strengthened with greater delegation of functions to local government.

Some countries have had positive experiences with active information campaigns that attempt to influence social norms to increase voluntary compliance by raising the "moral costs" of evasion. Information campaigns are designed to raise social awareness and nurture a culture of high tax morale and the rule of law. The campaigns typically inform the public about the negative implications of undeclared work for social insurance and the negative consequences of undeclared work for solidarity and fairness. In 2006, the United Kingdom focused on positioning tax evaders as a minority who damaged the interests of the majority. Some campaigns have targeted high-informality sectors. One example occurred in Canada, which focused on consumers in the construction industry, informing them of the legal and financial disadvantages of cash deals and linking quality and professionalism with registered contractors. Hungary's "Fair Play" campaign in 2007 emphasized, among other messages, the damage that tax evasion does to the country's financial situation. Tax morale specialists point out, however, that campaigns are usually more effective in countries that have made the broader efforts to improve governance, reduce corruption, and strengthen the rule of law. The sharply contrasting experiences of Chile and Argentina with similar national campaigns that encouraged consumers to demand a sales receipt with lottery prizes is a telling example (Bergman 2003). In Chile, where social norms of compliance were already strong, the campaign proved hugely effective at increasing tax compliance. In Argentina, where people hold a much dimmer view of institutions, its effectiveness was limited.

In summary, a growing body of empirical and policy literature clearly indicates the importance of accountability, governance, efficient and transparent legal structures, and therefore trust within the society to increasing tax compliance and tax morale. Citizens' perceptions of how government works and how compliant other citizens are have a strong impact on their willingness to comply. Although effective governance improvements and measures to strengthen institutional credibility and ultimately raise tax morale are obviously country and context specific, from the literature and case studies presented here, broad policy suggestions can be drawn:

- *Concentrate efforts to reduce corruption, increase transparency, and establish effective accountability structures on the tax administration.* It is through taxation that citizens feel the weight of their responsibilities in the social contract with the state. It is as good a place as any to focus efforts to strengthen that contract and is likely to be where those efforts can bring a quick and valuable return. Spain's example of ensuring that the "rules of the game" are enforced, even for the economically and politically powerful, was particularly effective.
- *Accompany institutional strengthening of tax administration with a shift in the stance of tax authorities from purely monitoring and enforcement, to client service.* When paying taxes is made easy, taxpayers will act in good faith.
- *Strengthen structures through which households can participate in decision making about how public resources are used.* Delegation of functions and responsibilities to locally elected government can be effective in reducing the distance between the taxpayer and the state, closely relating taxation to public choices about the provision of benefits and services.

References

Alm, J., G. H. McClelland, and W. D. Schulze. 1999. "Changing the Social Norm of Tax Compliance by Voting." *KYKLOS* 48: 141–71.

Alm, J., and B. Torgler. 2006. "Culture Difference and Tax Morale in Europe and the United States." *Journal of Economic Psychology* 27 (2): 224–46.

Bergman, M. 2003. "Who Pays for Social Policy? A Study on Taxes and Trust." *Journal of Social Policy* 31 (2): 289–305.

Brook, A.M., and W. Leibfritz. 2005. "Slovakia's Introduction of a Flat Tax as Part of Wider Economic Reforms." OECD Economics Department Working Papers No. 448, OECD, Paris.

Comín, F. 2007. "Reaching a Political Consensus in Spain: The Moncloa Pacts, Joining the European Union and the Rest of the Journey." In *Fiscal Reform in Spain*, ed. J. Martinez-Vazquez and J. Félix Sanz-Sanz. Cheltenham, UK: Edward Elgar.

Feld, L. P., and B. S. Frey. 2002a. "Trust Breeds Trust: How Taxpayers Are Treated." *Economics of Governance* 3: 87–99.

———. 2002b. "The Tax Authority and the Taxpayer. An Exploratory Analysis." Unpublished manuscript, University of Zürich, Switzerland.

Feld, L. P., and J.-R. Tyran. 2002. "Tax Evasion and Voting: An Experimental Analysis." *KYKLOS* 55: 197–222.

Frey, B. S. 2003b. "Deterrence and Tax Morale in the European Union." *European Review* (Cambridge University Press) 11 (3, July): 385–406.

Frey, B. S., and R. Eichenberger. 1999. *The New Democratic Federalism for Europe.* Cheltenham, UK: Edward Elgar.

Gambetta, D. 1988. "Can We Trust Trust?" In *Trust: Making and Breaking Cooperative Relations.* 213–37. New York: Blackwell.

Gorodnichenko Y., J. Martinez-Vazquez, and K. S. Peter. 2007. "Myth and Reality of Flat Tax Reform: Micro Estimates of Tax Evasion Response and Welfare Effects in Russia." IZA Discussion Papers No. 3267, December, Bonn, Germany.

Hanousek, J., and F. Palda. 2008. "Tax Evasion Dynamics in the Czech Republic: First Evidence of an Evasional Kuznets Curve." CERGE-EI Working Paper Series 360, Prague.

Hazans, M. 2011. "Informal Workers across Europe: Evidence from 30 European Countries." Background paper for "In from the Shadow: Integrating Europe's Informal Labor." Policy Research Working Paper 5912, World Bank, Washington, DC.

Horáková, M., and J. Kux. 2003. "Country Study on Informal Economy in the Czech Republic." Research Institute of Labor and Social Affairs, Prague. http://www.vupsv.cz/INFORMAL_ECONOMY.pdf.

Hughes, O. E. 1994. *Public Management and Administration.* New York: St. Martin's Press.

Ivanova A., M. Keen, and A. Klemm. 2005. "The Russian Flat Tax Reform." IMF Working Paper, January, International Monetary Fund, Washington, DC.

Job, J., and D. Honaker. 2003. "Short-Term Experience with Responsive Regulation in the Australian Taxation Office." In *Taxing Democracy: Understanding Avoidance and Evasion*, ed. V. Braithwaite. 111–30. Aldershot, UK: Ashgate.

Leibfritz, W. 2008. "Reducing Undeclared Work in Hungary—The Role of Tax Policy and Administration." Manuscript, World Bank, Washington, DC.

———. 2011. "Undeclared Economic Activity in Central and Eastern Europe: How Taxes Contribute and How Countries Respond to the Problem." Policy Research Working Paper 5923, World Bank, Washington, DC.

Levin, M., and G. Satarov. 2000. "Corruption and Institutions in Russia." *European Journal of Political Economy* 16: 113–32.

Martinez-Vazquez, J., and B. Torgler. 2009. "The Evolution of Tax Morale in Modern Spain. *Journal of Economic Issues* 43: 1–28.

Meriküll, J., and K. Staehr. 2008. "Unreported Employment and Tax Evasion in Mid-transition: Comparing Developments and Causes in the Baltic States." Bank of Estonia, Working Paper No. 6/2008.

OECD (Organization for Economic Cooperation and Development). 2008. *Reforms for Stability and Sustainable Growth: An OECD Perspective on Hungary*. Paris: OECD.

———. 2009. *Slovenia Economic Survey*. Paris: OECD.

Owsiak, S. 2007. "Taxes in Post-Communist Countries—Old and New Challenges." In *Tax Evasion, Trust, and State Capacities. How Good Is Tax Morale in Central and Eastern Europe?* ed. N. Hayoz and S. Hug. 187–225. Bern: Peter Lang.

Peter, Klara Sabirianova. 2008. "Falling Tax Evasion: How Much Can Tax Rates and Labor Regulations Explain?" Andrew Young School of Policy Studies Research Paper Series, Working Paper 08-10, February. W.J. Usery Workplace Research Group, Andrew Young School of Policy Studies, Atlanta, GA.

Pommerehne, W. W., and H. Weck-Hannemann. 1996. "Tax Rates, Tax Administration and Income Tax Evasion in Switzerland." *Public Choice* 88: 161–70.

Prusa, L., I. Bastyr, M. Brachtl, and J. Vlach. 2009. "The Socio-economic Status of Self-employed Persons in Czech Society." Research Institute for Labor and Social Affairs (RILSA), Prague.

Schaltegger, C. A., and B. Torgler. 2007. "Government Accountability and Fiscal Discipline: A Panel Analysis with Swiss Data." *Journal of Public Economics* 91: 117–40.

Staehr, K. 2009. "Estimates of Employment and Welfare Effects of Personal Labour Income Taxation in a Flat-Tax Country: The Case of Estonia." In *Microfoundations of Economic Success: Lessons from Estonia*, ed. David Mayes. 242–90. Cheltenham, UK: Edward Elgar.

Tanzi, V. 2002. "Corruption around the World: Causes, Consequences, Scope, and Cures." In *Governance, Corruption and Economic Performance*, ed. G. T. Abed and S. Gupta. 19–58. Washington, DC: International Monetary Fund.

Torgler, B. 2005. "Tax Morale and Direct Democracy." *European Journal of Political Economy* 21: 525–31.

———. 2011. "Tax Morale and Compliance: Review of Evidence and Case Studies for Europe." Background paper for "In from the Shadow: Integrating Europe's Informal Labor." Policy Research Working Paper 5922, World Bank, Washington, DC.

Torgler, B., and C. A. Schaltegger. 2005. "Tax Amnesties and Political Participation." *Public Finance Review* 33: 403–31.

Torgler, B., F. Schneider, and C. A. Schaltegger. 2007. "With or against the People? The Impact of a Bottom-Up Approach on Tax Morale and the Shadow Economy." School of Economics and Finance Discussion Papers and Working Papers Series 211, School of Economics and Finance, Queensland University of Technology.

Verhorn, C. L., and J. Brondolo. 1999. "Organizational Options for Tax Administration." *Bulletin for International Fiscal Documentation* 53 (11): 499–512.

World Bank. 2008. "Reducing Undeclared Employment in Hungary." World Bank Country Report No. 47777-HU, May, World Bank, Washington, DC.

World Bank, International Finance Corporation, and PricewaterhouseCoopers. 2009. "Paying Taxes: The Global Picture." www.doingbusiness.org/reports/thematic-reports/paying-taxes/~/media/FPDKM/Doing%20Business/Documents/Special-Reports/DB09-Paying-Taxes.pdf.

www.ingramcontent.com/pod-product-compliance
Lightning Source LLC
Chambersburg PA
CBHW071052280326
41928CB00050B/2272